The Korean Diaspora

The Korean Diaspora

Historical and Sociological Studies of Korean Immigration and
Assimilation in North America

Hyung-chan Kim, Editor

ABC-Clio, Inc.

SANTA BARBARA, CALIFORNIA
OXFORD, ENGLAND

Copyright © 1977 by Hyung-chan Kim
All rights reserved. No portion of this book may be reproduced in whole
or part in any form without prior written consent from the publisher.

Library of Congress Cataloging in Publication Data
The Korean diaspora.
    Includes bibliographical references.
    1.   Korean Americans—Addresses, essays, lectures.
2.   Americanization—Addresses, essays, lectures.
3.   United States—Emigration and immigration—Addresses,
essays, lectures.   I.   Kim, Hyung-chan.
E184.K6K63   301.45′11′957073   77-7080
ISBN 0-87436-250-4

American Bibliographical Center—Clio Press
2040 Alameda Padre Serra
Santa Barbara, California 93103

European Bibliographical Centre—Clio Press, Ltd.
Woodside House, Hinksey Hill
Oxford OX1 5BE, England

1 2 3 4 5

Manufactured in the United States of America

96669

To Charī, Kathy,
Lucy, and Phil

Contents

Preface

THIS ANTHOLOGY PRESENTS some results of recent research on Korean immigration to and assimilation in America. The essays were selected to illuminate three major questions which are frequently asked by those concerned with problems of immigration and assimilation.

First, what caused the immigration of Koreans to the Hawaiian Islands and the United States mainland? Little is known to date about Korea's domestic and international problems which ultimately spurred the immigration of approximately 7,000 Korean laborers and their families to Hawaii between 1902 and 1905. More studies are certainly needed before all the circumstances under which the immigration took place are revealed, but the first two essays of this anthology address the question with judicious scholarship.

Second, how has the Korean experience in America been essentially different from that of other immigrant groups, particularly the Japanese and Chinese? This question cannot be fully answered because we lack understanding of the personal and public life of early Korean immigrants and of the social and political organizations which they established in order to preserve and continue their own culture and institutions. We can only speculate on the sources of the uniqueness of the Korean experience. This uniqueness might have developed in relation to the Korean independence movement (1905–1945), which was strongly supported by most Korean immigrants in America. The Korean experience in America could have developed its unique characteristics because the immigration of Koreans did not last more than three years, and consequently the number of Koreans in America remained extremely small until 1965. There could be other factors which gave to the Korean experience in America unique qualities not shared by other immigrant groups. But perhaps it is premature at the the present stage of our knowledge to claim uniqueness. The remaining essays in Part One provide some insights into the development of social, religious, and political organizations in the Korean community in America. It is hoped that these studies will serve as a catalyst for further research into the question of uniqueness in the Korean experience.

Third, how successful have Korean immigrants and their descendants been in adjusting to American culture and society? For many years, sociologists and historians in America studied problems of assimilation from two major theoretical perspectives, i.e., acculturation, or cultural assimilation, and structural assimilation. The studies included in Part Two apply either or both of these perspectives to the investigation of social and cultural factors considered decisive in facilitating the assimilation of Korean immigrants. Many questions remain to be answered by further study using the same or different theoretical venues. Still to be explained are the relationship between generational differences and character, the relationship between the degree of assimilation of the Korean immigrant and the size of the Korean community of which he is a member, the degree of assimilation in relation to birth order of the individual within his family, and the degree of assimilation of the Korean immigrant in relationship to his strong need for Korean ethnic identity. The editor hopes that this anthology will encourage other concerned scholars to imaginatively research various problems of assimilation among Korean immigrants and their descendants.

In the romanization of Korean names and words, the McCune-Reischauer system, as amended by the Library of Congress to provide for hyphenation of given names, is employed. This system is not used, however, when the name of a particular individual is well known and familiar to the Western world, as in the case of Syngman Rhee, or when the individual repeatedly uses a different system of transliteration, as in the case of Lee Kyung. In the text and the notes, Korean and Japanese names are presented with the family name preceding the given name. However, when the given name is anglicized, it is given first. The names of the contributors to this anthology are given with their first names preceding their surnames. When their names are mentioned in the text or in bibliographical references, the usual Korean practice is observed.

During the preparation of this book, I received cooperation from individuals and institutions too numerous to mention. I thank the following individuals, who have given me their kind permission to reprint copyrighted material: Professor Kang Young-hoon, Director of the Research Institute on Korean Affairs, for permission to reprint the essay by Professor Cha Marn J.; William W. Cowan, Managing Editor, Oceana Publications, Inc., for permission to reprint the essay entitled "The History and Role of the Church in the Korean American Community," which appeared in *The Koreans in America, 1882–1974,* by the editor; and Choi Woon-sok, Associate Editor of *Korea Journal,* whose personal and professional interest in this project made it possible for me to reprint essays by Yu Chae-kŭn and by Yun Yŏ-jun.

I wish to express my sincere gratitude to Phyllis Bultmann for her excellent editorial assistance. The book is eminently more readable because of her unselfish effort to improve the text. My thanks go to Ann E. Drake, who typed the entire manuscript with patience and understanding. I am grateful to Jane Clark, Director of the Bureau for Faculty Research, Western Washington University, for financial assistance for typing, editorial service, and research.

HYUNG-CHAN KIM

Part One

Introduction

THE IMMIGRATION OF Koreans to the Hawaiian Islands in 1903 was primarily the result of Korea's internal and international problems, which radically changed the life of Korean people during the last three decades of the nineteenth century. Korea was a tributary state of China until 1876, when the Meiji government of Japan forced an unequal treaty. From that time until the defeat of China in the Sino-Japanese War (1894–1895), Korea was a bone of contention between the two nations. The period immediately following the Treaty of Kanghwa (1876) saw a sharp increase of trade and diplomatic relations between Japan and Korea. By the end of 1880, a permanent Japanese diplomatic mission was established in Seoul, and in 1881, a group of young Koreans were sent to Japan to study aspects of a modern nation.

Alarmed by Japan's aggressive policy toward Korea, Li Hung-chang, governor-general of Chihli province and de facto foreign minister of China, arranged a treaty between Korea and the United States to counterbalance Japanese influence in Korea. Through the mediation of Li, Korea and the United States signed the Treaty of Amity and Commerce in 1882, the first treaty Korea ever concluded with a Western nation. The treaty included a proviso pertaining to the immigration of Koreans to the United States. It stated that "subjects of Chosen (Korea) who may visit the United States shall be permitted to reside and to rent premises, purchase land, or to construct residences or warehouses in all parts of the country." Thus, the legal base was prepared for the immigration of Koreans to America.

Although the treaty between Korea and the United States paved the way for Koreans to immigrate, few took advantage of the opportunity. The actual immigration had to wait. In the meantime, a popular uprising led by a group of Tonghak followers broke out in the southern provinces of Korea. The Tonghak Rebellion of 1894 was essentially a political and social protest staged by masses of oppressed peasants against the corruption and evils of their rulers. As a political movement to overthrow a corrupt government, it failed because it lacked unity and discipline. But the Tonghak Rebellion accelerated the takeover of the Yi dynasty by ambitious Japanese imperial dreamers and served as a catalyst for the Sino-Japanese War.

As Western historian Homer Hulbert, eyewitness to much of what transpired in Korea in 1894, stated, that year marked the greatest crisis in Korean history since the seventh century. The Korean peninsula was converted into a battleground on which two foreign powers tried to settle their differences. The struggle ravaged the whole country, particularly the northwestern region. Many innocent Koreans lost their lives and property; many more were uprooted from their homes to drift from country to city in search of work. Japan's victory was confirmed in the Treaty of Shimonoseki (April 17, 1895). Through this treaty, China's recognition of Korea's political independence essentially conceded to Japan exclusive claim to Korea. Even before the end of the war, Japan forced upon the Korean government a series of sweeping political, economic, social, and educational reforms that were designed to change the traditional power structure in favor of Japanese interests.

However, Japan had to wait another decade, until November 17, 1905, to make Korea her protectorate, due to strong opposition from Britain, France, and Russia. However, Japan eliminated her traditional rival, China, as a contender, and she showed the remaining contenders her determination to go to war in order to secure her imperial interests in the Korean peninsula.

From 1895 to 1905, rivalry between Russia and Japan over Korea intensified, and the two nations had to resolve their differences through military confrontation. Japan defeated Russia in the Russo-Japanese War (1904–1905), officially concluded by the Treaty of Portsmouth on September 5, 1905. Through this treaty, Russia recognized Japan's predominant interests in Korea and renounced interference with Japan's policy there.

It is somewhat ironic that the emigration of Koreans took place during this decade of uncertainty and suspense as to the fate of Korea as a nation. One would normally suspect that a government in as much disarray as was the Korean government could not attend to policy matters concerning the emigration of its citizens. Once the destiny of Korea was determined and Japan forced protectorate status upon her, Japan put an end to the immigration of Koreans to America.

By the end of the Sino-Japanese War, two conditions favorable for the immigration of Koreans to America existed. First, the 1882 treaty between the United States and Korea offered Koreans an opportunity to go to America. Second, the Sino-Japanese War uprooted a large number of Koreans, and many of them moved to major port cities in hope of finding employment.

Two other conditions accelerated the immigration of Koreans to the Hawaiian Islands. As Wayne Patterson notes, in the first essay, the Hawaiian Sugar Planters' Association explored the possibility of employing Koreans as laborers on their plantations. Patterson suggests that the planters wanted to replace the Chinese and particularly the Japanese who had become militant in their demand for higher wages and better working conditions. He further suggests that the planters' inquiry was made possible by two conditions: first, one planter's opportunistic reading of an agreement between the planters and the Hawaiian government; second, the possibility of that planter's close relationship with the Russian government. Patterson provides circumstantial links between the Korean immigration request and Russian Far Eastern policy.

Another condition arose in 1901, when a long drought struck the country, as discussed in the second essay, by Yun Yŏ-jun. Anticipating a bad crop in the fall of 1901, the Korean government prepared to cope with a food shortage. Included in these preparations may have been a program for the immigration of Koreans to Hawaii, as later requested by the planters through Horace N. Allen, then American minister to Korea. Another prominent American who played a major role in bringing Korean laborers to the Hawaiian Islands was David Deshler, a friend of Allen and stepson of George K. Nash, governor of Ohio. Allen owed Deshler a political debt, since President McKinley, undoubtedly influenced by his friend Nash, appointed Allen minister to Korea. Deshler had asked Nash to help secure Allen's appointment.

It is not clear when the planters decided to employ Koreans as laborers on sugar plantations. In February 1902, William G. Irwin, a representative of the Hawaiian Sugar Planters' Association, met Allen, then in San Francisco on his way to Korea, to ask about the prospects of importing Koreans to work on the sugar plantations. Once the planters decided to import Korean workers, however, they were willing even to circumvent American immigration laws and pay Koreans to come to America. Many Koreans were unable to pay the nearly fifty dollars steamship fare from Korea to Hawaii. In the past, the planters assisted Japanese and Chinese laborers who wanted to come to Hawaii, but annexation of the Hawaiian Islands to the United States made the practice illegal. Therefore, the planters instructed Deshler to establish a bank in Inchon (the Deshler Bank), which received a steady flow of deposits from the Hawaiian Sugar Planters' Association. These funds were used to lend money to Koreans who wanted to immigrate to Hawaii.

The immigration of Koreans to Hawaii ended in 1905 as abruptly as it had started. Yun Yŏ-jun suggests in his essay a number of possible causes of the stoppage. One is Japanese pressure on the Korean government to discontinue sending Koreans to Hawaii. Given the initial motive of the planters to use Koreans in place of Japanese laborers who demanded higher wages and better working conditions, it is not surprising that the Japanese government wanted to end Korean immigration to Hawaii in order to protect Japanese citizens. However, Yun seems reluctant to conclude decisively that it was the Japanese who were responsible for ending Korean immigration. He suggests that the Korean government might also have been hard pressed by public opinion against its emigration program.

The next two essays, by the editor, describe the political, social, and religious institutions established by Korean immigrants in Hawaii. No matter what motivated them to enter an alien culture—and there were probably as many motives as there were social, religious, economic, and political differences between the immigrants—they all shared one thing: they had to work on sugar plantations for a living. Upon their arrival in Honolulu, Koreans were taken in groups to various plantations and placed in work camps, where they were allowed to maintain a semblance of community life. The first social organization to spring up from the Korean community in Hawaii was the church, established by Koreans converted to Christianity before their departure from their native land. Once established, the church became the organizational backbone of social and political activities in the Korean community. It also became the foundation for the political struggle for Korea's independence from Japanese colonialism. Leaders of the independence movement, such as Syngman Rhee, An Ch'ang-ho, and Pak Yong-man, received moral and financial support for their political activities from various church organizations established both in Hawaii and on the mainland. Therefore, from their inception until 1945, when Korea was liberated from Japan not by Koreans themselves but by external forces over which they had no control, political and religious organizations were inseparably tied to the important task of supporting political efforts to regain Korea's independence. However, this close relationship also served as a catalyst to dissension and conflict within the church. Differences began to develop among leaders of the Korean independence movement over political strategies to be employed against Japan. In retrospect, the independence movement, carried out by a small group of Korean immigrants in America, was insignificant because it failed to make even a dent in America's foreign policy toward Japan, in Japanese treatment of Koreans, or in Japan's international posture toward America. It is, however, remarkable that the leaders of the independence movement were able to keep the issue alive as long as they did by maintaining the flickering hope of returning someday to an independent Korea.

The fifth essay, also by the editor, discusses the historical development of small businesses by Korean immigrants in America. Particularly, it examines the tradition-of-enterprise hypothesis, which is presented by Ivan Light in his book *Ethnic Enterprise in America: Business and Welfare among Chinese, Japanese, and Blacks* as a possible explanation for the business success among Chinese and Japanese immigrants in America. Light suggests that a rotating credit system, which Japanese immigrants brought to their adopted country in the form of *tanomoshi* and Chinese immigrants brought in the form of *hui*, was largely responsible for their success. There are a number of problems with Light's hypothesis; one is the question of how much chance for success small business has in capitalist corporate America. A more crucial problem with the hypothesis, however, is determining how the rotating credit system was used to capitalize business and how much money was capitalized through *tanomoshi* and *hui*. Ivan Light has not provided concrete data on these two vital concerns. In research conducted to determine if Korean immigrants used *kye*, a traditional rotating credit system, it was found that they did not capitalize their businesses by this method. Instead, individual savings were used or the business was capitalized by means of selling stock certificates, a typical Western practice. This is not to discredit Light's hypothesis with regard to business success among Japanese and Chinese immigrants. It is an attempt to point out some of the major problems with a hypothesis which suggests that a cultural deficiency makes some individuals unable to conduct business successfully, while others are successful because of their culture. This kind of thinking puts the blame for failure squarely on the people rather than on the market system in the capitalist economy, where factors other than culture tend to determine success and failure in business.

The last essay, by the editor, attempts to provide some basic data on the number of Korean Americans and their salient demographic characteristics. Because of the nature of the history of Koreans in America, such basic data as birthrate, deathrate, and average size of household are unavailable. It is imperative that the 1980 U.S. census include persons of Korean ancestry as a separate category, so that more detailed information on Korean Americans may be provided to social planners as well as to students of demography.

The First Attempt to Obtain Korean Laborers
for Hawaii, 1896–1897

Wayne Patterson

KOREAN LABORERS FIRST arrived in Hawaii in 1903, to work on the sugar plantations and to substitute for the Chinese and offset the Japanese workers. Yet the first proposal for importing Koreans was made seven years earlier. This essay will focus on that ten-month period from November 1896 to August 1897 and will examine the development of events and attitudes which made Korean laborers sought after by the sugar planters. This initial, and ultimately unsuccessful, proposal contains some interesting ramifications.

After its discovery by Britain's Captain Cook in 1778, Hawaii became a new frontier for American missionaries, whalers, coffee growers, and sugar planters. While the missionaries attempted to change the spiritual climate, the prospering sugar industry was changing the nature of the Hawaiian economy from one of small independent growers to that of large-scale, labor-intensive plantations. By 1835, sugar had replaced coffee as the main crop, a transformation symbolized by the formation of Koloa Plantation on Kauai. From that time forward, sugar was king.

At first, the white sugar planters employed native Hawaiians on a contract-labor basis to man the cane fields. Because the demand for sugar was low in those early years, the growers were able to obtain enough workers. As time passed, two conditions operated

This essay is a revised version of a paper presented to the Columbia University Seminar on Korea, May 17, 1974.

to prevent this situation from becoming static.

The first of these was the decline in population of native Hawaiians and their general reluctance to perform plantation work. In 1836, the population was 108,579. By 1853, the population declined to 73,138. Seven years later, by 1860, only 69,000 Hawaiians remained.[1]

Second, the demand for Hawaiian sugar increased steadily. The market for sugar expanded as gold in California opened the West Coast and, later, as Civil War hostilities began. The result was ever-increasing sugar production.[2]

The decline in population and the increased demand for sugar produced a labor shortage destined to last for more than a century. This shortage, whether real or contrived, was to be the central causative factor in the social, economic, and political history of Hawaii for the next one hundred years. The search for additional sources of labor extended to other countries, and by the end of the century more than 400,000 immigrant laborers had been recruited from thirty-three countries.[3] Korean immigration was destined to play its own special role in this continuing story.

By mid-century the realization of a labor shortage was to bring together the planters and the government in a concerted effort to obtain foreign workers. As the Board of Immigration later reported:

> As early as 1850, it was recognized in Hawaii that the native population was neither willing nor able to supply the labor needed to expand agricultural enterprises, particularly the infant sugar industry, and both the Hawaiian government and the planters were prepared to assist in any way possible the procurement of immigrant workers who would build up a settled citizenry capable of maintaining these industries in the future.[4]

So in 1850, the planters formed the Royal Hawaiian Agricultural Society, to investigate outside sources of labor and promote plantation interests. That same year, the legal system was brought into line with the planters' wishes by the passage of a law to extend the contract-labor system to any foreigners who might enter Hawaii under contract to the sugar planters. The law's provisions—that contracts made in a foreign country for service in Hawaii were binding and that prison sentences would be imposed for failure to fulfill a contract[5]—rendered contract labor similar to indentured servitude in colonial America.

These developments made the sugar planters the single most powerful economic group in Hawaii—a status which continued even after annexation to the United States, when contracts became illegal—and were to leave a legacy of a century of economic, political, and social domination of Asian immigrants by white plantation owners.

Although the planters' society and the government arranged for the first immigrant laborers in 1852, when 293 Chinese from the Canton area came, serious searching for workers did not begin until

1864.[6] On December 30 of that year, the Act to Provide for the Importation of Laborers and for the Encouragement of Immigration was passed. This act created the Board of Immigration, which signified governmental supervision of immigration as a concession to the growing influence of urban centers. Later, in 1882, the growers reorganized, becoming the Planters' Labor and Supply Company, to act as a pressure group pushing the board for a sufficient supply of cheap plantation labor.[7]

Following Dr. William Hillebrand's trip to China in the spring of 1865, Chinese laborers in small numbers began arriving in Hawaii. In general, the planters were pleased with them, calling them "quiet, able and willing men."[8] The influx of Chinese remained relatively slight until 1876. In that year, the Kingdom of Hawaii signed a reciprocity treaty with the United States in which Hawaii was permitted to export sugar duty free to a previously tariff-protected American market. The treaty gave sugar its biggest boost, expanding production tenfold in the following decade.[9] With the new demand for sugar came an increased call from the planters for laborers. The decade between 1876 and 1885 witnessed the greatest influx of Chinese laborers—the total reached 46,000 by 1897.[10]

The arrival of the Chinese marked the beginning of a cycle of plantation labor in Hawaii which was to continue as each new group of immigrant laborers arrived. The Chinese received favorable comment initially, but by the early 1880s they became targets for criticism, mostly from townspeople. As their three-year contracts expired, more and more Chinese moved into the cities, looking for work at low wages, and tradespeople began to complain of unfair competition.

That the Chinese and subsequent immigrants failed to renew their contracts is not surprising. Sugar plantations, which operated as independent fiefdoms, were notorious for unfavorable working conditions: low wages; long workdays begun early; lack of opportunity for promotion; racial discrimination in the better jobs; work in the hot sun and in the rain; laborers' treatment by plantation foremen, police, and doctors; and, in general, a discipline that denied the worker's view of reasonable freedom.[11]

As new arrivals, the Chinese, like the succeeding peoples, were generally more amenable to plantation discipline than those who had been in Hawaii for some time. From the planter's point of view, a system of controls was necessary to keep the worker docile and to ensure the continuous performance of monotonous and physically exhausting labor. Accepting employment in a land several thousand miles from home and among aliens left the new laborer in a dependent state. In addition to language difficulties, immigrants faced ethnic segregation on the plantation, which prevented Americanization. Thus the economic interest of planters in keeping immi-grants on the plantations coincided with the natural inclinations of the immigrants to stick together.[12] Thus in the early years, the immigrants' racial traits were extolled and their critics were few. But once these immigrants responded to the American tradition of individualism and success, the plantation became associated with inferior status, and the immigrants began to leave.

As the Chinese moved to the cities, they became more visible to the urban middle class, who complained to the government that the Chinese were not doing what they were brought to Hawaii to do, that is, to work on the plantations. Other complaints were also registered: they were too different from the Hawaiian race; they smoked opium; they were disease-ridden; the ratio of men to women was too high for comfort; they hindered the Americanization of the Islands; and there were simply too many of them.

The planters were still generally happy with the Chinese laborers, who were docile and did not cause much trouble. Transportation costs were low and a worker's wages amounted to only ten dollars a month. The planters feared only that the Chinese might form a labor monopoly.[13]

But the serious objection was generated by public opinion. By 1882, only 5,000 of the 14,000 Chinese in Hawaii were on planta-tions,[14] and in 1884 they constituted 23 percent of the entire population.[15] Moreover, it was politically expedient, especially for those in power who favored annexation to the United States and who therefore took their cues from the mainland, to substitute another race for the Chinese. Even the planters saw how closely their interests were tied to their biggest market. Both planters and the politically powerful watched closely to see how the United States treated the Chinese.

Although the first Chinese who arrived in the United States in 1847 were students, the mid-1860s saw a great influx of Chinese labor for transcontinental railroad construction. When the railroad was completed, 25,000 Chinese lost their jobs and were dumped onto the western labor market, where they became convenient and highly visible scapegoats in the fluctuating political, social, and economic climate. By 1870, there were 63,000 Chinese in the United States and every tenth person in California was Chinese. The Chinese sought work in mines, farms, factories, and domestic services—jobs which whites scorned but which nonetheless gave the Chinese em-ployment while bonanza-seeking whites were out of work.[16]

The frustrations of the period led to anti-Chinese riots and the first hints of exclusion. Even though the Burlingame Treaty provided for "the inherent right of man to change his home and allegiance and also the mutual advantage of the free migration and emigration . . . from one country to another,"[17] the Chinese Exclusion Act was passed in 1882. The first legislative restriction against Chinese was passed in Hawaii in 1883, the first of four such laws. The pressure was on to find another source of cheap labor.

In 1878, South Sea Islanders were imported, but they did not take to plantation work. Six hundred Norwegians arrived in 1881, and three hundred Germans came between 1882 and 1885, but both proved too expensive to transport and recruit. The most promising non-Oriental laborers seemed to be the Portuguese, who first came in 1878 and eventually numbered about 14,000. Yet the Portuguese were also expensive to transport, demanded higher wages, and seldom renewed their contracts.[18]

While the planters were finding the Portuguese too expensive, others were glad to see white labor entering Hawaii. Those urging Americanization and annexation saw Portuguese workers as a means to offset the increasingly Oriental labor force in Hawaii. These voices became louder and louder as the 1880s drew to a close.

With legislative limitations placed on the number of Chinese permitted to immigrate, with the Portuguese temporarily out of the running, and with the Norwegians, Germans, and South Sea Islanders out of consideration for one reason or another, the planters turned to the Japanese as the most suitable to offset the Chinese. Like the Chinese before them and the Koreans who followed, the initial appraisals of the Japanese were highly flattering: "No better class of people for Laborers could be found than the Japanese race, so accustomed to raising Sugar, Rice, and Cotton, nor one so easily governed, they being peaceable, quiet, and of a pleasant disposition."[19]

The first Japanese arrived in 1868, when 148 were sent illegally by Hawaii's consul-general in Japan, Eugene Van Reed. Three years later Hawaii and Japan signed a treaty, but not until 1885 was emigration from Japan resumed. The first immigrants, aboard the Pacific Mail steamer *City of Tokyo,* landed on February 8, 1885. On board was Hawaii's new consul-general in Japan, Robert Walker Irwin. Irwin, who remained at this post until 1894, supervising immigration matters, formalized an immigration convention on January 28, 1886, which provided for systematic immigration during most of the following decade.[20]

In this way, by the late 1880s, the Japanese became the largest immigrant labor group. By 1890 there were more Japanese than Chinese in Hawaii, and by 1894 the 13,000 Japanese plantation workers represented about three-fifths of the total labor force.[21] The planters were pleased with the Japanese simply because they were so inexpensive to transport to Hawaii, as illustrated by the following figures:

Norwegian	$130
Portuguese	$112
German	$100

South Sea Islander	$ 78.50
Chinese	$ 76.85
Japanese	$ 65.85[22]

As these rates indicate, not only were Orientals less expensive to transport, but the Japanese were the least expensive. At first the Japanese were welcomed by the planters as substitutes for their predecessors, the Chinese, marking the beginning of a conscious policy by the planters of dividing and ruling to prevent a labor monopoly. Later, the Koreans were used in a similar role to offset the Japanese.

Like the Chinese before them, most of the Japanese originally intended to make money in Hawaii and then return home. Yet, like the Chinese, the Japanese stayed on in Hawaii because of weakening home ties, the pleasant climate, and the difficulty of saving enough for the return passage.[23] Also like the Chinese, the Japanese left the plantations and went into other trades, even more quickly, in fact, than the Chinese had.[24] As Japanese laborers moved to the cities, the townspeople, who had welcomed the move by the planters to bring in Japanese because of their apparent better qualities, found themselves in the midst of a proliferation of Japanese shops and food stores, Japanese-language newspapers and schools, and Buddhist temples.[25] By 1894, small businessmen began to complain about Japanese competition.[26]

The planters also became critical of the Japanese, but less so than the rest of the population was. For unlike the patient and docile Chinese, the Japanese were a proud and nationalistic people who would not be pushed around. Consequently, Japanese laborers were quick to take offense at plantation injustices. Even sympathetic accounts of plantation life acknowledge the abuses of the system:

> . . . [T]he employer furnished housing, food, a limited amount of plain furniture and medical attention. The housing was usually in barracks-like buildings and the food was of the plainest sort. If the laborer deserted his work he was likely to be hauled before a police magistrate and fined or imprisoned. On many plantations the laborers were treated with some degree of kindness and consideration, but at best plantation work under the contract system did not attract the better type of laborers nor did it keep them after their contracts had expired. The labor at Koloa Plantation with its military-trained German overseers did not have an easy time and desertions were many and frequent.[27]

The Japanese soon acquired the reputation of difficult and unreliable employees. One manifestation of this reputation was a phenomenon which had not previously occurred—strikes. Although under the contract-labor system strikes were illegal, work stoppages occurred from time to time as the Japanese workers began to stick together. Between 1890 and 1897 there were twenty-nine Japanese-inspired work stoppages,[28] and the rate of desertion reached 6 percent by 1895.[29]

While the planters recognized that the Japanese were cheap to import, the strike actions were a source of consternation. The planters began seeking a solution to the Japanese problem in the same way they had sought to solve the Chinese problem earlier—by pitting one race against another:

> The tendency to strike and desert, which their [Japanese] wellnigh full possession of the labor market fosters, has shown Planters the great importance of having a percentage of their laborers of other nationalities . . . [the Japanese] seize on the smallest grievance, of a real or imaginary nature, to revolt and leave work. . . . For this tendency to strike the only remedy possible is the introduction of some other class of labor to supplement the Japanese.[30]

It was further suggested:

> Strikes will continue as long as men combine, and the only measures that can be taken which may be effectual to any extent, are those which will reduce their opportunities for combination and their inclination for same. . . . It seems to me that this can be done by employing as many nationalities as possible on each plantation. If immigrants of various nationalities would come in until there are sufficient of them in the country to offset one nationality, we would then be better off.[31]

In addition to complaints from the planters, adverse public opinion forced the government to take notice of the problems. As the numbers of Japanese in Hawaii grew, the Hawaiian government became aware of the power of Japan, which was strong enough to make demands and protest vigorously in defense of its subjects in Hawaii—a role which the weaker Chinese government was unable to fulfill. Rumors that Japan wanted to annex Hawaii began to circulate.

The large Japanese population was also a threat to the political dominance of the white propertied class in Hawaii, which made its move for supremacy in the late 1880s and early 1890s. To this end, barriers to Japanese political participation were maintained, while the Japanese government suggested strongly in 1894 that the Japanese be given voting rights and more holidays. With the powerful Japanese navy lurking in the background, tensions rose, providing impetus to those who urged annexation as the only course to ward off this threat from Japan.

The white middle class and the annexationists had made their biggest move in 1887, when they forced the Hawaiian royalty to accept constitutional amendments limiting the power of the monarchy. Six years later, in 1893, the monarchy was overthrown and on July 4 of the following year the Republic of Hawaii was inaugurated with Sanford B. Dole as president.[32] When President Grover Cleveland advised the new government to restore the monarchy, the new government realized that annexation would not occur at least until after the 1896 American presidential election.

The change in government did not alter the problems faced by the planters and the (new) government concerning the Japanese. In 1894, following the departure of Irwin from his post of consul-general in Japan, emigration companies began to take over the sending of Japanese to Hawaii. These emigration companies had agents in Hawaii who dealt directly with the financial conglomerates involved in the sugar industry. Controversy raged over the unlawful sending of immigrants, and the consequent rejections of immigrants were a major issue in Hawaiian-Japanese relations. At the same time, a bill against sake added to the strain between the two countries.[33]

So it looked as if the Hawaiian government was taking the same attitude toward the Japanese in the mid-1890s as it had toward the Chinese in the mid-1880s. Yet the planters, who were not as anti-Japanese as the government, were wary of any plan which would deny them access to this supply of cheap labor. They wanted to make sure that there was always sufficient labor because the greater the supply of labor, the easier it was to keep wages low. The government vacillated as crosscutting interests were involved in the decision. This was because the government and the planters shared many of the same concerns and, often, even personnel. For among the proannexationists in Hawaii were the planters, who would profit from a further increase in the demand for sugar. While a segment of the public was convinced that annexation would bring a halt to the Orientalization of the Islands by encouraging white labor to come, the planters were to insist that they too wanted white labor for their plantations. But their economic interests interfered with their civic responsibilities as white labor would mean less profit. The interconnectedness of the government and the planting interests, which included the financial brokers behind the growers, often meant that governmental decisions were made with one eye on the planters.

The situation as defined called for the importation of other immigrant groups to offset the Japanese, just as the Japanese had been imported ten years earlier to offset the Chinese. So the government and the planters agreed that until the Japanese problem was settled, different laborers should be sought, principally from two groups: the Chinese, who had never really stopped coming to the Islands; and the whites, who could halt the increasing Orientalization of Hawaii.

In reopening Chinese immigration, the government and the planters were treading on thin ice. While the planters retained a certain nostalgia for the patient and industrious Chinese, especially in light of their more recent experiences with Japanese workers, political considerations made the new immigration of Chinese risky at best.

For one thing, annexation was almost a certainty, and the Chinese would be prohibited from immigrating by the laws of the United States, specifically the Chinese Exclusion Act.

Second, public opinion in Hawaii was not in favor of the renewed immigration. "Fort Street will come to resemble the business quarter of Amoy, Foochow, or Canton, and white civilization will be submerged," read an 1895 editorial.[34] Third, by advocating Chinese immigration the government was undercutting its own political support. The American Union Party, which was naturally proannexationist like the government, inserted an anti-Oriental immigration plank into its party platform.[35] Finally, statutory obstacles presented problems. An 1892 law limited the number of Chinese immigrants to 5,000 a year.

Nevertheless, the government and the planters agreed to a specific formula regarding the Chinese in April 1896. They agreed that the planters would try to import Asian laborers at the proportion of one-third Japanese and two-thirds Chinese, following President Dole's comment that "public opinion feels the competition of Japanese to be more keen than the Chinese and we should adopt a policy in which Chinese should be preferred to Japanese."[36]

The proportions agreed upon were generally adhered to as the planters began to ask for more Chinese. Between May 1, 1896, and May 1, 1897, 4,307 Chinese and 2,702 Japanese arrived. This two-to-one ratio obtained until the government had a change of heart and decided to halt all Chinese immigration in May 1897, one year prior to annexation, when it became mandatory. The Japanese again began arriving in full strength,[37] but by this time the troubles with the Japanese government had ended and with the election of William McKinley in November 1896, annexation and therefore white dominance were assured.

The second step toward counterbalancing the Japanese was a strenuous attempt to induce white labor to work on the sugar plantations. Naturally the planters, who wanted cheap Oriental labor, were not enthusiastic supporters of any government plan to obtain European labor, since transportation costs were higher and Caucasian field hands generally received higher pay than Asians doing the same work.[38]

Despite objections from the planters, the government felt constrained to attempt to bring in whites to placate a public which was generally critical of continued Asian immigration. To that purpose Europeans were offered better housing than Asians, with the former getting semiprivate rooms while the latter lived in barracks with six to forty men in a single large room.[39] In 1895, furthermore, Americans were even offered land as an inducement. Italians were approached as were Germans. But the latter were unwilling to work for such low wages (Europeans got eighteen to twenty dollars a month while Asians got fifteen). Other Europeans were unsatisfactory because they were not agricultural laborers.[40]

However, for one reason or another, the government decided that the best chance to get European labor lay with the Portuguese, who, we will remember, had been tried earlier. In May 1894 an attempt was made to reopen Portuguese emigration from the Azores. This involved an agreement with the government by the planters to pay $100 toward the total cost of $240 and half the cost for women, who would make up one-quarter of the total, and children. Families were preferred to single men, to promote stability and prevent moves to California, where wages were higher. Other inducements included a house worth about $400 and an acre of land, to encourage homesteading.

In a more far-reaching compromise, on August 20, 1895, the government persuaded the planters to agree to a proposal that 20 percent of the total number of immigrants be Portuguese laborers.[41] Yet just as before, problems arose. Cannavaro, the Portuguese commissioner, indicated that he would discourage Portuguese from immigrating because of the poor working conditions and low wages.[42]

As it became clear that the Portuguese would not be coming, the 20 percent agreement between the government and the planters was reduced to 10 percent and modified to include American or European laborers. The agreement stated:

> That permits hereafter granted to employers for the introduction of Asiatic agricultural laborers (*either Chinese or Japanese*) to be upon the following conditions: First. Before such permits are granted the employer shall bind himself to introduce into this country a number of European or American agricultural laborers equal in number to not less than ten percent (10%) of the number of permits for Asiatic laborers granted him at any one time or from time to time.[43]

On November 2, 1896, President Dole and two of his cabinet members, Samuel Mills Damon, minister of finance, and James A. King, minister of the interior and president of the Board of Immigration, met in a session of the Executive Council. To this meeting they had invited two men who had a proposition to make: Johann Friederich Hackfeld, vice-president of H. Hackfeld and Company; and Constantine M. Grunwaldt. According to Recording Secretary R. L. Marx. "The meeting was called for the purpose of discussing a proposition from Mr. Grunwaldt to import Koreans into the Hawaiian Islands to substitute Chinese and Japanese agricultural laborers."[44]

Although detailed records are not available, the session was presumably an informational one in which Grunwaldt indicated his ability to obtain Korean laborers and emphasized the benefits of using

Koreans instead of the Chinese, who would soon be prohibited entirely by annexation, and the Japanese, who were lately causing so much trouble. And as Orientals, the Koreans would still be cheap labor. According to the minutes, "The matter was discussed at length but no action taken in the matter."[45]

Later that day the Executive Council met again to consider the proposal and to make a decision. Hackfeld and Grunwaldt were absent from this meeting and a third member of Dole's cabinet, William Owen Smith, the attorney general, was present. Again, according to the recording secretary:

> The meeting was called for the purpose of discussing the decision of the Government in regard to Korean laborers.
>
> The following Resolution was adopted—
>
> Resolved, That the Government look favorably upon the proposition to import Korean laborers, but will await applications from the Planters.
>
> That the Government will assume no further responsibility than simply consenting to grant permits upon the same terms for which permits are granted for Chinese and Japanese.[46]

Following this favorable action, Hackfeld presumably would present applications for Koreans at subsequent meetings of the Board of Immigration. Yet in board meetings held in the year following that November 2 meeting—namely, meetings held on February 9, April 14, May 7, and August 2, 1897—although applications were made by Hackfeld for Chinese and Japanese as usual, there is no record of any request for Koreans, either from Hackfeld or from any other planter.[47]

How can we explain Hackfeld's sudden lack of interest in importing Koreans? At first glance, it appears that Hackfeld changed his mind when the government decided "to grant permits upon the same terms for which permits are granted for Chinese and Japanese." A careful reading of the agreement between the planters and the government reveals that Hackfeld might have avoided the 10 percent stipulation by importing Koreans, for they were not, after all, Chinese or Japanese. Hackfeld apparently thought that he could save himself the expense of bringing in more costly white labor by importing Koreans. But as the government saw through Hackfeld's plan, we might plausibly conclude that Hackfeld's subsequent noninterest was the result of the government's classification of Koreans as Asiatic agricultural laborers subject to the 10 percent rule. And so it seems, ironically, that the campaign to induce immigration of white laborers may have supplied at least part of the impetus for Hackfeld's Korean laborers proposal.

It will be instructive to examine more closely Hackfeld's company. H. Hackfeld and Company, the predecessor of American Factors

Ltd. or Amfac in modern Hawaii, was established in Bremen, Germany, by Heinrich Hackfeld in 1849. By the early 1880s, eighteen major sugar plantations, more than one-third of Hawaii's total, were being financed by German money from Hackfeld. The company was well on its way to becoming one of the celebrated Big Five, which were to dominate Hawaii's economy.[48]

By 1896, H. Hackfeld and Company, Sugar Factors, Importers and General Commission Agents, as it was known, operated a far-flung financial empire. For not only was the Hackfeld company the agent for numerous sugar plantations, it was also agent for two insurance companies and five intercontinental shipping lines, including Pacific Mail Steamship Company, Occidental and Oriental Steamship Company, and Toyo Kisen Kaisha—lines which specialized in transporting, among other things, labor immigrants from Asia to Hawaii. As agent for sugar plantations and shipping lines, including the interisland steamer service, Hackfeld was involved in all phases of procuring and transporting immigrant labor.[49]

From offices at the corner of Fort and Queen streets, the Hackfeld company determined the needs of sugar companies which it represented and relayed the labor request (after approval by the government) to recruiters in China or to the private emigration companies now operating in Japan.[50] So it was certainly within Hackfeld's usual functions to propose the importation of Korean laborers, especially if Hackfeld thought he could get around the 10 percent rule.

Hackfeld usually worked with the Japanese Emigration Company of Hiroshima[51] but occasionally corresponded with K. Ogura and Company and others. In addition to Honolulu, Ogura had offices in Osaka and Kobe, Japan, and Pusan and Inchon, Korea. Evidently, the Ogura company also dealt in the recruiting of Korean laborers to work in Japan.[52] Although there is no documentation linking Hackfeld's proposal to the Ogura company, we should not dismiss this possibility.

We must now turn to events which occurred eight months later, in July 1897, to examine in more detail the context in which the Koreans were discussed. Such examination may provide further clues for understanding the nature of Hackfeld's proposal. We shall see that in the period following Hackfeld's Korean proposal some planters and government officials had done some thinking about the Koreans.

At 2:10 on the afternoon of July 9, 1897, there was a meeting of the Advisory Council—a slightly larger decision-making body than the Executive Council. Present were Ministers Cooper and Smith and, by invitation, Swanzy, Tenney, Giffard, Houghtailing, Louisson, Robertson, and Hackfeld:[53]

> In the absence of President Dole, Minister Cooper stated: That it [is] the desire of the Executive to meet the Planters for the purpose of talking over

the labor proposition, and went on to say that the Executive would like to know about what would be the number of laborers required on the plantations for the next six months. Then Mr. Cooper stated that with the Treaty of Annexation signed by the Plenipotentiaries of the two countries the Government felt rather delicate in sending for any more Chinese;* so far as the Japanese are concerned there has been no intimation, officially, as to the stopping of laborers from Japan; as to what the future situation might be was not known, but it was desired to talk with these gentlemen on the subject and advise them fully of what might be before them.

President Dole then entered.

Mr. Smith cited the situation as set forth by Mr. Cooper and went on to state that in case a change had to be made in laborers why would it not be advisable to try Koreans? That Mr. Hackfeld some months ago had had some dealings or talk with a Russian Gentleman in regard to these laborers and this might be a wise move.

Mr. Tenney stated that he had heard that the Planters would be allowed to apply for Japanese laborers and that no restriction would be placed upon them.

Dole: Is this report authoritative that Japan has allowed immigration to begin again?

Hackfeld: I don't know. I only heard it from the representatives of the Japanese Emigration Company of Hiroshima.

Tenney: We have been approached by one or two of the members of the immigration companies informing us that they could secure us any number of Japanese laborers that we required.

Mr. Louisson stated that he had been approached by the agents of different companies in like manner.

The matter of the correspondence in regard to Chinese immigration exceeding that of Japanese, and the restrictions of such immigration being limited to the number that were in the country at the time the convention of 1886 was signed was brought up,** and President Dole stated that this might in itself necessitate the Government's not accepting any more applications for Chinese laborers.

Mr. Smith stated that Mr. Shimamura† had been informed that the resolution passed by the Executive some months ago that 2/3 Chinese and 1/3 Japanese was not now in force as there was no necessity for it now, the number being more equally divided.

Mr. Swanzy asked what action the Executive would be disposed to take in regard to the Planters importing American Negroes?***

Dole: I do not think the Government would interpose any objections if the experiment were made.

Swanzy: While no action at all has been taken by the Planters here for getting Negroes the subject has been brought up several times and we might try the experiment.

---

*The last request for Chinese had been approved three months earlier at the April 14 meeting of the Board of Immigration (see note 37).

**This refers to Irwin's 1886 immigration convention with Japan. Japan had complained to the Hawaiian government that the two-thirds and one-third ratio violated the treaty.

† H. Shimamura was the consul-general of Japan in Hawaii. He had served as secretary to the Japanese legation in Seoul. Fred Harvey Harrington, *God Mammon and the Japanese: Dr. Horace N. Allen and Korean-American Relations, 1884–1905* (Madison: University of Wisconsin Press, 1944), p. 22.

***There had been objections to suggestions of using blacks at least two years earlier. *Pacific Commercial Advertiser*, February 11, 1895.

Smith: Mr. Hackfeld, aside from the information received from that Russian Gentleman was there no other information to be obtained?

Hackfeld: We have no other information, but could write for it.

Cooper: Would the Japanese influence have any weight there?

Mr. Hackfeld and Mr. Swanzy both stated that they were quite sure it would not.

Cooper: How about the Japanese that have already been ordered? Are they coming?

Swanzy: I believe they are coming, yes.

Tenney: Mr. Boardman told me that he had received a communication from Japan to that effect.

Giffard: We have a letter from the Emigration Company here stating that Mr. Shimamura had stated that applications would be endorsed by him prior to being sent.

Cooper: Is there likely to be a very large demand for laborers during this next six months?

Swanzy: I do not know. That could be easily ascertained.

Giffard: We need about two hundred between now and January to fill our demands.

Dole: What becomes of all the Japanese laborers whose time expires in June? Do not a good many of these reship?

Swanzy: It is very seldom that they reship.

Dole: We wished to call you here today that we might have the benefit of your views on the subject as we wish in every way possible to assist the Planters in the ways of immigration.

Swanzy: I think a good many applications for Chinese have gone in lately, but if we understand that the immigration with Japan has not been interfered with, I think the Planters would be willing to withdraw these applications and send in applications for Japanese instead.

Mr. Smith asked if it would be practicable or desirable to try Portuguese again.

Dole: We think it is desirable to try these Koreans.

Swanzy: We have no reliable information, as far as we know, in regard to Negroes, *but have a letter or letters from a man who says he can supply us with such labor and I do not doubt but that he can.**

Mr. Smith favored the idea of making investigations in regard to getting Negroes in a limited number at first and trying them.

President Dole favored this plan also.

Hackfeld: Then the best plan would be for us to leave the applications in abeyance until the end of the month?

Dole: If you would do that we would notify you before the end of the month as to what our views are, or what changes, if any, the situation has taken.

Swanzy: Do you wish to know what the requirements in numbers are?

Dole: Any information you can give us we would be glad to have.

Mr. Hackfeld stated that he had recently written to this Russian Gentleman and would probably hear from him in the near future.

Adjourned.[54]

Seven weeks later, on August 27, 1897, the Executive Council

---

*In this statement by Swanzy, the phrase "such labor" here probably refers to Koreans in the context of a reply to President Dole's preceding statement in favor of trying Koreans. Notice that Swanzy is convinced that the man is in a position to deliver what he promised.

met to decide about importing Koreans. Present at this meeting were President Dole, Ministers Cooper, King, and Smith, and Francis M. Hatch, W.E. Rowell, and B.F. Dillingham.[55] The minutes record that "in the matter of the application of H. Hackfeld and Company to have the Board of Immigration approve the importation of Korean laborers under contract, a motion was made and carried that the Executive do not approve of the granting of such permits at the present time."[55]

Since no reason is given for this action and the person making the motion is not identified, we can only speculate on the reason for the disapproval. One logical guess is that, with annexation recently assured and the troubles with Japan over, it would be better not to begin importing another Oriental race into Hawaii.

At this point, further investigation into Hackfeld's proposal might seem pointless, for indeed there exists no additional documentation which would suggest any definite link between Hackfeld and the Koreans. Yet a close examination of that July 9 meeting and a look at simultaneous events in Korea will lead us to some rather surprising hypotheses.

One way to develop these hypotheses is to make some educated guesses about the identity of the mysterious Constantine M. Grunwaldt, where he came from, and his relationship, if any, to Hackfeld. We will remember that it was Grunwaldt who, in November 1896, with J. F. Hackfeld at his side, first proposed the importation of Koreans. During the July 1897 meeting Hackfeld indicated that he could write for more information, indicating that this person (Grunwaldt) was not in Hawaii. A check of all editions of Hawaiian directories from 1880 to 1900 shows that Grunwaldt was not a resident.

Where was Grunwaldt from and what was his nationality? His surname indicates that he could have been German. Yet if he were German and came from Hackfeld company headquarters in Bremen, Germany, it is difficult to suggest how he might have any ties with Korea. It is also conceivable that Grunwaldt was Russian. Here we might remind ourselves that at the July 1897 meeting Smith asked Hackfeld about a certain Russian Gentleman with whom he had had some dealings or talk some months earlier. If it had been eight months earlier (November 1896), then we might justifiably conjecture that this mysterious Grunwaldt was indeed that Gentleman.

Having established the Gentleman's identity, we must now determine his location. It is reasonable to assume that he came from and returned to, not Russia, but Korea; he had recently come to Hawaii to advertise the availability of Koreans for work on the plantations. So let us assume that Grunwaldt was a Russian who had just come from Korea.

Remembering Swanzy's comment during the July 1897 meeting

regarding his confidence in this person who promised to deliver Koreans, we might also surmise that Grunwaldt was rather prominent in Korea and in a position to make such an offer of Korean immigrants. Before turning to Grunwaldt's relationship with J.F. Hackfeld, let us pursue a second avenue of inquiry—that involving events transpiring in Korea at this time.

Japan had recently defeated China in a war over control of Korea. Yet the Japanese were having trouble consolidating their rule because of problems with the ruling family, especially Queen Min. The Japanese minister in Seoul, Miura, tried to rid Korea of Queen Min's influence by conspiring with Japanese soldiers in the city to raid the palace. During the raid, in 1895, Queen Min was killed.

Miura's responsibility was quickly ascertained and he was immediately replaced by Komura Jutarō.[57] The result of the entire affair was a distinct blow to Japanese hopes and prestige in Korea. King Kojong and the crown prince, fearing for their lives, accepted an offer of sanctuary from the Russian legation in Seoul and entered into residence there on February 11, 1896. The king was to remain there for a little more than a year, until February 23, 1897.

With Kojong in the Russian legation, the Japanese lost their hold on the Korean government and not surprisingly this Japanese decline coincided with a Russian ascendancy in Seoul. In March 1896, Russia negotiated an agreement with the Korean representative to the Tsar's coronation, Min Yŏng-hwan,[58] placing itself in a position, through advice, of directing the policies of the Korean government.[59]

As a result of this situation, the Russian minister to Korea, C. Waeber, became the most important man in Korea next to the king and inherited the advisory position previously held by the Chinese and Japanese ministers, respectively. One American diplomat stated, "I only know that the king and cabinet defer to Russian opinion in matters of consequence . . . the king seems to govern with Russia behind the throne."[60]

With the Russians firmly entrenched, the Korean government, undoubtedly spurred by Waeber's advice, began to make numerous economic concessions to various foreign powers, a turnabout from previous Korean policy. In late August 1896, Russia got a timber concession on the Tumen and Yalu rivers. The concession for the construction of the Seoul-Ŭiju Railroad went to the French. The Seoul-Inchon Railroad concession, originally scheduled to go to the Japanese, was given to Morse, an American, in 1896. Morse also received a mining concession in Hamkyŏng province. Another mining concession went to a German syndicate, an American was placed in charge of a normal school, and the British were named advisor to the police department.[61]

It was Waeber's policy to spread concessions around in order to counteract the influence of the Japanese—a policy which was to be advocated by Horace Allen several years later when he became U.S. minister to Korea; giving as many countries as possible a stake in Korea would prevent the domination of Korea by any one country. So liberal were Waeber and Kojong in doling out concessions that one historian has suggested that Waeber was replaced because despite the preponderance of Russian influence at the Korean Court, too many concessions were being given to other countries.[62] Consequently Waeber, who was pro-American and a good friend of Horace Allen, then secretary of the American legation,[63] was gradually eased out by the anti-American Alexis de Speyer, who stated that no Korean official friendly to the Americans would be retained in office.[64] Speyer's abusive tactics and manner caused Russian influence, which had been greatest while Waeber was in charge, to drop considerably.[65]

Such were the events in Korea when Hackfeld's Korean immigration proposal was being discussed in Hawaii. It is evident that Hackfeld's request in November 1896 came at a time when a pro-American Russian advisor, whose policies encouraged concessions to various foreign governments, became the paramount force in Korea. It is not inconceivable that Waeber would have granted an emigration concession to Hackfeld, a German company operating in the Republic of Hawaii, which would soon be annexed by the United States. Such a move would certainly have been consistent with Waeber's and, therefore, Russia's policy toward Korea.

Here it might be useful to recall the portion of the July 9 meeting dialogue in which Minister Cooper asked if the Japanese influence would have any weight in enabling Koreans to come to Hawaii. Both Hackfeld and Swanzy replied that they were quite sure that it would not. Their definite answer might well reflect knowledge, supplied by Grunwaldt, that Russia and not Japan was in the driver's seat in Korea.

This entire scenario becomes even more plausible when we combine the foregoing events in Korea and the probable identity of Constantine Grunwaldt as a Russian prominent in Korea with our final clue. Why was it the Hackfeld company that got the concession? Why not one of the other financial houses in Hawaii? The clue to Hackfeld's Korean-Russian connection lies in the role of J.F. Hackfeld himself.

J.F. Hackfeld was born in 1856 in Germany and came to Hawaii at the age of twenty-one to work as a cashier in his uncle's business. By 1881 he had risen to the position of partner with Paul Isenberg and H.F. Glade, who later became Hawaiian consul to Germany. By the mid-1890s, J.F. Hackfeld was best known as vice-president of H. Hackfeld and Company. Almost overlooked were a number of relatively minor political roles which he performed. Apparently Hackfeld served as the consul-general in Hawaii for several countries: Germany, Belgium, Austria-Hungary, and Russia.[66]

The confluence of these clues and incredible coincidences leads us to interpret Grunwaldt's visit offering Korean immigrants to Hawaii in late 1896 as a diplomatic mission from the Russian minister in Korea, Waeber, to the Russian consul-general in Honolulu, Hackfeld, for the purpose of furthering Russian Far Eastern policy.

This sequence of events may also help explain why the move to import Koreans was rejected in August 1897. As mentioned; the last item in the July 9 meeting was Hackfeld's statement that he had recently written to the Russian Gentleman (Grunwaldt) and that he would be hearing from him shortly. If Hackfeld had indeed heard from him within the seven weeks which elapsed between the July 9 meeting and the August 27 decision against importing Koreans, chances are that the news was negative; by that time Speyer had taken over in Korea and put an end to the concessions which had been flowing freely from the hands of Waeber the year before. If Hackfeld passed this presumably negative news on to the Executive Council, their negative ruling makes a little more sense.

Unfortunately, we will never know with certainty what transpired. Checking with Amfac revealed that the correspondence of Hackfeld no longer exists. Efforts to place Grunwaldt among the handful of Russians in Korea at that time (there were thirteen in 1892), by referring to the *Krasnyi Arkhiv*, were unsuccessful.[67] The minutes of the Hawaiian Sugar Planters' Association yielded no information. The Hatch papers in the Archives of Hawaii contain no mention of the Korean proposal. Finally, the diary and private correspondence of F.M. Swanzy, in the possession of his daughter, Mrs. James P. Morgan of Honolulu, contain no reference to Grunwaldt or Hackfeld's Korean proposal.

Notes

1. F. Hilary Conroy, *The Japanese Expansion into Hawaii, 1868–1898* (San Francisco: R. and E. Research Associates, 1973), p. 13. See also his *The Japanese Frontier in Hawaii, 1868–1898* (Berkeley: University of California Press, 1953).

2. Sugar production figures were:

1837	4,286 pounds
1847	594,816
1857	700,556

| 1863 | 5,292,121 |
| 1867 | 17,127,161 |

See Katherine Coman, "The History of Contract Labor in the Hawaiian Islands," *Publications of the American Economic Association* 4:3 (August 1903): 65.

3. Andrew W. Lind, *Hawaii's People*, 3d ed. (Honolulu: University of Hawaii Press, 1967), pp. 8, 19.

4. *First Report*, Board of Immigration to the Governor of the Territory of Hawaii (under act of April 24, 1905) for the period April 27, 1905, to January 31, 1907 (Honolulu, 1907), p. 3.

5. *Penal Code of the Hawaiian Islands* (Honolulu, 1850), pp. 174–75.

6. Conroy, *Japanese Expansion*, p. 16. The Chinese had five-year contracts which provided for wages of three dollars per month with free passage, food, and lodging.

7. The Planters' Labor and Supply Company was succeeded by the Hawaiian Sugar Planters' Association in 1895. The name remains the same today.

8. Coman, "History of Contract Labor," p. 12; Conroy, *Japanese Expansion*, p. 16.

9. *Third Report of the Commission of Labor in Hawaii, 1905* (Washington, D.C.: Government Printing Office, 1906). See also William A. Russ, Jr., "Hawaiian Labor and Immigration Problems Before Annexation," *Journal of Modern History* 15:3 (September 1943): 207–22.

10. Richard A. Liebes, "Labor Organization in Hawaii: A Study of the Efforts of Labor to Obtain Security Through Organization" (M.A. thesis, University of Hawaii, 1938), p. 11.

11. Andrew W. Lind, "Economic Succession and Racial Invasion in Hawaii" (Ph.D. diss., University of Chicago, 1931), p. 329. See also Romanzo Adams, *The Peoples of Hawaii* (Honolulu: University of Hawaii Press, 1933), p. 35.

12. Andrew W. Lind, *An Island Community: Ecological Succession in Hawaii* (Chicago: University of Chicago Press, 1938), p. 309.

13. Liebes, "Labor Organization in Hawaii," p. 12.

14. Conroy, *Japanese Expansion*, p. 82.

15. Lind, *Hawaii's People*, p. 27. For a good look at the Chinese in Hawaii, see Tin-yuke Char, ed. and comp., *The Sandalwood Mountains* (Honolulu: University of Hawaii Press, 1975).

16. Betty Lee Sung, *The Story of the Chinese in America* (New York: Collier Books, 1967), pp. 11–42. This book was originally titled *Mountain of Gold* (New York: Macmillan, 1967).

17. Sung, *Story of the Chinese in America*, pp. 47–49.

18. Liebes, "Labor Organization in Hawaii," p. 11.

19. Quoted in Masaji Marumoto, " 'First Year' Immigrants to Hawaii and Eugene Van Reed," in Hilary Conroy and T. Scott Miyakawa, eds., *East Across the Pacific: Historical and Sociological Studies of Japanese Immigration and Assimilation* (Santa Barbara: ABC-Clio, 1972), p. 14.

20. Yukiko Irwin and Hilary Conroy, "R. W. Irwin and Systematic Immigration to Hawaii," in Conroy and Miyakawa, eds., *East Across the Pacific*, pp. 47–48.

21. Conroy, *Japanese Expansion*, pp. 122–23.

22. Coman, "History of Contract Labor," p. 35.

23. Conroy, *Japanese Expansion*, pp. 126–27. That the Japanese came with the intention of remaining in Hawaii is suggested by the higher ratio of women to men than among the Chinese. See Lind, *Hawaii's People*, p. 26.

24. Lind, *An Island Community*, p. 254.

25. Conroy, *Japanese Expansion*, pp. 145–46.

26. Russ, "Hawaiian Labor," p. 213.

27. Arthur C. Alexander, *Koloa Plantation, 1835–1935: A History of the Oldest*

Hawaiian Sugar Plantation (Honolulu: Honolulu Star-Bulletin Ltd., 1937), p. 99.
28.   The breakdown of the strikes is:

1890	2	1894	4
1891	5	1895	3
1892	2	1896	3
1893	4	1897	6

See John E. Reineke, "Labor Disturbances in Hawaii, 1890–1925: A Summary," typescript (Honolulu, 1966).

29.   Lind, *An Island Community*, p. 225.

30.   *Planters Monthly*, 1894, p. 493.

31.   Republic of Hawaii, *Report of the Labor Commission on Strikes and Arbitration* (Honolulu, 1895), pp. 23–24. The speaker is an unidentified plantation manager. The report recognized that injustice and bad treatment existed under contract labor and that the employer had the advantage.

32.   Dole became governor of the Territory of Hawaii upon annexation and presided over the successful importation of Koreans in 1903.

33.   For more on the sake law and rejections of immigrants, see Conroy, *Japanese Expansion*, ch. 11.

34.   *Hawaiian Star*, February 1, 1895.

35.   *Hawaiian Star*, April 9, 1894.

36.   Foreign Office and Executive (hereafter F.O. and Ex.), *Immigration, 1896*, Archives of Hawaii (Honolulu). Dole said this at a meeting of a committee of the planters and the Executive Council on March 11, 1896. Representing the planters were Edward D. Tenney, C. Bolte, and J.F. Hackfeld, who formed the Committee on Labor of the Hawaiian Sugar Planters' Association (HSPA). See C. Bolte, Secretary of the HSPA, to Cooper, Minister of Foreign Affairs, March 28, 1896, in F.O. and Ex., *Immigration, 1896*. The March 11, 1896, meeting was called to urge the planters to ask for more Chinese—presently more Japanese than Chinese were being applied for. Hackfeld, speaking for the planters, agreed and said they would cooperate.

37.   The following figures were reported at subsequent meetings of the Board of Immigration:

Date	Japanese	Chinese
March 26, 1896	0	920
May 1	1001	901
May 7	0	0
Aug. 5	550	997
Oct. 31	426	824
Feb. 9, 1897	334	626
April 14	391	959
Aug. 2	1298	0
Nov. 5	822	0
Dec. 13	795	0

See Board of Immigration, *Minutes, 1879–1899*, Archives of Hawaii, pp. 321–34. Notice that no requests were made for Chinese after May 1897 in accordance with the government decision. Thus a two-to-one ratio of Chinese to Japanese was maintained as per the planter-government agreement. Compare the 2,702 arrivals noted with the previous year period, which saw 9,195 Japanese arrive. See Conroy, *Japanese Expansion*, pp. 165–66. Although no Chinese arrived after May 1897, this was not the last heard of the Chinese. In 1921, the planters wanted to import Chinese to relieve another labor shortage. When the request was denied by the U.S. Congress, the planters tried to import Filipinos. See Liebes, "Labor Organization in Hawaii," pp. 38–39; Lind, "Economic Succession and Racial Invasion in Hawaii," p. 295; John

E. Reineke, "Feigned Necessity: Hawaii's Attempt to Obtain Chinese Contract Labor, 1921–1923," typescript (Honolulu, 1968).

38.   Liebes, "Labor Organization in Hawaii," p. 23. Compare transportation costs table, Liebes, p. 6.

39.   Wray Taylor, Secretary of the Board of Immigration, to E.A. Mott-Smith, Minister of Foreign Affairs, November 20, 1899, in "Conditions of Hawaiian Labor," Archives of Hawaii, pp. 1–12.

40.   F.O. and Ex., *Immigration, 1896*, March 11, 1896.

41.   Conroy, *Japanese Expansion*, p. 162.

42.   F.O. and Ex., *Immigration, 1896*, March 11, 1896.

43.   Emphasis added. This revised proposal, which first appeared with the title "The Proposition to be Made to the HSPA," indicates that the agreement was initiated by the government. It appeared as an undated separate sheet following the minutes of an Executive Council meeting on March 11, 1896, and preceding the next entry, dated March 28. The March 28 document was a letter from C. Bolte to Henry Cooper, and it contained a similar version of the agreement. F.O. and Ex., *Immigration, 1896*. There is no way to determine exactly when the revised agreement went into effect. For example, the 20 percent agreement was apparently still in force at the March 26 Board of Immigration meeting. Board of Immigration, *Minutes, 1879–1899*, p. 321. A reference in a letter from Bolte to Cooper dated September 23, 1896, states that the agreement was reached on September 17 at an Executive Council meeting. Interior Department, *Immigration, 1865–1899*, Archives of Hawaii, Miscellaneous, File 51. The agreement appears again in a letter from William O. Smith, Attorney General, to C. Bolte, dated October 27, 1896. F.O. and Ex., *Immigration, 1896*. See also Interior Department, *Immigration, 1865–1899*. On October 31, 1896, the agreement was put into operation for the first time at a Board of Immigration meeting. Board of Immigration, *Minutes, 1879–1899*, pp. 326–27. The planters had to submit requests to the Executive Council for permission for labor entry permits. The Executive Council decisions were carried out by the Board of Immigration. The president of the board, James A. King, was a member of the Executive Council as minister of the interior. Although the planters posted bonds to guarantee a white labor inflow of 10 percent, they were unable to reach that figure and forfeited their bonds in 1898. Two days after the October 31, 1896, meeting of the Board of Immigration, the first request for Koreans was made to the Executive Council.

44.   Executive and Cabinet Council, *Minutes, April 16, 1895–December 3, 1896*, Archives of Hawaii, p. 174 (November 2, 1896).

45.   Executive and Cabinet Council, *Minutes, April 16, 1895–December 3, 1896*, p. 174.

46.   Executive and Cabinet Council, *Minutes, April 16, 1895–December 3, 1896*, p. 174.

47.   Board of Immigration, *Minutes, 1879–1899*, pp. 328–32. Hackfeld was present at the May 7 meeting.

48.   Jared G. Smith, *The Big Five* (Honolulu: Advertiser Publishing Company Ltd., 1944), ch. 6, unpaginated. See also William A. Simonds, *Kamaaina—A Century in Hawaii* (Honolulu: American Factors Ltd., 1949). In addition to Amfac (Hackfeld), the other companies comprising the Big Five were Alexander and Baldwin, Theo. H. Davies and Company, C. Brewer and Company, and Castle and Cooke Ltd.

49.   Hackfeld's holdings included the following:

Sugar Companies: Lihue Plantation Company
Grove Farm Plantation Company
Hanamaulu Sugar Plantation
Koloa Sugar Company
Kekaha Sugar Company
Meier and Kruse Plantation

H.P. Faye and Company's Plantation
Hawaiian Commercial and Sugar Company
Pioneer Mill Company
Kipahulu Sugar Company
Kukaiau Plantation Company

Insurance Companies: Trans-Atlantic Fire Insurance Company
North German Fire Insurance Company

Steamship Lines: Pacific Mail Steamship Company
China
City of Tokyo
City of Peking
City of Rio de Janeiro
Occidental and Oriental Steamship Company
Doric
Coptic
Gaelic
Toyo Kisen Kaisha
American Maru
Hong Kong Maru
Nippon Maru
Hawaiian Line of Packets to San Francisco
Bremen and Liverpool Line of Packets

F.M. Husted, ed., *Directory and Handbook of Honolulu and the Hawaiian Islands* (San Francisco, 1896), Archives of Hawaii, p. 14 (Hackfeld Advertisement).

50. After 1894 the systematic immigration overseen by Irwin was taken over by a number of private emigration companies which maintained liaison with the Big Five to supply them with Japanese immigrants.

51. Conroy, *Japanese Expansion*, p. 170 (n. 38).

52. Ogura to Cooper, April 23, 1896, in F.O. and Ex., *Immigration, 1896*. For links between Ogura and Hackfeld, see Board of Immigration, *Minutes, 1879–1899*, p. 316.

53. *Henry E. Cooper* was a lawyer and judge who served as minister of foreign affairs between 1895 and 1899. *William Owen Smith* (1848–1929) was a lawyer who became attorney general of the Republic of Hawaii. Smith was present at the meeting of the Executive Council on November 2, 1896. In that year "public business" took him to China and Japan. After annexation he became secretary and treasurer of the HSPA and president of the Guardian Trust Company. He also served as secretary and auditor of Alexander and Baldwin Ltd. Smith, as well as Dole, was apparently convinced of the desirability of importing Koreans. *Francis M. Swanzy* was director of Theo. H. Davies and Company and secretary and treasurer of the HSPA. He later became president of the HSPA and presided over the arrival of Koreans from 1903 to 1905. *Edward D. Tenney* was secretary and director of Castle and Cooke Ltd. and vice-president of the HSPA. *Walter M. Giffard* was vice-president and manager of the William C. Irwin Company, another financial house which controlled sugar plantations. *George S. Houghtailing* was silent throughout the meeting. *Morris Louisson* was president of the Heeia Agricultural Company. *George H. Robertson*, a lawyer and manager of C. Brewer and Company, was silent during the meeting.

54. Executive and Advisory Councils, *Minutes, 1897*, Archives of Hawaii, July 9, 1897. This document contains a most detailed account of the meeting and is reproduced here in its entirety, emphasis added. Summaries of the meeting appear in William O. Smith, *Correspondence, 1895–1899*, Archives of Hawaii, Miscellaneous, File 133, July 9, 1897; Executive Council, *Minutes, December 4, 1896–July 19, 1898*, Archives of Hawaii, pp. 99–100. Each has identical summaries of the July 9, 1897,

meeting concerning Koreans: "The question of importing American Negroes and Koreans was discussed."

55. Francis March Hatch (1852–1923) was the Hawaiian envoy to Washington and had just returned after successfully completing negotiations for annexation. W.E. Rowell was director of public works. Benjamin F. Dillingham was general manager of the Oahu Railway and Land Company.

56. Executive Council, *Minutes, December 4, 1896–July 19, 1898*, p. 115 (August 27, 1897).

57. Komura became involved in Korean immigration when he assumed the post of foreign minister of Japan and exchanged diplomatic messages with his successor in the Seoul post, Hayashi Gonsuke. See C.I. Eugene Kim and Han-kyo Kim, *Korea and the Politics of Imperialism 1876–1910* (Berkeley: University of California Press, 1967), p. 88.

58. Min Yŏng-hwan was later appointed president of the Emigration Bureau, which oversaw Korean immigration to Hawaii.

59. M. Frederick Nelson, *Korea and the Old Order in Eastern Asia* (New York: Russell and Russell, 1967), p. 233.

60. John M.B. Sill, American Minister to Korea, to Richard Olney, Secretary of State. Quoted in Nelson, *Korea and the Old Order*, p. 232.

61. Kim and Kim, *Korea and Politics*, p. 93; see also Han Woo-keun, *The History of Korea* (Seoul: Ŭl-yu Publishing, 1970), p. 435; Homer B. Hulbert, *The Passing of Korea* (Seoul: Yonsei University Press, 1969), p. 155; Nelson, *Korea and the Old Order*, p. 234.

62. Hulbert, *Passing of Korea*, pp. 150, 156. Hulbert in his role of journalist in Korea in the 1900 to 1905 period became involved in the issues surrounding Korean immigration to Hawaii, defending it vigorously.

63. Allen later took personal charge of several aspects of Korean immigration to Hawaii.

64. Nelson, *Korea and the Old Order*, p. 234.

65. Kim and Kim, *Korea and Politics*, p. 94. There is some question as to when Speyer actually succeeded Waeber. Nelson, *Korea and the Old Order*, pp. 230–31, says Speyer arrived on January 12, 1896; Han, *History of Korea*, p. 433, concurs. But Kim and Kim, p. 94, imply that Speyer replaced Waeber *after* the king left the Russian legation, that is, after February 1897, and Han, pp. 433–34, says that after Speyer's arrival in January 1896, Waeber did not leave but stayed on to advise Speyer. From the dates of the concessions granted it is clear that Speyer's influence and policies did not become fully operative until the spring or summer of 1897. The timing may be important when compared with simultaneous events in Hawaii.

66. Husted, *Directory and Handbook*, p. 28. For a biography of Hackfeld see the *Pacific Coast Commercial Record*, May 1892, p. 10. H. Hackfeld and Company's assets were seized in 1918, when the United States entered the First World War. J.F. Hackfeld died in Bremen, Germany, on August 27, 1932.

67. Harrington, *God, Mammon and the Japanese*, p. 340. *Krasnyi Arkhiv* (historical journal of the Central Archives of RSFSR, Moscow, translated into English in *Chinese Social and Political Science Review*, 1933–1936), "First Steps of Russian Imperialism in Far East (1888–1903)," *Chinese Social and Political Science Review* 18:2 (July, 1934): 236–81.

Early History of Korean Immigration to America

Yŏ-jun Yun

IN DECEMBER 1902, twenty years after the Korea-United States Treaty of Amity and Commerce, the first group of Koreans, 121 immigrants, left for Hawaii, and during the next three years a total of 7,226 Koreans in 65 groups left Chemulpo, now Inchon, for Hawaii. In April 1905, 1,033 Koreans immigrated to Mexico.

The immigration of Koreans to the Hawaiian Islands was a major event in the long history of Korea. The adventure of sailing across the Pacific to settle in a totally strange land, whatever the reason, provided Korean immigrants with an opportunity to see the world beyond the Hermit Kingdom, where their ancestors had lived for centuries. The immigrants, once settled, contributed much to the independence movement in their home country, opening a new era in modern Korean history. They donated funds to the Provisional Government of Korea, exiled in Shanghai, and they themselves launched various diplomatic campaigns for Korean independence. In fact, their struggle for, and contributions to, Korean independence paralleled the direct, armed resistance of Korean immigrants in Manchuria and China against Japanese rule in Korea.

This study is based on research data available both in Korea and the United States and on interviews with first-generation Korean immigrants in the United States. It is undertaken to investigate the motivation for Korean immigration to Hawaii, the social classes and social consciousness of immigrants, the cause for suspension of Korean

33

immigration to Hawaii, the reason for Korean immigration to Mexico, and the Korean view of immigration in the first decade of this century.[1]

Existing records indicate that Korean immigration to Hawaii was a result of the open door policy and the enlightenment movement in Korean society during the late nineteenth century.[2] During the declining period of the Yi dynasty, a small group of intellectuals launched various campaigns of enlightenment, encouraging an open door policy in order to provide the people with knowledge about the world beyond the borders of Korea. Through editorials and articles in such vernacular newspapers as Tongnip Shinmun (The Independent), Hwangsŏng Shinmun (The Imperial Palace News), and Cheguk Shinmun (The Imperial News), they stressed that the only way for Korea to develop as a strong, independent power was to introduce Western civilization to the country as soon as possible. Having opportunities to make contact with Western civilization through tours of Western countries or by way of China, these intellectuals strongly felt the need for diplomatic and trade relations with Western countries. However, the subject of Western civilization was far from the average Korean's mind in those days.

Instead, the view of the West as barbarian, an attitude that had been developed by court scholars in the 1860s, was deeply rooted in the minds of the Korean people. Moreover, the fact that most Korean immigrants to Hawaii were peasants and workers, and that 65 percent of them were illiterate, makes it hard to believe that they went to Hawaii in order to help reform and modernize Korean society through the introduction of Western civilization.

In view of the bad crops and the ensuing hardships Koreans experienced around the turn of this century, the motivation for Korean immigration to Hawaii must be sought in the economic rather than political aspect of society. In 1901, just one year before immigration to Hawaii started, a long spell of dry weather struck the country. On July 23, King Kojong, anticipating a bad crop in the autumn, ordered the government to suspend all civil engineering projects and to halt the export of rice. The government immediately suspended rice exportation and decided to import 300,000 sŏm of rice from Indochina.[3]

On October 9, King Kojong ordered the government to establish a relief office for starving people, and on December 4, the king ordered the establishment of an office to distribute to needy people the rice and other grains that were collected in taxes. The royal family donated 20,000 wŏn as a relief fund, and the government decided to deduct one-fifth to one-third of the stipends of all government officials for six months as donations to starving people.

Provincial reports showed an ever-increasing number of needy families and agrarian revolts in many places. However, the government had no effective means to control the social confusion that resulted from famine. Of the total budget of 7,585,877 wŏn for 1902, the relief budget for starving people amounted to only 6,466 wŏn, excluding the donations from the royal family and government officials. At this juncture, the U.S. government asked for Korean immigration to Hawaii, and the Korean government agreed. Thus, the food crisis in Korea combined with the labor shortage in Hawaii brought about Korean immigration to the Islands.

Horace N. Allen, chief of the U.S. legation in Seoul, and the official who negotiated with the Korean government for Korean immigration to Hawaii, said that the economic situation in Korea necessitated the immigration. In a letter to Secretary of State John Hay dated December 10, 1902, Allen described the famine of the previous year and said, "There has been talk of organizing an emigration bureau ever since last winter."[4] In a different letter, to Governor Sanford B. Dole of Hawaii, Allen said, "The severe famine of the past winter made the matter seem all the more attractive to the people, while the fact the government had to import large quantities of rice to feed the starving seems to have turned the attention of the officials favorably. . . ."[5]

No Korean government record on early immigration to Hawaii is available now, but Allen's letter is evidence that the Korean government began to consider organizing an emigration office in the winter of 1901.[6] In fact, the government established the Emigration Office, to handle emigration and overseas tours by Koreans, on November 16, 1902.[7]

Hwangsŏng Shinmun also noted that immigration to Hawaii was due to economic reasons. On December 29, 1902, just a week after the first group left Chemulpo, an editorial said that some people went north to Russia and others went to Hawaii because famine and starvation had reached a point beyond their endurance.

The first Korean immigrants to Hawaii came from various classes of society. Chinese and Japanese immigrants to Hawaii were mostly peasants, but only one-seventh of the Korean immigrants were peasants, the others were common laborers, coolies, low-grade government officials, ex-soldiers, students, house servants, mine workers, and political refugees.[8] Peasants were a very small portion of the immigrant group because Korean peasants were conservative and indifferent to emigration in those days. For all those who emigrated it was a matter of resolute determination and adventurousness to cross the Pacific, leaving behind the land they and their forefathers had tilled for generations, however hard their living might be, and however well off they might be in Hawaii. Awaiting them all in Hawaii was work on the sugar cane farms.

Under the centuries-old influence of the Confucian way of living, the Korean people tended to consider settling overseas, which meant departure from home and family, a thoughtless undertaking, even immoral conduct. With such a view of emigration, it was very hard for them to go abroad or seek contact with Western civilization.[9] This tendency was particularly strong among peasants, who were very attached to the land.

Another reason for the small proportion of peasants in the group immigrating to Hawaii was that emigration was advertised in big cities and port cities only—Seoul, Inchon, Pusan, Wonsan, and Chinnampo. The East-West Development Company, responsible in Korea for recruiting immigrants to Hawaii, had a main office in Inchon and branch offices in Wonsan, Chinnampo, Pusan, and Mokpo. As a result, many people in these cities, who had a progressive outlook and many more opportunities to observe Western civilization than rural people, applied for emigration permits.

As mentioned earlier, 65 percent of Korean immigrants to Hawaii were illiterate. This is a rather low illiteracy rate in view of the extremely limited opportunity for education in Korea in the late nineteenth century. Of course, this rate was based on knowledge of Korean letters, not of the English alphabet. The immigrants did not understand a single English word and had to have the help of Korean interpreters.

David W. Deshler, president of the East-West Development Company, advertised for Korean interpreters in *Hwangsŏng Shinmun.*[10] Korean interpreters boarded the ship with the immigrants and worked on sugar cane farms in Hawaii. Hyŏn Sun, one of the Korean interpreters recruited by Deshler, said that he and his wife went to Hawaii because he had been told that he had to live in Hawaii with Korean immigrants.[11]

Before their departure, Korean immigrants prepared themselves for adaptation to the new life; they knew that they would be total strangers to Hawaiian life. In 1895, the Korean government had promulgated the haircut decree demanding that all adult males cut their topknots, but the immigrants at first refused to comply because they believed that cutting off the topknot would be worse than killing themselves. Thus applicants for immigration to Hawaii, all except a few young Christians, wore topknots and Korean clothes. However, while going through procedures with the emigration company they cut off the topknot in order to prepare themselves for adaptation to Hawaiian customs.

Before leaving Korea, the men changed into Western work clothes, probably their first experience with the West. After leaving Korea, the emigration ship stopped at Kobe or Yokohama, where with the help of interpreters, the immigrants took physical examinations.

Aboard the emigration ship, they began to experience a transition from a closed to an open society. The ship was not a passenger ship but a freighter. Men and women were put into the same cabin; a new experience for people who had just left a society where even a seven-year-old boy was not allowed to share a seat with a girl of his age. However, they had to adapt quickly to this new situation by divesting themselves of the Confucian distinction between the sexes.[12]

The early Korean immigrants had a weak national consciousness. However, the new life in a land of strange historical and cultural background made them feel a strong love for Korea and her people which inspired them to organize self-governing bodies on the Hawaiian farms. The head of this autonomous organization was elected in a meeting of all members, and he inspired in all Korean immigrants of his farm a strong sense of solidarity. The rules of this organization called for the love of fellow Korean immigrants, respect for and protection of women, and prohibition of gambling and alcohol, and they provided a fine of one to two dollars for violations.[13] The qualifications for election as head of this self-governing body were mature age, courage, decisiveness, honesty, sincerity, and education.[14] Of course, only men were eligible to head this organization. The leader had a broad range of authority: he represented the Korean community in the social life of Hawaii, and he mediated all conflicts between members of his organization. Korean immigrants new to his farm were required to report to him.

The loyalty of Korean immigrants was clearly reflected in their request for a permanent Korean government representative in Hawaii. In a letter to the foreign minister of Korea, dated May 1, 1905, the Korean community in Hawaii asked for a Korean consul in Hawaii, saying that they would provide all funds for establishing and operating a consulate.[15]

However, on May 5 the Korean government appointed the Japanese consul in Hawaii, Saito Kan, as honorary Korean consul under the excuse of financial problems.[16] In view of the Korea-Japan relationship at the time, it can be said that this was done under pressure from the Japanese government. Under the Korea-Japan protectorate treaty signed November 17, 1905, Japan was authorized to meddle in the foreign affairs of Korea, and it had begun to interfere with the domestic affairs of Korea, by having the Korean government appoint Japanese advisors to all cabinet ministries, even before this coerced treaty.

It was about this time that Japan began to press for Korea's appointment of the Japanese consul in Honolulu as honorary Korean consul. Japanese minister to Korea, Hayashi Gonsuke, visited the Foreign Ministry and asked why it had not yet appointed the Japanese consul in Honolulu as honorary Korean consul, in spite of the fact

that King Kojong had already approved such an appointment.[17]
On April 21, 1905, the Japanese chargé d'affaires, Hagiwara Morika-
zu, demanded that the Korean government appoint the Japanese
consul in Hawaii as honorary Korean consul.[18] As a result, Foreign
Minister Yi Ha-yŏng formally appointed Saito Kan as honorary
Korean consul on May 5, 1905.

However, the Korean community in Hawaii did not accept the
action and continued to request the sending of a Korean consul.
In August 1905, the Korean community sent Yi Tong-ho to Seoul
as its representative, to appeal directly to the Korean government
for a Korean consul. Yi visited the Foreign Ministry, but it is not
known whom he met at the ministry and what reply he received.[19]

Hwangsŏng Shinmun carried in its August 15, 1905, issue the
following petition of the Korean community to the Korean government:

> Although we the Korean emigrants in Hawaii have shallow knowledge of the
> world, we are well aware of the fact that as there cannot be two suns in
> the heaven, so there cannot be two kings in a country. We take pride in
> our loyalty to the king of Korea, though we are far away from the country.
> There are some 7,000 of us in Hawaii, but the home government does not
> take care of us. Are not we Koreans?
>
> Some 10 ethnic groups in Hawaii have their own consuls for the protection
> of their lives and property, except us Korean emigrants. We feel as if we
> were a flock of sheep without shepherd and a boat without an oar. We have
> requested on several occasions the home government to send our consul. . . .
>
> Should the home government appoint a foreigner as a Korean consul, we
> will never accept him as our consul. Is it because of financial problems that
> the government is moving to appoint a foreigner as Korean consul in Hawaii,
> in spite of the fact that Korea is an independent country? If this is the reason,
> we are ready to raise the money necessary for establishing and operating a
> Korean consulate. . . .[20]

Considering the fact that the Korean immigrants in Hawaii were
of the lower class in Korea, their loyalty to the king and Korea
as seen in the above petition is striking. However, the king and
his government were too weak politically and economically to accept
the request. King Kojong was but a figurehead, and Japan held
the actual power of his government. The government was drained
of financial resources and had to rely on Japanese loans.

Korean immigration to Hawaii came to a halt two years and five
months after it started. On April 1, 1905, the Foreign Ministry
instructed the mayors of such port cities as Inchon, Pusan, and
Pyongyang to stop sending immigrants to Hawaii. In the instructions,
the ministry ordered the mayors to issue passports to those going
abroad to study but not to those emigrating.[21]

The Passport Office, established within the Royal Household
Ministry on November 16, 1902, was abolished on October 11, 1903,

because of the financial difficulties of the government.[22]

There is no record available that explains why the government suddenly stopped sending immigrants to Hawaii. But *Hwangsŏng Shinmun* reported on April 5, 1905, that many Korean immigrants in Hawaii were unable to return home because they could not save enough money to buy steamship tickets, though they wanted to return because of the hard labor required in Hawaii and the difficulty in adapting themselves to the Hawaiian mode of life.

But historical records suggest that Japanese pressure upon the Korean government was one of the factors responsible for the end, in 1905, of Korean immigration to Hawaii. The Japanese government filed a protest with the Korean government against continued emigration after the April 1, 1905, decree of the Foreign Ministry banning emigration.[23]

On May 8, 1905, Hagiwara Morikazu, Japanese chargé d'affaires in Seoul, urged Vice-Foreign Minister Yun Ch'i-ho to stop sending Korean immigrants immediately, calling his attention to the fact that many Koreans had immigrated to Hawaii after the April 1 decree. Yun told Hagiwara that all of these immigrants had been issued passports before the decree and that when they left the country there would be no more emigration from Korea. Hagiwara again met Yun on May 10 to ask about the departure of 92 emigrants from Chinnampo on May 7. Hagiwara called for strict enforcement of the ban on emigration.[24]

On May 31, Japanese Minister Hayashi Gonsuke told Foreign Minister Yi Ha-yŏng that passports were still being issued to many emigrants in Inchon; those without passports were also being allowed to leave the country aboard emigration boats. Hayashi urged Yi to strictly enforce the decree banning emigration. Judging from the repeated Japanese requests for strict enforcement of the Foreign Ministry's decree, we can reasonably believe that the Korean government stopped emigration under pressure from the Japanese. Early in June 1905, Hayashi lodged with Yi a formal request that the Korean government instruct the mayor of every port city to stop sending emigrants to any foreign country, in view of the situation in Korea "at this juncture, which does not warrant emigration of Koreans. . . ."[25] Japan said that there was no Korean diplomatic mission in Hawaii which could protect Korean immigrants in disputes with their Hawaiian employers caused by the language barrier.[26]

But this seems to have been only an excuse. Japan's real reason for discouraging Korean immigration to Hawaii was a desire to protect Japanese in Hawaii. In 1902, there were 31,029 Japanese immigrants working on sugar cane farms in Hawaii, 73.5 percent of the total 42,242 sugar cane workers on the Islands.

Sugar cane farmers of Hawaii began recruiting Korean workers in the face of this big number of Japanese workers on their farms in order to keep a racial balance among their workers. With the increasing number of Korean workers on the farms, Japanese workers pressed their government to influence the Korean government to suspend Korean immigration to Hawaii.[27]

The Japanese resident-general in Korea, installed under the protectorate treaty of November 17, 1905, believed that Japanese workers could dominate the labor force in Hawaii if the Korean government stopped sending immigrants. In fact, it attached great importance to the Korean government's decree banning immigration to Hawaii because this greatly reduced the competitors to the Japanese.[28]

Another reason for Japan to require the Korean government to stop immigration to Hawaii was her economic and military interests in Korea. Japan needed Korean workers to construct military facilities, including roads, for her expansionist policy on the Asian continent and to increase Korea's rice production for export to Japan.[29]

It is also quite possible that the Korean government itself put an end to the immigration of its citizens to North America. The government had been informed of the hardships to which its citizens had been subjected in Yucatán, Mexico.

Korean immigration to Mexico was arranged by the Continental Settlement Company, an emigration firm set up by John G. Meyers, a British citizen, and Ōniwa Kwanichi, a Japanese citizen, in Seoul. Under a contract with major haciendas or large farms in Mexico, Meyers supplied Asian workers. He tried to recruit workers in Japan and China for Mexican farms but failed. He then went to Korea for the same purpose.[30] He set up branch offices of his company in Inchon, Kaesong, Pyongyang, Chinnampo, and Suwon to recruit farm workers. He also ran seven advertisements for immigrants to Mexico in *Hwangsŏng Shinmun* between December 17, 1904, and January 13, 1905. The gist of the advertisement is as follows:

> Mexico is a civilized and rich country bordering on the United States. It is known for fertile land, beautiful nature and warm weather. There is no bad disease in this country. Because there are many rich people but few poor people, it is very hard to recruit workers. Recently, many Japanese and Chinese people went to Mexico, some with their families, to make money and they are all rich now. Koreans can also become rich in Mexico if they emigrate. Although Korea and Mexico have not yet concluded a trade agreement, Mexico will accord Korea the most-favored-nation treatment and Korean emigrants will be allowed to visit Korea whenever they want to.[31]

The advertisement also contained the following nine terms of contract for Korean immigrants to Mexico:

> 1. Emigrants to Mexico should go with their families. While single emigrants cannot enjoy the pleasure of homes, those with families will benefit from their family members in tilling land, raising chickens and hogs, and making food and clothes.

2. Travel expenses, including steamship tickets and food expenses aboard the ship, will be provided by Mexican farms.
3. No tax will be imposed on houses and land in Mexico.
4. Peasants will be accorded special treatment and medical care will be free of charge.
5. Emigrants will be given rental houses with free supply of fuel, and children seven years of age or older will go to school free of charge.
6. Workers will have a nine-hour working day for $1.30 (equivalent to ₩ 260 in Korean money) to $3 in wages against $0.20 to $0.25 in food expenses a day.
7. Wages will be paid once a month, on the seventh of every month, to workers themselves, and not to others for the workers.
8. The initial contract will terminate in five years, and those who have finished this period are free to return to Korea. Those returning to Korea after finishing the five-year contract will be paid a bonus of $100.
9. The voyage to Mexico will take about a month, and the date of departure will be announced in advance.

The Continental Settlement Company recruited a total of 1,039 emigrants from Seoul and other cities through these advertisements. According to Japanese Consul Kato in Inchon, the 1,033 immigrants to Mexico consisted of 702 men, 135 women, and 196 children. They were recruited from 18 cities—454 from Seoul, 225 from Inchon, 73 from Pusan, 55 from Mokpo, 37 from Pyongyang, 33 from Masan, 26 from Wonsan, 25 from Kaesong, 24 from Yŏng-dŭngp'o, 22 from Chech'ŏn, 18 from Taegu, 12 from Pongsan, 9 from Kwangju, 7 from Kyŏngju, 6 from Suwon, 6 from Ulsan, 4 from Hwangju, and 3 from Miryang.[32] Although the company had branch offices in five cities only, the emigrants came from almost all cities of the country, including remote Chech'ŏn and Pongsan, and this is believed to have been because information was available throughout the country on the life of Korean immigrants to Hawaii.[33] Like the immigrants to Hawaii, immigrants to Mexico were workers, peasants, ex-soldiers, ex-civil servants, and others from the lower classes of society.

The ship to Mexico left Inchon early in April 1905.[34] Because the government decreed a ban on emigration just before the departure of this ship, she was the first and last ship carrying immigrants to Mexico from Korea.

After a voyage of about one month, the ship arrived at Salina Cruz on May 15.[35] Two died during the voyage and 1,031 Koreans landed in Mexico.[36] They went to Mérida, the capital of the State of Yucatán, by way of Coatzacoalcos and Progreso. Yucatán, a peninsula in the Gulf of Mexico, is in the tropical zone. When the Korean immigrants arrived there, it was the rainy season. With the sultry air and scorching sun, Yucatán was by no means a paradise to the Korean immigrants.

The Korean immigrants were divided among 24 farms, of which 22 were Chenché, Az-Kora, Zu-Ku, Buenavista, Chin-ki-la, Ti-zi-min,

San Enrique, Za-cil, San Francisco, Santiago, Kan-kap-chen, Ku-ka, No-ge-yong, It-zin-kap, San Antonio, San-ak-tah, Chun-chu-ku-mil, Yaz-ché, Cho-cho-lá, Ko-bop-cha-ká, Santa Rosa, and Temo-zón.[37]

On the first day of their work on these farms, Korean immigrants knew that they had been totally deceived by the Continental Settlement Company. Not only the stifling weather but also the wages and working hours were totally different from what the immigrants had been told in Korea. They worked twelve hours a day, cutting henequen leaves with a knife, for a wage of thirty to thirty-five cents.[38]

Henequen rope was a major industry of Yucatán, which exported some $30 million worth a year. Korean immigrants worked on henequen farms which recruited Asian workers, including Koreans, and exploited them under bad working conditions. Some Korean immigrants ran away from these farms only to be caught in a few days because they were totally unfamiliar with the local geography. Farm managers beat the runaways with wet rope, and in order to keep them from running away, their barracks were locked and watched by guards.

The miserable enslavement of Korean immigrants in Yucatán was first revealed to the world by a Chinese named Ho Hui, who lived in Mérida. He wrote letters to four Koreans in San Francisco, Shin T'ae-gyu, Hwang Yong-sŏng, An P'il-su, and Pang Hwa-chung, describing to them the life of Korean workers at henequen farms in Yucatán. The gist of Ho's letters is as follows:

> In rags and worn sandals, the Koreans are laughed at by Mexicans. You can't watch them without tears, going in groups to henequen farms, men holding the hands of their children and women carrying their babies on their backs. They are worse than animals. Here in Mexico, the aborigines are called the fifth or sixth grade slaves in the world, but Koreans are called the seventh grade slaves. When they fail to finish the assigned work, they are made to kneel down and are beaten until their flesh is torn and bloody.[39]

The four Koreans sent Ho's letters and an article on the life of Korean immigrants in Mexico from the Chinese newspaper *Wenhsing Ipao,* published in San Francisco, to the Young Men's Christian Association of Sangdong church in Seoul. Chŏng Sun-man, an employee of the YMCA, wrote an article based on Ho's letters and the *Wenhsing Ipao* story and published it in *Hwangsŏng Shinmun,* in order to spread the news in Korea of the miserable life of Korean immigrants in Mexico.[40]

The YMCA also sent a letter to the Korean government, demanding that it take steps to bring Korean immigrants in Mexico home immediately, while charging that it failed to protect them from slavery.[41] On July 31, 1905, *Hwangsŏng Shinmun* carried an editorial on the misery of Korean immigrants in Mexico, accusing the government of failing to protect the lives and property of Koreans in Mexico and demanding immediate ameliorative steps for them.

Accordingly, the government began to investigate those who had arranged the immigration to Mexico and asked the Mexican government to take measures to protect Korean immigrants. King Kojong ordered the government to negotiate with the emigration company for the return of Korean immigrants from Mexico and condemned the government for failure to prevent immigration to Mexico.[42]

On August 11, 1905, Foreign Minister Yi Ha-yŏng sent a cable to the Mexican government requesting that it protect Korean immigrants until the Korean government could send officials to Mexico, though the two governments had not yet established diplomatic relations. On August 17, Yi instructed the Korean embassy in Washington to negotiate with the Mexican government for the protection of Korean immigrants in Mexico and requested Japanese Minister Hayashi Gonsuke in Seoul to interrogate Ōniwa Kwanichi concerning the conditions under which he and Meyers recruited immigrants to Mexico. Yi also asked Minister Hayashi to recommend to his government that it request that the Mexican government protect Korean immigrants. On August 22, Minister Hayashi notified the Korean government that the Japanese government had instructed the Japanese embassy in Mexico to take steps to protect Korean immigrants.[43] In reply to Minister Yi's cable of August 11, the Mexican government notified Yi, on August 22, that it was not true that Korean immigrants in Mexico were leading a life of slavery.[44]

The YMCA sent Yi Pŏm-su and Pak Chang-hyŏn to Mexico on August 24, 1905, to survey conditions, but they went to Mexico City and not to Yucatán, for reasons not known.[45] The government sent Vice-Foreign Minister Yun Ch'i-ho to Hawaii and Mexico on August 27, 1905, but he went to Hawaii only, because of financial problems.[46]

The miserable life of Korean immigrants in Mexico was reported in Korea two months after the immigrants left for Mexico, but the Korean government could do nothing to help them. When the Korean government was deprived by Japan, under the protectorate treaty concluded on November 17, 1905, of its right to conduct its own foreign affairs, the problems of Korean emigrants overseas came under the control of the Japanese resident-general in Korea.

During the decline of the Yi dynasty Koreans responded negatively to emigration. The centuries-old Confucian way of thinking regarded emigration overseas as a crime, for it left the graves of ancestors and members of the clan unattended. This attitude was expressed in the two progressive newspapers, *Hwangsŏng Shinmun* and *Cheguk Shinmun,* which at the time represented the reform movement. They advertised for and reported on immigrants to Hawaii and Mexico, but they used the word "laborers" instead of "immigrants." This suggests that Korean society was not yet able to see emigration as a means of introducing advanced civilization into the country for social and political reforms. *Cheguk Shinmun* ran an editorial on emigration in the May 12, 1903, issue urging its suspension:

> They [emigration firms] must recruit many ignorant and stupid people, such as the Negro people of Africa and the peasants of Korea, as workers. But they have already brought many Negroes to the United States, and Africa is far, far away. They have an eye on Koreans because Korea is nearer than Africa and because Koreans are strangers. They lured stupid Koreans with sugar-coated words and many Koreans have crossed the sea. . . . It is lamentable that our brothers and sisters have become slaves like African Negroes in a strange land. Let's all tell each other how miserable the life is there in the strange land so that we may not hear the sad story again.

Immigration to Hawaii and Mexico between 1902 and 1905 was very different from Korean immigration to the United States since 1965. Early immigrants were peasants and laborers who had lost their means of livelihood in Korea as a result of continued bad crops, inflation, and exploitation by corrupt government officials. In contrast, recent immigrants to the United States are well educated and skilled in their professions. Whereas emigration at the turn of the century was motivated by the impoverished economy of the country, recent emigration has resulted mainly from military tension and political and social unrest in Korea. However, the two waves of emigration have one aspect in common, they were products of changes in Korean society, though the changes differed in nature.

Notes

1. Representative works on the history of early Korean immigration to America include Kim Wŏn-yong (Warren Y. Kim), *Chae-Mi Hanin osimnyŏn-sa* [Fifty-year history of the Koreans in America] (Reedley, California: Charles Ho Kim, 1959); Sŏ Kwang-un, *Miju Hanin ch'ilsimnyŏn-sa* [Seventy-year history of Korean emigrants in the United States] (Seoul: Kyop'o Munje Yŏn'guso, 1973); and Ko Sŭng-je, *Han'guk imin-sa yŏn'gu* [A study on the history of Korean emigration] (Seoul: Changmungak, 1973).
2. According to Kim Wŏn-yong, *Chae-Mi Hanin*, and Sŏ, *Miju Hanin ch'ilsimnyŏn-sa*, the immigration to Hawaii was a result of the enlightenment movement, designed to introduce Western civilization and pave the way for trade with Western nations.

3. Kuksa P'yŏnch'an Wiwŏn-hoe (National History Compilation Committee), *Kojong sidae-sa* [The history of King Kojong's era], vol. 5 (Seoul: National History Compilation Committee, 1971), p. 388. Foreign Minister Pak Che-sun told the Japanese, Chinese, U.S., British, German, Russian, and French legations in Seoul of King Kojong's measure banning the export of rice and exempting duties on the import of rice, on July 24, 1901.

4. Allen to Hay, December 10, 1902, in United States, Department of State, U.S. Embassy, Korea, *Dispatches from United States Ministers to Korea, 1883–1905* (Washington, D.C.: National Archives and Records Service, 1949–1951). This is the first record of the U.S. government's actions regarding Korean immigration to Hawaii.

5. Allen to Hay, December 10, 1902.

6. It is not clear whether the need to set up the Emigration Office was discussed in the Korean government or in the negotiations between the Korean government and the U.S. minister.

7. According to Kuksa P'yŏnch'an Wiwŏn-hoe, *Kojong sidae-sa*, p. 680, the Emigration Office was responsible for issuing passports to students going abroad for study, citizens going on overseas tours, and farmers, merchants, and industrialists going abroad on business.

8. See, for example, Bernice B.H. Kim, "The Koreans in Hawaii" (M.A. thesis, University of Hawaii, 1937).

9. Koh Byong-ik, "Korean Concept of Foreign Countries during the Yi Dynasty," *Paeksan Hakpo* [Paeksan Review] 8 (June 1970): 231–32.

10. *Hwangsŏng Shinmun* [Imperial Palace News], December 6–16, 1902. The advertisement was in the name of the *Taesira* (Deshler) Bank in Inchon and said that the bank needed interpreters, when actually interpreters were needed for Korean immigrants.

11. Hyŏn Sun, *P'owa yuram-ki* [Memoirs of my Hawaiian sojourn] (Seoul: Hyŏn Kong-yŏm, 1909).

12. Bernice B.H. Kim, "Koreans in Hawaii," p. 84.

13. According to Hyŏn Sun, the fines collected were used for the celebration of King Kojong's birthday, New Year's Day, and U.S. Independence Day. On these days, Korean immigrants were allowed to drink wine and whiskey.

14. Bernice B.H. Kim, "Koreans in Hawaii," p. 119.

15. *Hwangsŏng Shinmun*, January 25, 1905.

16. *Hwangsŏng Shinmun*, May 6, 1905.

17. *Hwangsŏng Shinmun*, September 6, 1904.

18. Yun Yŏ-jun, "Miju imin ch'ilsim-nyŏn," [Seventy years of immigration in America], *Kyŏnghyang Shinmun* [Kyŏnghyang Daily], November 20, 1973.

19. *Hwangsŏng Shinmun*, August 10, 1905, reported that Yi Tong-ho's petition was so touching that all the people shed tears while reading it.

20. *Hwangsŏng Shinmun*, August 15, 1905, carried the full text of Yi's petition but did not say anything about the petition's origin. It is believed, however, that the text was prepared in Hawaii and brought to Seoul by Yi Tong-ho.

21. *Hwangsŏng Shinmun*, April 3, 5, 1905.

22. *Kyŏnghyang Shinmun*, October 24, 1973. The Passport Office could not pay salaries to its officials in 1903 because it could not get the budget for its operation.

23. *Hwangsŏng Shinmun*, April 7, 1905. The decree banning emigration drew a strong protest from the emigration firm, Inchon Singmin ch'ongtae hoesa (Inchon Emigration Representative Company), which threatened to request compensation for losses caused by the ban, with the result that the decree could not be enforced for the time being.

24. *Kyŏnghyang Shinmun*, November 20, 1973.

25. *Hwangsŏng Shinmun*, June 9, 1905.

26. *Kyŏnghyang Shinmun*, December 25, 1973.

27. *Kyŏnghyang Shinmun,* November 29, 1973.
28. *Kyŏnghyang Shinmun,* November 29, 1973.
29. Shin Sŏk-ho et al., *Han'guk hyŏndae-sa* [History of modern Korea], vol. 4 (Seoul: Ch'ŏnggu Munhwa-sa, 1974), pp. 138–52.
30. Kim Wŏn-yong, *Chae-Mi Hanin,* p. 10. Meyers said in a letter to Japanese Governor-General Terauchi, dated June 24, 1910, that he came to Korea to recruit immigrants to Mexico.
31. *Hwangsŏng Shinmun,* December 17, 20, 22, 24, 28, 1904, and January 9, 13, 1905. According to Kim Wŏn-yong, in *Chae-Mi Hanin,* and Sŏ Kwang-un, in *Miju Hanin ch'ilsimnyŏn-sa,* immigrants to Mexico were recruited in secret, but actually the recruitment was done openly through newspaper advertisements.
32. *Kyŏnghyang Shinmun,* December 4, 1973. Of the 1,039 Koreans recruited, 1,031 reached Mexico.
33. Kim Sun-min, who returned to Korea on July 26, 1922, after two years of study in Mexico, said in his article, in *Tong-a Ilbo* [East Asia Daily] August 5, 6, 7 and 9, 1922, that many immigrants went to Mexico because they were told they could become rich there in three years of three hours work a day, and that they could immigrate to Hawaii from Mexico after three years.
34. *Hwangsŏng Shinmun,* April 4, 1905, reported that the emigration ship left Inchon at 11:00 a.m., April 2, 1905, but in Japanese Government-General in Korea, *History of Inchon City,* and documents on immigration to Mexico in the government archives, the departure date is said to be April 4.
35. *Hwangsŏng Shinmun,* July 29, 1905.
36. Kim Wŏn-yong, *Chae-Mi Hanin,* p. 11. Several first-generation immigrants were quoted as saying that three—one adult and two children—died on the ship to Mexico.
37. Jose Sanchez Pac, *Memorias de la Vida y Obra de los Coreanos en Mexico desde Yucatán* (Mexico City: Secretaria de Educacion Publica, 1973), pp. 12–13.
38. Historical records differ on the daily wages received by Korean emigrants in Mexico—twenty-five to thirty-five cents.
39. *Hwangsŏng Shinmun,* July 29, 1905.
40. *Hwangsŏng Shinmun,* July 29, 1905. According to Kim Wŏn-yong, in *Chae-Mi Hanin,* and Sŏ Kwang-un, in *Miju Hanin ch'ilsimnyŏn-sa,* however, the life of Korean immigrants in Mexico was first made known in Korea by ginseng dealer Pak Yŏng-sun on May 11, 1905. The fact was that it was reported in Korea four months earlier.
41. *Hwangsŏng Shinmun,* July 29, 1905.
42. *Kyŏnghyang Shinmun,* December 15, 1973.
43. *Kyŏnghyang Shinmun,* December 19, 1973.
44. *Hwangsŏng Shinmun,* August 23, 1905.
45. No historical record is available on the two YMCA men who returned from Mexico City without visiting Yucatán. *Hwangsŏng Shinmun* only reported their departure from Korea, and *Shinhan Minbo* [New Korea], published by the Korean National Association in the United States, ran an article on April 7, 1907, criticizing them for not visiting the Korean community in Yucatán.
46. Yun returned to Seoul on November 6 without going to Mexico because his request for travel expenses was turned down by Japanese financial advisor Megata Shutaro in Seoul.

The History and Role of the Church in the Korean American Community

Hyung-chan Kim

WHEN THE FIRST large group of Korean immigrants arrived in Honolulu, Hawaii, on January 13, 1903, there were among them some who had already embraced Christianity as their religion.[1] These Christians became active in establishing churches in the Korean community in Hawaii and on the mainland of the United States. That there were Christians among the first emigrants from Korea was certainly not a historical accident; the situation related closely to the history of evangelism in Korea and in part caused the immigration of Koreans to the Hawaiian Islands.

As early as 1784, Christianity came to Korea in the form of Catholicism, when Yi Sŭng-hun, the son of an ambassador to China, returned to Korea with books, crosses, and Christian artifacts. He had gone to China to study and was baptized in Peking. In 1794 a Chinese priest came into Korea, crossing the Yalu River border in secrecy in response to Yi Sŭng-hun's plea for more priests.

Catholicism began to gain converts shortly after its arrival in Korea. Many persons dissatisfied with their lot in the present life turned to the teachings of Catholicism that promised a better life in the next world, no matter how vaguely they understood the real meaning of life after death. Others embraced the religion because it symbolized Western scientific knowledge. At any rate, as many Koreans turned to Catholicism, the Yi Court (1392–1910) became deeply concerned over the doctrine of the Catholic church that preached equality of men and the brotherhood of mankind. The doctrine was considered dangerous to the preservation of the Confucian system of loyalties and ancestor worship, which was the foundation of the kingdom. Therefore, the Yi Court issued an edict in 1785 banning Christianity. Shortly after the ban, many Korean Christians, along with the Chinese priest, were put to death. The persecution of Christians continued. In 1839, three French missionaries and their Korean followers were executed. The incident so angered the French government that it sent two ships to Korea in 1846 with demands for an explanation. As late as 1866, three bishops, seventeen priests, and numerous Korean Christians were martyred.

The 1882 Treaty of Amity and Commerce between Korea and the United States, and other treaties the Yi Court had been compelled to conclude with other Western nations, brought more Western missionaries to Korea. Although most of them sought the wealth of the earthly kingdom upon their arrival in Korea, a few were dedicated to the cause of the heavenly kingdom.[2] Among them was Horace N. Allen, who was sent to Korea in 1884 by the Presbyterian Board of Foreign Missions of the United States. Shortly after his arrival in Seoul, an incident occurred that helped him gain the confidence of the king of Korea. During a coup d'état involving the conservatives and progressives of the Yi Court, the queen's nephew was seriously wounded and Allen, a doctor as well as a missionary, was called upon to give him immediate medical attention.[3] His successful treatment of the queen's nephew won him the position of the king's personal physician and resulted in royal approval of Christianity.

For a number of reasons, more Koreans in the north accepted Christianity than did their countrymen in the south. First of all, Koreans in the northern provinces had been discriminated against by the Yi Court, which was constantly plagued by regional factionalism. The Yi Court sent to the northern provinces government officials who were considered dangerous to the security of the court. It also denied the people from the northern provinces access to high positions in the central government. This policy of discrimination produced the popular insurrection of 1811, led by Hong Kyŏng-nae. The rebellion was strongly supported by the people in the north, who were also suffering from a severe famine. Second, during the Yi dynasty, the Koreans of the north developed a less rigid social structure than their countrymen in the south because they lacked sufficient arable land. The northern Koreans were therefore exposed to more egalitarian values that made them more amenable to the acceptance of Christian doctrine.

Third, several decisive battles were fought in the northwestern region of Korea, particularly in the vicinity of Pyongyang, during the Sino-Japanese War of 1894–1895. Koreans became caught between the retreating Chinese soldiers and the advancing Japanese army, and much of their property was destroyed in the war, the outcome of which was to determine the political fate of the Korean people in the years to come. Several missionaries stationed in the vicinity of Pyongyang gave their time and effort to alleviate the sufferings of the people caught innocently in a war created by foreign powers. Such unselfish devotion of missionaries to the care and cure of Koreans afflicted by war gradually endeared them to the Korean people, who flocked to churches to learn of a better world, both spiritual and material, to live in.

American missionaries encouraged Koreans, by deed or word, to immigrate to the Hawaiian Islands as they saw "an opportunity for Koreans to improve their condition and to acquire useful knowledge and to better themselves financially . . . ," as David W. Deshler wrote to Huntington Wilson, chargé d'affaires of the American legation in Tokyo, in a letter asking Wilson to intervene on his behalf after the Korean immigration had been terminated by the Korean government in 1905.[4]

Commenting on the influence of American missionaries on Koreans who made the decision to immigrate to the Hawaiian Islands, Yi Tae-sŏng, executive secretary for the Korean Student Christian Movement of Hawaii, once stated:

> It was at this critical stage in her history that the great and good missionary, Dr. and Mrs. H.G. Underwood, and Rev. and Mrs. Henry G. Appenzeller, appeared in Korea and began telling the wonderful story of the Cross and what it could do for those who will accept it and undertake to carry it through life. To the timid, stoical Korean the message was one of hope and life. Eagerly he asked of its power and a sample of its results. The one was told him by the missionaries, the other was pointed out to him in the advanced life of the United States. Soon the United States was the hope of Korea, for was it not there that the wondrous Cross had brought beneficient results? Was it not worth the while of any timid, downtrodden Korean laborer to make the attempt of reaching this haven of peace and plenty? As the Korean embraced Christianity he began to look for a place where it might be lived in peace.[5]

Missionaries were not the only reason for Korean immigration to the Hawaiian Islands. There was widespread famine in the northwestern region of Korea during the winter of 1901, and the government tried to save the people from starvation by allowing them to emigrate. Also, there were agents who recruited laborers to work on Hawaiian sugar plantations. One of them was David W. Deshler, who was responsible for the immigration of the first group of Koreans to Hawaii in 1903.[6]

Of all American missionaries, Reverend George Heber Jones of the Methodist missions was most influential with Korean emigrants. He came to Korea in 1887 and was sent to Chemulpo in 1892 to

succeed Reverend Appenzeller. Chemulpo, now Inchon, was a port
city where Deshler was stationed to recruit Korean laborers. Partly
because of his geographical location and partly because of his
compassion for Koreans leaving their homeland for a strange place,
Jones felt the need to encourage them by telling them about life
in Hawaii. He also gave some leaders among them letters of introduction to the superintendent of Methodist missions in Hawaii so that
they would be greeted by someone upon their arrival in Honolulu.
Reverend John W. Wadman, superintendent of the Hawaiian missions
of the Methodist Episcopal church, in his report, "Educational Work
among Koreans," described the role Jones had played in the immigration of Koreans to Hawaii:

> While encamped at the seaport of Chemulp'o, awaiting the transport to bear
> them away into a strange land, Rev. George Heber Jones, a Methodist Episcopal
> Missionary, became interested in their welfare, and held large tent meetings
> in order to inspire them with laudable ambitions and prepare them for the
> strange experiences so soon to overtake them. He also handed a few of the
> leaders among them letters of introduction to the Superintendent of Methodist
> Missions in Hawaii, and gave them in parting his heartfelt blessing.[7]

Later, in 1906, when Jones published an article under the title,
"The Koreans in Hawaii," in the *Korea Review,* the missionary
mentioned that he met in Hawaii a Korean and his family whom
he had baptized in Korea.[8]

As has been pointed out, some Korean immigrants were converted
to Christianity even prior to their departure for the Hawaiian Islands.
Therefore, the history of the church in the Korean American
community may be considered a continuing saga of Korean Christianity which may be divided into four major periods: the period of
beginning and growth (1903–1918); the period of conflicts and
divisions (1919–1945); the period of status quo (1946–1967); and
the period of revival (1968–1976).

The period between 1903 and 1918 saw a rapid growth in the
number of Koreans professing Christianity as their religion. It has
been estimated that during the period, approximately 2,800 Koreans
were converted to Christianity and thirty-nine churches were established in the Hawaiian Islands alone. This numerical growth is a
remarkable achievement in view of the fact that the total number
of persons of Korean ancestry in the Islands during this period
was less than 8,000. A number of factors seem to have contributed
to such phenomenal growth. First, Korean society in the Hawaiian
Islands lacked strong social groups established on the basis of
traditional ties. Although clan associations and organization by sworn
brotherhood existed,[9] they proved ineffective in dealing with white
Americans. Second, Christianity may have been used as a means

of gaining sympathy from white Americans. This particular point was alluded to by Jones:

> One third of all the Koreans in Hawaii are professing Christians. They dominate the life in the camps on the Islands of Oahu, Kauai and Maui where they are stamping out gambling and intoxication. The Koreans have fallen into sympathetic hands in Hawaii.[10]

Third, the church offered those who were not members of either clan association or sworn brotherhood their only opportunity to engage in social intercourse outside their work camps. Fourth, there seems to have been a certain degree of group pressure on non-Christians, particularly after a significant number of Koreans had become converts. Thus parents who were not Christians would send their children to church.

During this period several churches of different denominations were established in Hawaii. The first group to establish a church were Korean Christians of Methodist persuasion. Efforts to establish a congregation began on November 3, 1903, when a group of Koreans in Honolulu chose An Ch'ung-su and U Pyŏng-gil to negotiate with a superintendent of the Methodist mission for a place of worship. As a result, the Korean Evangelical Society was organized a week later and church services were held at a rented house. The society did not receive regular church status until April 1905, when John W. Wadman was appointed superintendent of the Hawaiian missions of the Methodist Episcopal church by Bishop John W. Hamilton.[11] Wadman contributed much to the growth of the Methodist church in the Korean community in the Hawaiian Islands from the time of his appointment until his resignation on January 1, 1914.[12] He was instrumental in purchasing a piece of property situated on the corner of Punchbowl and Beretania streets, Honolulu, at a sum of $12,000 for the purpose of organizing a boarding school for Korean boys. While serving as superintendent of the mission, Wadman also supervised the boarding school which was directed by his wife until June 1913, when Syngman Rhee, later first president of the Republic of Korea, was appointed principal of the school.

It is alleged by Kim Wŏn-yong (Warren Kim), author of *Chae-Mi Hanin osimnyŏn-sa* [Fifty-year history of the Koreans in America], that Rhee was given this position by Wadman as an expression of his gratitude to Rhee, who had helped settle a dispute between Wadman and the people of the Korean community in the Islands. The dispute began with a local newspaper report, on October 4, 1912, that Wadman had received a sum of $750 from a certain Japanese consul in Honolulu, who had donated the money ostensibly to help poor Koreans. When he was confronted by a group of angry Koreans who hated anything symbolic of Japan, Wadman acknowledged receiving the money, but he gave a reason different from that reported by the newspaper. He said that he had accepted money for maintenance expenses for the boarding school.

Koreans felt it was their moral duty to oppose the acceptance of financial assistance from an official of the government that had deprived them of their nation since 1910. Wadman was further embarrassed when Korean students refused to attend school. At this time Syngman Rhee arrived in Honolulu at the invitation of the Korean National Association. When he was asked by Wadman to intervene in the dispute, he gladly accepted the request and worked toward a solution. With assistance from Rhee, Wadman managed to avoid a confrontation of a more serious nature, but he also sowed seeds of conflict and dissension by appointing Rhee principal of the boarding school.[13]

The second Methodist church grew out of the Korean Evangelical Society, organized by a group of Korean residents in San Francisco on October 8, 1905. Mun Kyŏng-ho assumed the responsibility of conducting church services until July 15, 1906, when Pang Hwa-chung succeeded him as evangelist for the group. The society was expanded after Yang Chu-sam arrived in San Francisco on his way to Nashville, Tennessee, where he was to attend the Divinity School of Vanderbilt University. Upon his arrival Yang saw everywhere around him the life of adversity and poverty to which his countrymen were subjected. He was so moved emotionally by what he saw that he decided to postpone his study in order to take on the work of helping his countrymen spiritually and materially. The society rented a building on California Street and held a church service dedicating the house of worship. The building had three floors. The first floor was used as a dining hall for Korean boarders, who were accommodated on the third floor. The second floor was used for church services. The society was granted its present church status after Reverend Yi Tae-wi was appointed pastor on August 5, 1911. The congregation moved to the present church building located on Powell Street in June 1928. Today, the Korean Methodist Church of San Francisco is the oldest such church on the mainland of the United States and has a membership of three hundred. Its annual budget as of April 1974 is approximately $21,000 and its total assets are estimated at $500,000.[14]

During the first period, an Episcopal church was organized in Honolulu by the efforts of Chŏng Hyŏng-gu and Kim Ik-song, also known as Isaiah Kim. On February 10, 1905, a church service dedicating the Korean Episcopal church was held at Saint Andrew Episcopal Church in Honolulu, and the church rented a classroom at a local elementary school as a place for church services. On October 16 of the same year, the church was permitted the use of a part of Saint Elizabeth Episcopal Church, a local Chinese church.

The first period also saw the establishment in Los Angeles, in 1906, of the first Presbyterian church ever established in the United States by Korean Christians. A group of Korean residents of Los Angeles sent a representative to negotiate with the Presbyterian Missionary Extension Board for a place of worship. The board responded by dispatching Reverend Richard, who became instrumental in establishing the Korean Presbyterian mission. The group rented a house on Bunker Hill Street for services but did not receive church status until April 1921.

The second period in the history of the church in the Korean American community was marked by disputes over policy on church administration, church financial business, and operation of the Korean boarding school which was later known as the Chungang Hakwŏn, or the Central Institute. As has been noted, Syngman Rhee was able to secure principalship of the Central Institute in 1913. No sooner had he become principal than he requested use of a lot on the corner of Emma and Punchbowl streets, purchased by the Korean National Association of Hawaii at $1,500, on which to build a dormitory to accommodate students at the Central Institute. However, his request was denied by the delegates to the annual convention of the Korean National Association in 1915, and Rhee decided to use a less legitimate but more effective means, that of threat and coercion, to take the property away from the association. Rhee learned that there had been some irregularities in the business of running the association. It had been said that Hong In-p'yo, treasurer of the association, and Kim Chong-hak, its president, dipped into the till entrusted to them. Upon learning of the irregularities, Rhee demanded that he be given the power to supervise the treasury of the association and that the controversial property be turned over to him for use by the Korean school. Rhee seems to have orchestrated his demand with another high-handed method. A group of students from the Central Institute led by Yang Yu-ch'an came to the association's annual convention in May 1915 to beat up Yi Hong-gi, Kim Kyu-sŏp, Yi Chong-gun, and Kim Chong-hak for opposing Rhee's request.[15] The *Honolulu Advertiser* ran an article concerning this incident in July 1915 under the title, "Korean Trouble Gets into Court," which included the following:

> . . . An Hung Kyong, [An Hŭng-gyŏng] General Manager, charged Hong in Pio [Hong In-p'yo] for embezzling $120 from membership fees, and Kim Chong Hak [Kim Chong-hak] for embezzling $1,300. Yi Hong Ki [Yi Hong-gi] who was maltreated a month ago by a mob at Korean National Association brought a trial of 19 men in court. . . .[16]

The beating incident and the revelation of embezzlement of funds by officers of the association changed the mood of most members of the association. When the request was brought up for reconsideration, the delegates reversed their previous decision and thirty-five of thirty-eight voted for the free grant of the land.

Rhee was not only a catalyst to disputes among Koreans, but a sharp wedge between the Hawaiian Methodist mission and some Korean Methodist Christians. When William H. Fry was appointed to succeed Wadman as superintendent, on January 1, 1914, he learned that church financial matters had been dealt with in a less than businesslike manner. Fry wanted to correct past mistakes in the mission administration by means of his close personal supervision of both the church and the school. Also, it was alleged that Fry was opposed to the use of the church and school as training centers for political leaders and as centers of political activity related to the Korean independence movement against the Japanese Empire. Rhee, on the other hand, wanted to use church and school for these purposes. Furthermore, Rhee refused to take orders from Fry and challenged him to turn the governance of the school and church over to Koreans. Rhee was of the opinion that Koreans should have complete control over the church and school, since they were supported entirely by Koreans in Hawaii. Proponents of such diametrically opposed positions were certainly destined to travel separate courses sooner or later.[17]

The inevitable separation came in the fall of 1916, when a group of seventy or eighty people left their Methodist church in order to follow Rhee's leadership toward autonomy and self-determination of the church in the Korean community. The first church service after their separation was held at the residence of Pak Nae-sun, and the separatists decided to hold their church services at the Korean Girls' Seminary building. In 1918 the place of worship was moved to the school building located at Wailaie Street and 7th Avenue. At the beginning, the congregation was known simply as the Sillip Kyohoe, or the New Church, which was changed to the Korean Christian church sometime in 1917. This was not the only New Church in the Islands. A New Church was established at Koloa, Kauai, as early as 1915, and there were as many as fifteen when the separatist movement reached its zenith.

An important event in the development of the New Church took place on December 13, 1918, when the first Annual Delegates Conference of the Korean Christian Churches was held to establish an organization to coordinate various church activities and to discuss methods of combating the established Methodist church. Out of this conference emerged the Korean Christian missions known as the Central Korean Christian church. The delegates seem to have agreed on a major weapon against the well-established Methodist church, supported by a strong missionary organization. The idea of independence and self-government was to be their effective weapon, as Rhee expressed in a letter to Kingsley K. Lyu dated December 12, 1944:

> . . . When I founded the Korean Christian Church with you people, I was sure I would lose my Korean and American friends in the Methodist Church. But I was resolved that we Koreans should control our own church administration without depending upon the foreign missions; that we should govern our own affairs. It was natural that the Methodists criticized our Christian people and were bitter to us. . . .[18]

From the beginning of the separatist movement to August 1945, when Korea was freed from Japanese colonialism, the members of the Korean Christian church were an indispensable part of the Korean national independence movement abroad. Ideologically, they advocated as strongly as they could that Koreans were ready to exercise self-government and independence. As evidence, they pointed to their Korean church as a symbol of independence from foreign domination and of self-government in administering their own affairs. Financially, they made contributions from their meager earnings as workers on sugar plantations or as manual laborers.

The rapid growth of the Korean Christian churches in Hawaii seems to have had an adverse effect on the quality of the spiritual care received by members of the churches. There were in the Korean Christian churches no persons trained in the Christian ministry until 1919. Those who had taken on the responsibility of church pastorates were people acquainted with some Bible lessons and the written Korean language, hardly acceptable qualifications for the difficult task of caring for man's spiritual needs. Sometime in 1919, after he had been ordained and admitted into the California Synod of the Presbyterian Church, Min Ch'an-ho arrived in Honolulu. As an ordained man of God, however, Min did not live up to standards commensurate with either the training that he had received or the ministerial ethics that he had pledged to uphold. According to Kingsley K. Lyu, Min began to perform the duties of a bishop immediately after he had become pastor of the Korean Christian church in Honolulu, and ordained men into the ministry of the Korean Christian churches. It is alleged by Lyu that Min ordained more than ten of Rhee's supporters by laying his hands on their heads. Therefore, when the charter of the Central Korean Christian Church of Honolulu was obtained on December 9, 1924, the churches on the islands of Oahu, Maui, and Hawaii had pastors ordained by Min.[19]

These "ordained pastors," handpicked for their political and personal loyalty to Rhee, soon began to turn churches into clubhouses for political lectures. Church services officiated by them usually began with a lecture on a political topic and ended with an announcement of political activities in connection with the Tongji-hoe, the Comrade

Society, a political organization which according to Kim Wŏn-yong was established by Rhee on July 7, 1921, to support his Korean national independence movement. Kingsley K. Lyu gives the date as November 1920. It is said that during church services the pastors seldom neglected to praise Rhee, who was remembered by them in their prayers. Those who neglected such decorum soon found themselves without a job. According to Lyu, a pastor formerly of the Presbyterian faith accepted the pastorate at the Korean Christian church but was soon relieved of his duties because he forgot to repeat the name of Rhee in his prayers.[20]

It is not surprising, in retrospect, that those ordained to the Christian ministry in such a hollow manner confused personal loyalty to a political leader with services to mankind, and an ideological message for an earthly kingdom with the universal message for the heavenly kingdom.

Conflicts and disputes did not end with the separation of Rhee's followers from the Methodist church. The Korean Christian church had a series of its own internal dissensions. The first occurred soon after Min's resignation in 1929. Min was forced to resign, as he had been accused of misappropriating a $15,000 church-building fund. His successor, Yi Yong-jik, was anxious to enforce the church regulations originally written by Syngman Rhee in the hope that the church would become a house of worship rather than a place for supporting Rhee's political activities. Soon the congregation was divided into two groups, one group supporting Yi and the other determined to oust him. Charges and countercharges were made, and thousands of dollars were spent as legal fees paid to determine the legitimate owner of the Korean Christian Church of Honolulu. Almost every Sunday the local police were called in to protect the church service, officiated by Yi, against the violence of the anti-Yi faction.

Another controversy arose in the summer of 1946, when the pastor of the Korean Christian church attempted to separate politics from church affairs. With the approval of the church board, the pastor announced that no person or group would be allowed to use the church building for purposes other than church-related activities. This announcement touched off a series of verbal attacks against the pastor and members of the church board. A small group, led by a former assistant treasurer, accused the pastor of being anti-Rhee, as he had failed to repeat the name of Rhee in his prayers. On September 29, 1946, when the church board refused to recognize such a characterization of the pastor, the group attempted to take over the church administration by force. The controversy over which group was the orthodox congregation of the Korean Christian church was finally decided by the court, which ordered the two groups to unite in October 1948.[21]

Several churches of different denominations were established on the mainland of the United States during the second period. As many Koreans began to move from the Hawaiian Islands to such metropolitan areas on the mainland as Oakland, Los Angeles, Chicago, and New York, there was an increasing need to establish local churches. As early as June 1914, a small group of Koreans in Oakland met at the residence of Mun Wŏn-ch'il to conduct church services. They were officiated by Reverend Hwang Sa-yong, who worked for the Methodist Episcopal Church South. On August 10, 1917, the group moved its place of worship to the residence of Cho Sŏng-hak and invited Im Chong-gu, a student at the Pacific School of Religion, Berkeley, California, to serve as evangelist for the group. After Im had become an ordained minister, the group negotiated with the Methodist Episcopal mission for a place of worship. The mission sent Reverend David, who appointed Im Chong-gu and No Sin-t'ae as evangelists for the church, which was officially established on March 2, 1929. In 1938 the group purchased a building located on Webster Street and dedicated it as a place of worship on December 20. In July 1940 the congregation was moved to another building located on Harrison Street in order to accommodate the increasing membership.

A group of Korean residents in New York negotiated in February 1923 with a Methodist mission for a place of worship. The mission extended its help by providing a large sum of money for the purchase of a building located on West 21st Street. The church building was dedicated on April 23. The congregation moved to a larger building located on West 115th Street in order to accommodate an expanding church membership in October 1927. During the same year, the Korean Methodist Church of Chicago, which had been established in July 1924, moved to a new building situated on Lake Park Avenue.

A conflict developed within the Korean Presbyterian Church of Los Angeles soon after its establishment, and on October 14, 1924, a group of church members severed their relations with the church and established their own church known as the Free Church. On July 10, 1930, the members of the Free Church sent their representatives to the Methodist Episcopal mission to ask for assistance in establishing a church. The mission sent Reverend David, who officiated over the establishment of the Korean Methodist Church of Los Angeles on October 16, 1930. Today, the church building, which was dedicated on October 7, 1945, is located on West 29th Street.[22] Besides these Methodist churches established in major metropolitan areas, there was a Presbyterian church in Reedley, California, which was organized in June 1936. Also, a Christian church, modelled after the Korean Christian Church of Honolulu, was established by members of the Tongji-hoe in September 1936.

Compared with the second period in the history of the church in the Korean American community, which was replete with controversial disputes and conflicting interests, the third period, between 1946 and 1967, was characterized by efforts on the part of the *Ilttae* (first generation) to maintain the status quo, and by an attitude of indifference and rebellion on the part of *Itae* (second generation, Koreans born in America of immigrant parents) and *Samtae* (third generation, children of the second generation). A number of social, cultural, and political factors seem to have contributed to this intergenerational conflict. First, the *Ilttae* had seen their national sovereignty gradually eroded by the Japanese Empire, prior to their departure for the Hawaiian Islands and the mainland of the United States. After their arrival in America, most of them kept a burning patriotism for Korea intact, and they participated directly or indirectly in the effort to regain Korea's national independence. The *Ilttae* as a whole had a political cause to fight and live for throughout their lives.

However, to the *Itae* and *Samtae* the political independence of Korea was more ideological rhetoric than a political imperative. After independence came to Korea in 1945, that issue no longer served as a rallying point for Koreans in America. Second, to *Ilttae* the church was a place of both social interaction and cultural identification. After all, they spoke the same language and shared the same values and customs, and much of their unique cultural behavior was mutually reinforced in the social contacts provided by the church. Although the *Itae* had been under strong cultural influence from the *Ilttae*, they must have felt strange at times and somewhat alienated when they were taken to church by their parents, who spoke only Korean to their contemporaries. So far as the *Samtae* were concerned, they could hardly identify themselves with the *Ilttae* religiously, for they did not understand either their language or their culture. As pointed out by Cho Kyŏng-suk Gregor, the *Itae* "show a complete lack of interest in the matter of politics and religion."[23] Third, the exclusion law and the quota system in American immigration policy from 1924 to 1968 prevented more Koreans from coming to the United States.[24] Had they been allowed to enter, they would have provided their ethnic church with more vitality and spiritual leadership.

The fourth period in the history of the church in the Korean American community began with a new influx of immigrants from Korea, which has sent more than 200,000 nationals to the United States, particularly to large metropolitan areas, since 1965. It is estimated that there are now as many as 80,000 Koreans in the

Los Angeles area alone, and more new arrivals are expected to join their countrymen in this area. This new wave of immigration promises resources and leadership long needed badly for a revival of the ethnic church in the Korean American community. However, it also portends potential problems for the church. There are already some signs of the stress and strain to which the church in the Korean American community has long been subjected. One such sign is the proliferation of churches founded on the bedrock of denominationalism. A number of historical and social forces seem responsible for the emergence of the denominational church within the Korean community today. New immigrants arrive in the United States with their own religious preferences, and not surprisingly, they look for the church of their choice or try to establish their own denominational church. This seems to be a major cause for the proliferation of churches. For instance, there are today in the city of San Francisco a total of nine churches attended almost exclusively by Koreans. Of these only two share the same denominational affiliation. These churches were originally established as denominational churches.[25]

Other churches professing different brands of Christianity seem to have less than clear philosophies for their denominational affiliation. Whether or not these churches have been established separately because of fine differences in the theological interpretation of the Bible is yet to be clarified. What seems clear to those who have carefully watched the painful and long metamorphosis of the Korean ethnic church is that disputes over petty individual interests and honors rather than theological concerns have been predominant reasons for divisions within the church since its inception in the Korean American community. The recent dispute between two pastors of the Korean Missionary Church located on 11th and New Hampshire streets, Los Angeles, is a case in point.

Apparently the church had been established under the leadership of Reverend Ko Wŏn-yong. Ko was elected chairman of the church board, and the responsibility for running the church fell on his shoulders. Ko later invited one of his friends, Reverend Chang Yun-song, to take care of his congregation while he was away for missionary duty. When Ko returned from his mission work to take up his position as pastor of the church he had helped to build, Chang refused to relinquish the post and claimed that the congregation had recognized him as legitimate chairman of the church board. Chang continued to conduct church services and even refused to call upon Ko to officiate at Sunday services. As Ko said in an interview with a newspaper reporter later, he felt that he was alienated from his own congregation.

One Sunday Ko decided to lock the door of the church building where Chang was to hold his church service. Then he led a group of his sympathizers to the residence of a church elder for their own church service. Angered by Ko's action, which had left approximately one hundred people stranded on the street, a group of four or five representatives from among Chang's followers came to protest against Ko and disrupted the church service in progress. Irritated by the unexpected visitors, someone from Ko's group called in local police to intervene in the dispute. Today the congregation remains divided without a hope for reunification.[26]

As has been observed, the new influx of large numbers of Korean immigrants into the United States also promises growth and development for the Korean ethnic church. The number of churches is increasing by leaps and bounds. There are more than twenty churches in the Los Angeles area alone. There are three Korean churches in the vicinity of Seattle, where there was not even a single church for Koreans prior to 1968.[27]

The quality of sermons delivered from pulpits has improved, and the sermons have demonstrated deliberate efforts of pastors to interpret and teach the Bible without influencing the laymen's secular interests, a practice which had plagued the church in the Korean American community during the first and second periods of its history.

In spite of the conflicts and problems within the church, it has served the Korean American community in a number of important areas which would otherwise have been neglected. It is unfortunate, retrospectively speaking, that during its embryonic stage the church was swept into a vortex of political controversies over philosophical arguments and over strategies for the Korean national independence movement. It is tragic, particularly in view of the fact that so much of the energy and resources of the church were diverted to an unrealistic and naive notion that the leaders and followers of "Christian America," when sufficiently supplicated by their fellow Korean Christians, would assist the Koreans in their fight against Imperial Japan. The leaders of the Korean national independence movement were largely ignorant of American foreign policy toward Imperial Japan, particularly during the early period of the movement. They were also too ignorant of the dynamics of American domestic politics of accommodation to utilize it for their cause. Given the historical conditions under which the Korean independence movement was undertaken, however, the church played an active role in supporting propaganda and diplomatic efforts to restore Korea's independence.

The Korean independence movement was supported financially by a great number of small contributions made largely by Korean residents in the Hawaiian Islands,[28] most of whom were members of local churches, particularly Korean Christian churches. When the Korean Commission, established sometime in the autumn of 1919 in Washington, D.C., issued bonds, during the same year, to generate the first $250,000 of the $5 million to be used for diplomatic and propaganda purposes, many Korean Christians purchased them.[29]

The church also played an active role in educational and journalistic efforts to maintain and perpetuate Korean culture. Most of the Korean immigrants seem to have sent their children to Korean-language schools for practical as well as patriotic reasons. First of all, they wanted to bring up their children as Koreans. In order to achieve this goal in an alien culture, they needed an educational institution devoted to the teaching of Korean history, language, and culture. The church was chosen primarily for three reasons. First, there were already churches established in various work camps, and therefore there was a basic organizational structure for the task. Second, most of the people qualified to teach children anything about Korea were pastors, who were literate enough to instruct them.[30] Third, due to lack of instructional materials, the Bible and Christian hymnbooks were used as textbooks.

Korean immigrants established their language schools as a symbol of their national independence. There were already foreign-language schools operated by Japanese and Chinese in the Islands, and the Koreans were determined not to be surpassed in this crucial area of national culture. Further, they saw an opportunity to put the Korean language to the practical use of educating their children, who were attending English-language schools. They hoped that their children would serve them as interpreters.[31] Various bulletins were also published by a number of churches, and they were used both as newspapers and instructional materials, since they carried Bible lessons in Korean. An important one, published by the Korean Methodist Church of Honolulu, was called the *Honolulu Korean Church Bulletin* and was published from November 1904 to October 1940.

Available reports on the projects sponsored by the church in Korean American communities today seem to indicate that recreational and social activities for group cohesion are being emphasized more than are educational and political programs, though there are on the mainland a few Korean-language schools supported by the local churches. This is certainly in accord with the needs of the Korean ethnic community today, and it is highly desirable that the church detach itself from controversies over Korea's internal politics.

There is, however, a vital need waiting to be filled in the Korean American community by either the church or other grass-roots social organizations. If Korean immigrants in America are to share fully with other Americans what their adopted country has to offer to its citizens, then they have to participate sooner or later in American domestic politics of accommodation, separatism, or radicalism. Whatever their choice of political style, the Korean immigrants will soon be in need of an organizational base for their participation in American politics. In the past, Irish and Italian Americans have used their ethnic affiliation with Catholicism rather effectively to gain political power.[32] Whether or not Korean Americans will use their church as a political weapon remains to be seen.

Notes

1. Bernice B.H. Kim, "The Koreans in Hawaii," *Social Science* 9:4 (October 1934): 410. In her later work, "The Koreans in Hawaii" (M.A. thesis, University of Hawaii, 1937), p. 209, Kim states that "the Koreans were told that they were going to America, a Christian country, and that it would be the proper and advantageous thing to become Christians. All the young Koreans were eager to succeed in their venture, so one and all professed to become Christians."

2. Fred Harvey Harrington, *God, Mammon and the Japanese: Dr. Horace N. Allen and Korean-American Relations, 1884–1905* (Madison: University of Wisconsin Press, 1944) pp. 103–08.

3. Harrington, *God, Mammon and the Japanese*, pp. 19–25.

4. Deshler to Wilson, Governors' Files, *Carter–U.S. Depts.*, Archives of Hawaii (Honolulu), October 1905–June 1907.

5. Yi Tae-sŏng, "The Story of Korean Immigration," *The Korean Students' of Hawaii Yearbook, 1932* (Honolulu: Korean Students' Alliance of Hawaii), p. 47.

6. Deshler's biography is incomplete. According to Ch'oe Song-yŏn, author of *Kaehang kwa yangkwan yŏkchŏng* [Opening of Korea and history of western-style buildings], as reported by Yun Yŏ-jun in "Miju imin ch'ilsim-nyŏn" [Seventy years of immigration in America], *Kyŏnghyang Shinmun* [Kyŏnghyang Daily], October 13, 1973, Deshler had joined the Orient Consolidated Mining Company, and lived in Chemulpo, now Inchon, with a Japanese woman.

7. John W. Wadman, "Educational Work among Koreans," Reports of Public Instruction, December 31, 1910–December 1912 (Honolulu: Department of Public Instruction, 1912), pp. 146–49.

8. George Heber Jones, "The Koreans in Hawaii," *Korea Review* 6:11 (November 1906): 405.

9. Linda Shin, in "Koreans in America," *Roots: An Asian American Reader* (Los Angeles: University of California, Asian American Studies Center, 1971), pp. 201–06, stated that "most of the emigrants who came to Hawaii before 1906 were relatively unorganized in traditional social groups." This seems to be an overstatement in view of the fact that Korean immigrants had maintained their traditional social organizations in Hawaii for the first few years. For a discussion of these organizations see Kingsley K. Lyu, "Korean Nationalist Activities in Hawaii and America, 1901–1945," manuscript in possession of Professor Donald D. Johnson, Graduate Division, University of Hawaii, 1950.

10. Jones, "Koreans in Hawaii," p. 405.

11. Kim Wŏn-yong (Warren Y. Kim), *Chae-Mi Hanin osimnyŏn-sa* [Fifty-year history of the Koreans in America] (Reedley, California: Charles Ho Kim, 1959), p. 47.

12. Kim Wŏn-yong, in *Chae-Mi Hanin*, claims that Wadman was relieved of his duties in June 1914. However, according to a letter from William Henry Fry, Wadman's immediate successor, to L.E. Pinkham, Governor of the Territory of Hawaii, dated July 27, 1915 (Archives of Hawaii), Wadman was relieved of his duties on January 1, 1914.

13. Kim Wŏn-yong, *Chae-Mi Hanin*, pp. 42–43.

14. *Miju Tong-a* [Tong-a Daily in America], April 18, 1974.

15. Lyu, "Korean Nationalist Activities," pp. 52–53. Yang Yu-ch'an was appointed by Syngman Rhee as Korean ambassador to the United States when Rhee became the first president of the Republic of Korea.

16. *Honolulu Advertiser*, July 3, 1915.

17. Lyu, "Korean Nationalist Activities," p. 64.

18. Quoted in Lyu, "Korean Nationalist Activities," p. 68.

19. Lyu, "Korean Nationalist Activities," p. 71.

20. Lyu, "Korean Nationalist Activities," p. 75.

21. Lyu, "Korean Nationalist Activities," p. 76.

22. Lee Kyung, "Settlement Patterns of Los Angeles Koreans" (M.A. thesis, University of California, Los Angeles, 1969), p. 35.

23. Cho Kyŏng-suk Gregor, "Korean Immigrants in Gresham, Oregon: Community Life and Social Adjustment" (M.A. thesis, University of Oregon, 1963), p. 54.

24. Although the act of October 3, 1965, (P.L. 89–236) repealed the national origin quota system established in 1924, the act included a three-year phase-out period.

25. *Miju Tong-a*, April 4, 1974.

26. *Miguk Sosik* [American News], February 26, 1973.

27. *Miguk Sosik*, April 23, 1974.

28. A careful count of the people who promised to make contributions, as reported in the *Korean Pacific Weekly*, an official bulletin published by Tongji-hoe indicates that a total of sixty-nine persons promised a sum of $1,026, or less than $15 per person. See *Korean Pacific Weekly* (June 14, 1941): 19.

29. Kim Wŏn-yong, *Chae-Mi Hanin*, p. 379.

30. Helen Lewis Givens, "The Korean Community in Los Angeles County" (M.A. thesis, University of Southern California, 1939), p. 38.

31. Lyu, "Korean Nationalist Activities," p. 33.

32. Edgar Litt, *Ethnic Politics in America* (Glenview, Illinois: Scott, Foresman and Company, 1970), pp. 60–80.

Korean Community Organizations in America:
Their Characteristics and Problems

Hyung-chan Kim

THE HISTORICAL DEVELOPMENT and current conditions of Korean community organizations in America present historians and social scientists with a number of problems. First, documentation on Korean community organizations is scarce in spite of the fact that it has been over seventy years since the first group of Korean immigrants arrived in America. Second, the large number of Korean immigrants entering America every year makes it almost impossible to study their organizations, which change kaleidoscopically in response to the flow of new immigrants and their needs. Third, with the influx of new immigrants, new organizations are created, like mushrooms after a spring shower, by those dissatisfied with established organizations or determined to offer their compatriots social services and collective security not well provided by older organizations. Fourth, there is at present no central organization to coordinate efforts of those groups in Korean communities in different parts of the United States to which a majority of Korean immigrants give voluntary allegiance as regular members. The absence of a centralized agency responsible for gathering and disseminating data relevant to the experience of Korean immigrants, both old and new, further complicates the task of researchers.

Korean community organizations in selected areas, including San Francisco, Los Angeles, and Honolulu, will be studied here for the following reasons. First, these urban centers have the oldest settlements established by Korean immigrants. Although the activities of Korean community organizations in these areas have not been systematically and continuously documented, basic documentation in the form of journalistic reports has been published intermittently by *Shinhan Minbo* (New Korea), which has been in existence for more than six decades. This source of information, along with diaries, anecdotes, interviews, and a few published as well as unpublished studies, allow a preliminary analysis of Korean community organizations. Second, these selected areas are major centers of organizational activities among Koreans. Much of the organizational effort for the Korean independence movement was undertaken in these areas. It is also in these areas that social, cultural, and religious groups have worked to sustain and promote Korean culture and identity. Third, of an estimated 200,000 Koreans who have entered the United States since the beginning of Korean immigration to America in 1903, most of them since 1965, more than 120,000 reportedly reside in these three cities. Los Angeles alone is believed to have more than 80,000 Korean immigrants, who have established 250 social, cultural, religious, economic, and political organizations. Fourth, although there is no central organization with which a majority of Korean residents in the three cities is willing to be affiliated, the Korean Association of Southern California in Los Angeles has tried to coordinate activities of groups by establishing within the association a board of directors, members of which represent the organizational purpose and interests of their own groups.

Numerous theoretical and conceptual approaches have been employed by social scientists in their study of characteristics of social organizations. Some representative approaches are the theory of administration, perhaps better known as the scientific management theory; the theory of human relations, which gave rise to the concept of informal organization; and the decision-making theory.[1] None of these approaches seems suited as a methodological tool to the present study, as information on the organizational behaviors of Korean immigrants is lacking. Inasmuch as the study is exploratory, intent on stimulating further research by providing basic information and conceptual models, an historical and analytical approach is employed. It is necessary to describe historically the development of Korean community organizations, since Korean immigration took place under special circumstances. For the purpose of analyzing characteristics of Korean community organizations in these urban centers, the concept of *urban ethnic organizing*, recently developed by Daniel Reidy in his study of the ethnic people of Cleveland,[2] is applied, to illustrate the basis of Korean community organizations and how they promote the interests of the Korean ethnic group.

Urban ethnic organizing refers to the processes whereby an operative utilizes urban ethnicity to bring about planned social change for group development in an urban community. Urban ethnicity is "the basic cultural patterns that establish and maintain the distinctness of non-Anglo-conforming population groups in cities."[3] By this definition, Korean immigrants settled along a two-mile stretch on Olympic Boulevard in Los Angeles demonstrate urban ethnicity. Cultural patterns which set them off from other non-Korean groups are their heritage, national origin, language, and religion. The various organizations in the Korean community in Los Angeles are agents of social change promoting group development of Korean residents. Group development, therefore, has two essential features: it is based on ethnicity and directed toward social change. Planned social change focuses on three areas: electoral politics, economic development, and "new social issues." Although, depending on changing circumstances, other social concerns of the residents of an urban ethnic community may be grouped under the rubric of "new social issues," the following are representative concerns: education and culture, social services, security, community control, land use and planning, consumer protection, and environmental enhancement. Figure 1 illustrates urban ethnic organizing and its conceptual scheme.

Social organizations abound in the Korean community. However, none seems comprehensive enough in its organizational philosophy and purpose to encompass all of the needs of Korean residents, particularly the needs of recent immigrants who lack social services of many kinds. Consequently, in analyzing Korean community organizations based on ethnicity whose purpose is to promote group development by effecting social change, we must identify community organizations with services they have provided or proposed. Given their common base and purpose, the only differentiating characteristic between groups is the kind of social change each has brought about or plans to effect.

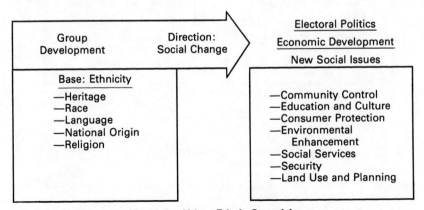

Figure 1.   Urban Ethnic Organizing

Few organizations are capable of bringing about planned social change, no matter how lofty and encompassing their philosophy and purpose, unless they have resources within their reach. Resources required by ethnic organizations for effectiveness are: constituency development, planned social change, and organizational maintenance. By constituency development is meant the ability of an organization to broaden its ethnic base within the community it purports to serve by utilizing ethnic symbols, ideological resiliency, and strong leadership. In order to work toward social change an ethnic organization needs: 1) clear goals for social change, 2) orientation toward the future in the program it initiates or sponsors, 3) communitarian scope in the number of participants and the manner in which they participate, 4) ability to use confrontation as a means of effecting social change, and 5) ability to build coalitions with other organizations within the ethnic community or across ethnic lines in order to strengthen its position. Organizational maintenance refers to the concern of an organization for its very survival. An organization with a long history of continuing programs tends to be efficient and multi-issue in scope, and capable of raising funds for its projects. Figure 2 illustrates the twelve characteristics of an effective organization.

The history of Korean community organizations in these selected areas may be divided into three major periods: the independence movement (1903–1945); organizational dormancy (1946–1965); and organizational resurgence, which began after enactment of a new immigration law in America in 1965. The history of the church

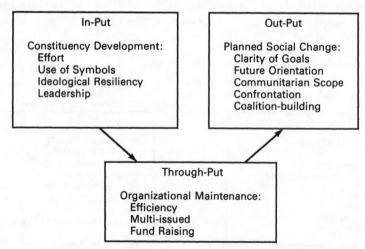

Figure 2. Characteristics of an Effective Ethnic Organization

in the Korean community will not be discussed here unless it is directly related to the topic under study. The church in the Korean community in America was treated in the preceding essay.[4]

Immediately after their arrival in Hawaii in 1903, Korean immigrants began to form community organizations. From 1903 until just before the annexation of Korea by Japan in 1910 four types of community organizations, three of which were indigenous Korean organizations, developed. They were religious, political, and social in their basic characteristics. As discussed in the preceding essay, Koreans converted to Christianity prior to their immigration established a number of churches in Hawaii. As a social institution the church was not an indigenous Korean organization. It is significant, however, that when Koreans banded together to establish a religious organization, they founded it on a relatively new religion they had recently embraced rather than on Korea's traditional religions.

The second community organization developed in Hawaii was Tonghoe or the village council, a self-governing body installed on each plantation having more than ten Korean families. The Tongjang, the village chief, was head of the Tonghoe and was elected once a year by popular vote before an assembly of all adult male Koreans on the plantation. The village council was a law-enforcing agency authorized by its members to arrest, prosecute, and punish any Korean found guilty of breaking the community's code of ethics. To enforce the community's code of ethics the Tongjang was assisted by Sach'al, the sergeant at arms, and Kyŏngch'al, the police. Any Korean accused of having broken the code of ethics was brought before the Tongjang, who reviewed the case with the Sach'al. If the accused was found guilty, he was fined or flogged, depending upon the nature of the offense.[5]

The sworn brotherhood, which was more subterranean in its organizational structure than the church or the village council, was the third organization developed in Hawaii. The sworn brotherhood was organized by individuals in need of protection against foreigners. Some Koreans had fifty or sixty sworn brothers, each tattooed for membership identification. Although the sworn brotherhood was initially organized to protect members from foreigners, it eventually became a source of community conflict, as members of one brotherhood were pitted against those of another.[6]

The fourth type of community organization grew out of special political situations in Korea. Although Korea did not officially become a colony of Japan until 1910, when Japan annexed Korea, for all practical purposes, Korea became a colony of Japan in 1905. In September 1905 Russia, defeated by Japan in the war of colonial interests, agreed by the Treaty of Portsmouth to leave Korea to Japan for her colonization.[7] In November of the same year, Japan maneuvered Korea into signing a treaty establishing the residency-general in Seoul to take charge of Korea's external affairs. However, Japan did not limit itself to supervising Korea's international relations. Matters of domestic policy came increasingly under Japanese control, thus making Japan de facto ruler in Korea.[8]

As early as 1903 a political organization, Shinmin-hoe (New People's Society) was established in Honolulu by a number of Koreans who were concerned with Japanese penetration into Korea.[9] The society was organized for the purpose of resisting Japanese aggression and rebuilding Korea with people of regenerated spirit at home and abroad. The society did not receive much support from the community. In fact, the leaders of the society were branded traitors because of their radical ideas.[10] Another organization, Ch'inmok-hoe or the Friendship Society, was established in 1903 by An Ch'ang-ho with a small group of Korean students in San Francisco. The number of members remained small until 1905. When the news of the Protectorate Treaty signed on November 17, 1905, reached the Korean communities in Hawaii and San Francisco, a political awakening occurred among Koreans who saw a need for organizing for Korea's political independence.

From December 1905 to September 1907, Koreans in Hawaii established more than twenty organizations, the purposes of which included, without exception, resistance against the Japanese colonial policy and political independence for Korea.[11] Soon after the emergence of various political clubs and societies, many community leaders saw a need to integrate them into a stronger, unified organization. In September 1907, the leaders established Hanin Hapsŏng Hyŏphoe or the United Korean Society, headquartered in Honolulu. Community leaders in California consolidated small organizations scattered throughout the state: Kongnip Hyŏphoe, the Mutual Assistance Society, was formed in 1905. By 1908, the society had 130 members and chapters in Oakland, Los Angeles, Redlands, Riverside, Boyd, and Rock Spring.[12]

The efforts to consolidate and mobilize growing numbers of political organizations in Korean communities in America did not come to an end with the establishment of the Hanin Hapsŏng Hyŏphoe in Hawaii and the Kongnip Hyŏphoe in California. Leaders of the two organizations continued to develop close cooperation, which was greatly accelerated by the Stevens case of 1908. Durham Stevens, an American who was employed by the Japanese Foreign Office and subsequently appointed by the Japanese government as an advisor on Korea's financial and foreign affairs, was sent by Itō Hirobumi, the Japanese governor-general in Korea, to explain Japan's policy to the American government. On his way to Washington, D.C., he arrived in San Francisco on March 20, 1908, where he stated in an interview with a *San Francisco Chronicle* reporter that Japanese control of Korea was working for the good of Koreans. The Korean community was outraged by the statement and held a mass joint meeting of the Kongnip Hyŏphoe and Taedong Poguk-hoe, the Great Unity Fatherland Protection Society. The meeting selected four representatives, Mun Yang-mok, Ch'oe Chong-ik, Chŏng Ja-kwan, and Yi Hak-hyŏn, to confront Stevens and demand a public apology.[13] The four went to Stevens at the Fairmont Hotel and asked him to retract his statement and publicly apologize. When Stevens refused, he was severely assaulted, until other hotel guests intervened. On the following morning, March 23, Stevens, accompanied by the Japanese consul, Koike Chōzō, arrived at the Ferry Building to make his railway connection. As Stevens stepped down from a limousine, he was fatally shot by Chang In-whan, a member of the Taedong Poguk-hoe. Stevens was taken to a nearby hospital for emergency treatment, but he died on March 25 from the wounds he had received. Chang In-whan was arrested and arraigned a week later. The Korean community in California and Hawaii hired lawyers and interpreters, collected evidence, and solicited defense funds. A total of $7,390 was contributed by the Korean residents in Hawaii,[14] Mexico, China, Japan, and the United States for Chang's defense.

Tae-Hanin Kungmin-hoe or the Korean National Association, was organized on February 1, 1909, when the Kongnip Hyŏphoe and the Hanin Hapsŏng Hyŏphoe merged. The purpose of the association was to represent Korean interests in the United States. Headquarters were in San Francisco and chapter headquarters in Hawaii, Siberia, and Manchuria. The association required all Korean residents in America to become members and pay dues. The association took over the role of the Tonghoe and the sworn brotherhood as protector of the interests of Korean residents in the United States. It was alleged that the president of the association assumed the duties of a consul-general and of a chief of police. By 1910, when Korea became a colony of Japan, most political organizations established by Korean residents in America were consolidated into the Korean National Association.

The unity of the association did not last long, as conflicts arose among leaders of the Korean independence movement over the philosophies and strategies to be used in achieving Korea's independence. An Ch'ang-ho, one of the most active political leaders, along with Syngman Rhee and Pak Yong-man, saw achieving the independence of Korea as a long process requiring the spiritual regeneration of each Korean citizen. An rejected revolutionary methods; instead, he chose the patient approach of educating individuals. Syngman Rhee saw diplomacy as a means of achieving Korea's independence. He believed that pressure from a sufficient number of major powers of the world could force Japan to give up Korea. Pak Yong-man was the most radical activist of the three. He believed that Japan would give up Korea only if she were forced or defeated militarily. The three leaders were unable to work together within the organizational structure provided by the Korean National Association, and each decided to seek his own followers and win their support.

An Ch'ang-ho established Hŭngsa-dan, the Corps for the Advancement of Individuals, in San Francisco on May 13, 1913. With "virtue, intellect, and health" as its organizational philosophy, the Hŭngsa-dan concentrated on improving the lives of Korean residents in America. An was particularly interested in the well-being of Korean students. He aggressively recruited them for the Hŭngsa-dan, visiting many at their schools or places of work in order to persuade them to join his organization. Many students were impressed with An's philosophy for Korea's independence, and with his personal appearance and conduct. Among those who joined the Hŭngsa-dan were Yi Kwang-su, now considered the father of modern Korean literature, and Cho Pyŏng-ok, who later ran against Syngman Rhee as a presidential candidate.[15] Some Korean students avoided An because they had been warned by Rhee not to stay too long in San Francisco. One such student was Im Pyŏng-jik, who held a number of illustrious diplomatic posts under Rhee's administration.[16] The Hŭngsa-dan continued to build its organizational strength by expanding its membership and offering cultural and educational programs. When Korea gained independence in 1945, however, much of Hŭngsa-dan's philosophy lost its meaning for Koreans in America. For all practical purposes the corps is now defunct.

In April 1914 Pak Yong-man recruited 300 ex-soldiers of the Korean army from among the immigrants to Hawaii and organized them into Kun-dan or the Military Corps. From this organization eventually developed Tae-Chosŏn Tongnip-dan or the Korean National Independence League, which was formally established on March 3, 1919. The Tongnip-dan collected independence funds for Pak when he was in China to help him organize and train 3,000 Korean soldiers. It was reported that some of his followers, including Kim Yun-bae and Yang Mun-sŏ, sent Pak $1,000.[17] The organization was short lived as its leader was assassinated on October 17, 1928.

Tongji-hoe, the Comrade Society, was established, according to Kingsley K. Lyu, by Syngman Rhee in November 1920,[18] when Rhee was on his way to Shanghai to preside over cabinet meetings of the Korean Provisional Government as its president. En route to Shanghai from Washington, D.C., Rhee met in Honolulu a number of his ardent followers who were eager to organize a new group to support him exclusively. It is alleged by Kingsley K. Lyu that Rhee wanted, at first, to form Ch'ŏngnyŏn Tongji-hoe, the Youth

Comrade Society, but he was persuaded to accept the formation of the Tongji-hoe, which included both young and old members.

Upon his return to Honolulu from Shanghai in 1921, Rhee changed the name of the Hawaiian chapter of the Korean National Association to Kyomin-dan, the Korean Residents Association. Rhee reasoned that the objectives of the Korean National Association had been achieved by the establishment of the Korean Government-in-Exile and that the independence movement should be carried out by the government in Shanghai, of which he had been elected president on April 16, 1919. This was a move by Rhee to strengthen his position among the Korean residents in the Hawaiian Islands. Rhee believed that he would receive active support from organizations loyal to the Korean Provisional Government in Shanghai. Members of the Tongji-hoe continued to support Rhee in his effort to achieve Korea's independence through diplomatic channels. Many followers who were also members of the Korean Christian church contributed money to the Tongji-hoe until 1945.[19] After 1945, Rhee went to Korea, and the Tongji-hoe became practically defunct, although it still maintains offices in Los Angeles and Honolulu.

During the second period, between 1946 and 1965, no significant steps were taken toward the establishment of organizations for Korean immigrants. Korea's independence, a major motivating force behind the political activities of Korean community organizations, had been achieved, and no major issues were in the offing. Most of the early immigrants had died and those remaining had no vested interests in Korean politics. Occasionally political activists opposed Syngman Rhee's rule in Korea, but they were effectively checked by Rhee, who kept a long arm on Koreans in America. Also, due to American immigration policy, no large groups of new Korean immigrants came to America until 1965. Every year a few hundred Korean students were allowed to enter America on student visas, but most of them did not develop a keen interest in either American or Korean politics, although some of them participated in local Korean students' associations.

Interest in organizational activities emerged from second generation Koreans. In 1960, a group of second generation Koreans born in California and Hawaii gathered to establish a nonpolitical and nonreligious civic organization. The organization was the American-Korean Association, and its headquarters was at 4033 Don Felipe Drive, Los Angeles. Its main purpose was to promote Korean culture and tradition. However, the limited number of Korean specialists available forced the organization to invite as speakers non-Koreans including a mayor, governor, congressman, and NASA space scientists. Today, one of the more significant programs of the organization provides scholarships for local high school students.[20]

The third period of organizational resurgence began almost simultaneously with the influx of large numbers of new Korean immigrants into America after 1965, when the American government repealed the national origin quota system, which had been the basis for American immigration policy since 1924. Since 1970, an average of 15,000 Koreans have immigrated to America every year. The swelling Korean population in Los Angeles and its vicinity has developed fifty community organizations which claim to be nonprofit, fifty church groups, four Buddhist temples, and over fifty high school and college alumni associations.[21] Figure 3 identifies the "nonprofit" organizations and their professed goals.

Of these organizations, the Korean Association of Southern California now enjoys wider participation by community people than any other group. Since 1968, when it was officially organized, the association has tried to legitimatize its existence by holding an annual

Focus on Issues	Names of the Organizations

Electoral Politics: Korean-American Political Association of Southern California.

Economic Development: Korean-American C.P.A. Society, Korean Travel Agency Association of California, Korean Petroleum Dealers Association of California, Korean Hair Products Association of America, Korean Food Association of Southern California, Korean Commonwealth Credit Union of California, Korean Town Development Corporation, Na U Club, Korean Photographic Association of California, Tae Kwon Do Federation of California, Hwa Rang Do Association of California, Korean Nurses Association of California, Korean Dental Association of California, Korean Medical Association of California, Korean Oriental Herb Doctor Association of U.S.A., American Korean Businessmen's Association, Korean Chamber of Commerce of Southern California, Korean Association of Southern California.

New Social Issues:
  Education and Culture: Christian Youth Association of California, Korean Philharmonic Orchestra, Los Angeles Korean Opera Company, Korean Musician Association of California, Korean Artist Association of Southern California, Korean-American Youth Foundations, Korean American Sport Association of A.A.U., Korean Musician Union Association, Korean Culture and Film Association of California, All Korean University Alumni Association of Southern California, Korean Golf Club, Korean Church Federation of Southern California, Korean Amateur Sport Association Branch, U.S.A., Korean Student Association of California, Korean Youth Academy, Korean Fishing Club, Korean Society of Engineering Science and Professional Management of Southern California.

  Social Services: Senior Citizens Association of California, Korean Ministers' Association of Southern California, Korean-American Student Guidance Center, Korean Planned Parenthood Association of California, Community on Aging Association of California, Oriental Christian Counselling Center, Oriental Service Center, Asian Community Service Center, Korean Christian Service Center of California, Korean American Social Health Education Society of Southern California, Korean Senior Citizens Association of California.

Figure 3. Korean Community Organizations in Los Angeles[21]

election to elect its president and his staff. In 1972, the association revised its constitution in order to induce Korean residents to participate in and cooperate with its organizational affairs and to consolidate various community groups under its organizational umbrella. Through the new constitution the association created a board of directors consisting of representatives from each of the Korean community organizations which met three qualifications: organizational purpose commensurate with that of the Korean Association of Southern California, nonprofit status, and recognition by the association that the organization could cooperate and work together with other groups. On the basis of these characteristics, sixteen community organizations were allowed to send representatives: the Korean National Association, Tongji-hoe, Hŭngsa-dan, the Korean Women's Patriotic League, the Chamber of Commerce, the Korean-American Political Association of Southern California, the Korean Women's Association of Southern California, the Korean Society of Engineering Science and Professional Management of Southern California, the Korean-American Youth Foundations, the Christian Youth Association of California, the Korean Community Center Fund, the Korean Church Federation of Southern California, the Senior Citizens Association of California,[22] the Korean Culture and Film Association of California,[23] and two other groups, one representing education and culture, and the other representing athletics.

Efforts toward organizational consolidation and unity have had little effect on the perennial problem of divisiveness in the community. The establishment of the Korean Senior Citizens Association of California is a case in point. The association was established by An Min-hong during a meeting at the Korean Cultural Center on April 7, 1973. The professed goal of the association was to promote the interests of the aged in the community. The association soon proved counterproductive as it fought with the already existing Senior Citizens Association of California over acquisition and control of state and federal funds. An attempt in early July to bring the two organizations together was unsuccessful because leaders of each group insisted on following their own proposal for merger.[24] In the meantime, vital service for the aged was unavailable because there was no organization to deal with state and federal agencies. The organizations were eventually merged on January 12, 1974, when Ch'oe Sŏng-gon, chairman of the Senior Citizens Association of California, conceded to An Min-hong the chairmanship of the new organization by taking a vice-chair position.[25] By July 1975, unity had ended and four organizations contended for control of $17,500 to be allocated to the aged of the Korean community by the city of Los Angeles. According to a city employee in charge of funds, municipal authorities were ready to disburse the funds as soon as an organization in the

Korean community in Los Angeles was ready to administer the funds.[26]

Two organizations challenging the legitimacy of the Korean Association of Southern California were recently established in Los Angeles. The first group was established on February 26, 1974, when fourteen of the twenty founding members met to create Kyop'o Munje Yŏn'gu-hoe or the Research Association for Korean Problems in America. According to Kuk Yŏng-il, who was elected chairman of the association during the meeting, the purpose of his group was to study and examine various political, economic, social, educational, cultural, and scientific problems pertaining to the Korean community in Los Angeles, in order to show a direction for the Korean residents to follow. There were five committees established within the association: the political affairs committee, headed by Chŏng Jae-mun; the economic affairs committee, chaired by Shin Yong-hak; the cultural affairs committee, led by Pae Hyo-sik; the social affairs committee, directed by Pak Chong-sam; and the scientific affairs committee, chaired by Song Pu-sŏk. Frank Chang, Kim T'ae-cho, Kim Ki-sŏng, and Kim Sin-ch'an were elected to the executive committee. Other important members attending the meeting were Song Yŏng-ch'ang, chairman of the Tongji-hoe, Chin Hyŏng-ki, Song Ch'ŏl, and Ko Chong-ku.[27]

One of the first tasks the research association took on as a part of its ostensive purpose of giving Korean residents a direction was the appointment of an eleven-member committee to study ways and means whereby an organization with a wide communitarian scope of interest and participation could be established in the Korean community of Los Angeles.[28] Of the eleven appointed to the study committee, five were members of the research association—Kim Ki-sŏng, Song Yŏng-ch'ang, Kim Sin-ch'an, Song Pu-sŏk, and Frank Chang. The remaining members were Sonia Sŏk, Kwŏn Hwi-sang, Sŏk Chin-yong, Ŏm Il-u, Yi Chong-son, and Kwŏn Yong-bae.[29]

The committee met on July 10, 1974, with one member absent, to discuss two main questions: whether or not there was a need for an all-Korean residents' association, and whether or not the present Korean Association of Southern California could be restructured. During the meeting a minority opinion suggested that the committee wait to see recommendations by the nine-member committee which had been appointed by the Korean Association of Southern California for a self-study. Despite this cautious opinion, the membership decided to establish yet another organization in the name of consolidation and unity. Five days after this decision to establish Kyop'o Yŏnhap-hoe, the Federated Association of Koreans in America, *Miguk Sosik* (American News) ran an editorial on the very subject of unity under the title, "One is Better than Two." Warning against the tendency among Korean residents and their leaders toward divisiveness, the editorial called upon the research association committee and the Korean Association of Southern California to develop a workable program of cooperation. Concluding its acid criticism of the people who harbor "an invisible interest in honor, personal reputation and desire for high positions," the editorial stated that the Korean community did not want to see two Korean associations.[30] The warning, mixed with a strong plea for unity, was not heeded, and the Federated Association of Koreans in America came into being on September 29. Ch'oe Hang was elected chairman of the association. In an interview with a *Miguk Sosik* reporter, he stated, "[I] will forsake personal interests and desire for fame, and will work for the Korean community."[31]

One of the most recent conflicts between the research association and the Korean Association of Southern California developed over the question of who should control the building to house the Center of the Korean Association of Southern California. Through its consulate in Los Angeles the Korean government sent $100,000 to the Korean Community Center Fund, an independent committee appointed to solicit funds and select a building to house the center.[32] The committee decided to acquire a building located at 981 South-western Avenue, Los Angeles, for a price of $200,000. Apparently, the government in Seoul wanted to have the building registered as a common property owned both by the Korean Association of Southern California and the Republic of Korea. Explaining the government's position, Yang Hoe-jik, president of the Korean Association of Southern California, made a statement to the effect that the government in Seoul wished to take the action as a precautionary measure against the possibility of Communists taking over the center.[33]

Responding immediately, Frank Chang, chairman of the Research Association for Korean Problems in America, characterized Yang's statement as "an act of selling the nation," and demanded a public apology. Chang also proposed a public hearing on the question of control.[34] The fund committee met on September 9 to consider the government's request for common ownership. During the meeting the committee decided unanimously to reject the request.[35] It was reported that the committee would recommend to the government in Seoul that the building be registered under the name of the Korean Association of Southern California as the sole owner.

When the history of Korean community organizations from 1903 to 1945 is examined in light of Reidy's conceptual scheme, it reveals a number of characteristics which eventually led to the demise of these organizations. It is true that the organizations were based on Korean ethnicity and that they worked toward the interests of Korean residents in America. However, there were very few issues they dealt with which were vital to the improvement of the lives of Korean immigrants in America. The issue, Korean independence, on which they expended so much energy and money was impractical and misdirected, and it was beyond the ability of Korean immigrants, who had no substantial power to change the direction of American foreign policy toward Japan to any significant degree. The Koreans were a small, invisible minority who did not even have the right to participate in American electoral politics. Barred from participation in American political processes by ineligibility for American citizenship, they were deprived of one of the most effective means of influencing American domestic and foreign affairs. Their dream of achieving Korea's independence, either by means of diplomatic pressure on Japan or by military force, was built on sinking sand. A number of factors certainly influenced their active support of the Korean independence movement. Many of the Koreans who went to Hawaii between 1903 and 1905 were not true immigrants, but sojourners wishing to return to their native land at the first opportunity. The leaders of the Korean community in America were, almost exclusively, young students who were unable to find employment commensurate with their educational accomplishments, due to racial discrimination in America. Only three alternatives were open to them—go back to a Korea ruled by Japan, stay in America and take menial jobs, or seek Korean immigrants of sufficient numbers to support their political activities. Several of them were successful in converting their countrymen, who supported the movement with their hard earned money. However, because of the difficulty in raising funds for their livelihood and political activities, leaders of the independence movement became jealous of each other. When an individual was more successful than others, there soon developed rumors attacking his integrity and reputation.

Second, leaders of the Korean community organizations, as well as their followers, were too politically and socially inexperienced in democratic group processes to accommodate a wide variety of opinions and ideas with much ideological resiliency. They had seldom participated in organizations beyond their family, clan, or club meetings prior to their coming to America, and their physical removal from their native culture did not alter significantly their particularistic and exclusive social values, which were neither receptive to building organizations on a communitarian scope nor conducive to coalition-building.

Third, the community organizations, almost without exception, were built around the single issue of achieving Korea's independence.

In view of the fact that Japan's colonial administration in Korea lasted until 1945, it is rather remarkable that these single-issue-oriented organizations continued to sustain the interest of their supporters. On the other hand, heated arguments and unresolved conflicts protracted for over four decades undoubtedly contributed to the division and erosion of the organizations, and finally to their demise.

The short period of organizational resurgence, which began in the Korean community in 1966, is already marked with controversies and conflicts. When characteristics of present Korean community organizations are examined in light of Reidy's conceptual model for effective organization, major organizational weaknesses that may prove fatal become obvious. Most Korean community organizations are suffering from lack of participation by Korean residents, which points up their inability to develop a significant number of constituents. Also, their organizational purposes are rather dubious. Most of them include promotion of fellowship, unity between members, and protection of members' interests among their purposes, but most have not made clear what these goals mean in terms of specific organizational programs. Very few organizations in the Korean community have a communitarian scope, either of interests or participation, as they have failed to develop a large constituency. Almost without exception, organizations have shown inability to develop coalitions with organizations within the Korean ethnic community or across ethnic lines.

In order to illustrate the problem of organizational weaknesses in the Korean community, the Korean Association of Southern California, the largest Korean organization in California and perhaps in America, will be examined. The association has been in existence since 1968. During its existence it has barely built a membership of 1,000,[36] hardly a significant number considering the total Korean population of Los Angeles and its vicinity. It is true that more people register as members of the association when the annual election of its president and his staff is held. But there is a serious question as to whether they are actual people, with good membership standing who come out to vote, or "people on paper" whose dues are paid by candidates who are willing to use purchased ballots.[37] Irregularities in elections are directly related to the lack of financial resources, from which the association has suffered since its inception. During 1974 the association received $8,490 in membership dues, $4,504 in contributions from the president of the association and his staff, and $7,600 in registration fees from candidates who ran for various offices of the association.[38] The source of revenues is questionable, amounts are too small for an organization that claims to represent 80,000 Korean residents in Southern California.

Lack of funds is not confined to the association. Most Korean community organizations in Los Angeles are plagued with this problem. In order to secure funds they beg contributions from various Korean business establishments. It is reported that a certain Korean shopkeeper in Los Angeles was asked for contributions by an average of ten organizations a month.[39]

Irregularities in elections and lack of funds are not the only problems in building a constituency. There is a great deal of ideological rigidity among leaders, who possess particularistic value systems that tend to exclude their opponents from participating in the decision-making process.

The Korean Association of Southern California has no clear and specific organizational purpose. Its constitution states that the association was established to promote fellowship and unity among members, to protect their rights and interests, thereby developing a sound Korean society, and to facilitate cultural exchange and friendship between Korea and America.[40] This lofty purpose has not been followed by concrete programs. To date, the association has failed to put together programs to achieve its professed objectives. The protection of the rights and interests of Korean residents will not be achieved through empty phrases. What is urgently needed is a concrete program of action which will send strong messages to municipal, state, and federal government agencies concerning specific social needs of the Korean community. For this purpose the association should launch a rigorous campaign to organize persons of Korean ancestry who are American citizens by birth or through naturalization. The sooner the Korean community realizes that it has to work as a strong political pressure group to influence American political processes, the better for its future in America. In this regard, it should be pointed out that Koreans who have come to America since 1965 are not sojourners but immigrants. Therefore, they are not looking forward to going back to their native land; instead, they are here to stay and make America home for themselves and their children. This single factor, coupled with the fact that Korean immigrants are now eligible for American citizenship, makes it imperative that community organizations build their strength and vitality around political issues, the outcome of which Koreans could successfully influence. Electoral politics is still the most effective system in America for delivering to people what they demand.

In the past, various minority groups in America have used confrontation as a means of achieving their goals. Most of them, however, had franchise to exercise against their opponents, who had vested interests of their own. It would be naive to think that the Korean minority could use the same strategy to accomplish its goals. Without the right to vote, their confrontation with well-established interest groups would be less than effective. Coalition politics in America is politics based on the strength of an organization to deliver votes.

The more votes an organization can deliver, the better chance it has of finding groups willing to build coalitions. Unless and until the Korean minority can deliver a bloc of votes that influences the outcome of local electoral politics, very few groups will be inclined to join its forces. Therefore, one of the first tasks the Korean Association of Southern California needs to take on is influencing qualified Koreans to exercise their franchise, and building organizational strength around them. In order to accomplish this, the association could hold classes to prepare Korean immigrants for their citizenship test. Once they are qualified to vote, the association should initiate a strong voter registration program and encourage Koreans to vote for candidates the association endorses.

As previously pointed out, most of the organizations built on the single issue of Korea's independence met their demise. When the Korean Association of Southern California finally emerges from its organizational problems to deal with practical concerns of the community, it should develop its goals on the basis of many issues that encompass comprehensive community needs. It should also continue to examine old goals and seek new ways of serving changing community needs.

In conclusion, a certain amount of confusion and conflict is expected of Korean community organizations as their members go through a period of transition from sojourners to immigrants to settlers. It is hoped that they will come out of their confusion better organized and more united, to develop a national organization comparable to the Japanese American Citizens League or the National Association for the Advancement of Colored People in its communitarian scope and programs.

Notes

1. Amitai Etzioni, *Modern Organizations* (Englewood Cliffs, New Jersey: Prentice-Hall, 1964), pp. 20–31.
2. Daniel Reidy, *Urban Ethnic Organizing* (Ann Arbor, Michigan: University Microfilms, 1973), pp. 140–57.
3. Reidy, *Urban Ethnic Organizing*, p. 141.
4. Also in *Korea Journal* 14:8 (August 1974): 26–37.

5. Kingsley K. Lyu, "Korean Nationalist Activities in Hawaii and America, 1901–1945," manuscript in the possession of Professor Donald D. Johnson, Graduate Division, University of Hawaii, 1950, pp. 31–33.

6. Lyu, "Korean Nationalist Activities," pp. 29–30.

7. Hilary Conroy, *The Japanese Seizure of Korea, 1868–1910* (Philadelphia: University of Pennsylvania Press, 1960), p. 329.

8. C.I. Eugene Kim and Han-kyo Kim, *Korea and the Politics of Imperialism, 1876–1910* (Berkeley: University of California Press, 1967), p. 121.

9. Kim Wŏn-yong (Warren Y. Kim), in *Chae-Mi Hanin osimnyŏn-sa* [Fifty-year history of the Koreans in America] (Reedley, California: Charles Ho Kim, 1959), states that the organization was established on August 7, 1903, in Honolulu, Hawaii, but Chŏng Tu-ok, in "Chae-Mi Hanjok tongnip undong silgi" [The real story of the independence movement of Koreans in America] *Han'guk Ilbo* [Korean Times], February 28, 1961, says that it was established sometime in 1904. Chŏng's claim is corroborated by Kingsley K. Lyu, who interviewed Yi Hong-gi, an eyewitness to many Korean independence activities in Honolulu. According to Yi, the Shinmin-hoe was established in December 1904 at Kappa, Kauai.

10. Lyu, "Korean Nationalist Activities," p. 38.

11. Kim Wŏn-yong, *Chae-Mi Hanin*, pp. 81–95.

12. Kim Wŏn-yong, *Chae-Mi Hanin*, pp. 98–102.

13. Lee Houchins and Chang-su Houchins, "The Korean Experience in America, 1903–1924," *Pacific Historical Review* 43:4 (November 1974): 556–57.

14. Kim Wŏn-yong, *Chae-Mi Hanin*, pp. 318–26.

15. Cho Pyŏng-ok, *Na'ŭi hoego-rok* [My memoirs] (Seoul: Minkyosa, 1959), pp. 75–77. According to Cho, An came to see him in a small town in California where he was employed as a farmhand. He and An spent three days together, An doing most of the talking, to persuade Cho to join his organization. At the end of their short meeting, Cho joined the Hŭngsa-dan.

16. Im Pyŏng-jik, "Na'ŭi iryŏk-sŏ" [My resumé], *Han'guk Ilbo*, November 13, 1973. Im stated that he was met by a number of An's followers upon his arrival in San Francisco. Later they came to his apartment to persuade him to join the Hŭngsa-dan during his short stay. He refused to join, excusing himself on account of his expected study.

17. Lyu, "Korean Nationalist Activities," pp. 46–59.

18. According to Kim Wŏn-yong, the Tongji-hoe was established on July 7, 1921. This is corroborated by No Chae-yŏn in his *Chae-Mi Hanin saryak* [A concise history of Koreans in America], 2 vols. (Los Angeles: American Publisher, 1951, 1963).

19. Walter Jhung, "Korean Independence Activities of Overseas Koreans," *Korean Survey* (December, 1952): 8.

20. Lee Kyung, "Settlement Patterns of Los Angeles Koreans" (M.A. thesis, University of California, Los Angeles, 1969), p. 42.

21. *Hanin ŏpso chŏnhwa-pu* [Business telephone directory of the Korean community] (Los Angeles: Korea Times, Los Angeles Bureau, 1974), pp. 4–20.

22. *Miguk Sosik* [American News], December 19, 1972.

23. *Miguk Sosik*, February 15, 1973.

24. *Miguk Sosik*, July 4, 1973.

25. *Miguk Sosik*, January 15, 1974.

26. *Miju Tong-a* [Tong-a Daily in America], July 12, 1975.

27. *Miguk Sosik*, February 27, 1947.

28. *Miguk Sosik*, July 5, 1974.

29. *Miguk Sosik*, July 12, 1974.

30. *Miguk Sosik*, July 15, 1974.

31. *Miguk Sosik*, September 30, 1974.

32. *Joong-ang Daily News,* September 3, 1975.

33. *Joong-ang Daily News,* September 4, 1975.

34. *Joong-ang Daily News,* September 8, 1975.

35. *Joong-ang Daily News,* September 10, 1975.

36. *Miguk Sosik,* January 28, 1974. A regular meeting of the association was held on January 27, 1974. Only 220 members were present to discuss organizational affairs. The number of members required to constitute a quorum was 191, one-fifth of the total membership.

37. *Miguk Sosik,* March 19, 1974. During a meeting held on March 18, a member of the board of directors charged one of his colleagues with volunteering to pay $500 to cover $5 dues for 100 members.

38. *Miju Tong-a,* December 31, 1974.

39. *Joong-ang Daily News,* June 26, 1975.

40. *Miguk Sosik,* January 18, 1974.

Ethnic Enterprises
among Korean Immigrants in America

Hyung-chan Kim

THE PRESENT STUDY has three major purposes: it describes historically the growth and development of small business enterprises in the Korean community in America; it presents a short summary of a survey the author conducted on randomly selected business firms owned and operated by Koreans in Los Angeles, the San Francisco Bay area, Honolulu, and Chicago; it analyzes in light of past and present conditions of Korean ethnic enterprises the tradition-of-enterprise hypothesis. The hypothesis was originally formulated by E. Franklin Frazier in his attempt to explain the failure of blacks in small business enterprises in America, and is further developed by Ivan Light in his recent study, *Ethnic Enterprise in America: Business and Welfare among Chinese, Japanese, and Blacks.*[1]

The marked underrepresentation of blacks in small business enterprises in their neighborhoods has been a subject of considerable interest and study among historians and sociologists in America. Basically, two major theories have emerged from their attempts to account for blacks' failure in business. According to the discrimination-in-lending theory, blacks have been effectively prevented from securing business loans from institutional lenders, especially banks, due to white racism. Even if blacks were able to borrow money, they were often charged higher interest rates than whites, and thus risked failure from the beginning.

The special consumer-demands theory argues that blacks in America did not have culturally derived consumer demands which could not be satisfied by people outside their community. As a result, whites established small businesses in black communities and supplied blacks with goods they wanted to buy. Unlike blacks, however, foreign immigrants such as Chinese and Japanese had culturally derived consumer demands which white tradesmen were unable to satisfy. "Since the immigrants spoke little English and had their own ethnic culture, they needed stores to supply them with ethnic foods and other services."[2] Special consumer demands based on culture, therefore, created protected markets for ethnic businessmen who knew what their countrymen wanted.

Light dismisses these two theories, as they have been found inadequate. According to him, the discrimination-in-lending theory is inadequate, as it fails to explain the preponderance of small businesses among Japanese and Chinese, who have been as much the target of white racism as blacks. Light also finds the special consumer-demands theory essentially inadequate. Although it is correct that Chinese and Japanese small business proprietors had protected markets due to their respective cultures, ethnic consumer demands do not explain the diversity of their markets. Light argues that Chinese and Japanese tradesmen dealt not only with their countrymen but also with non-Oriental customers. In fact, so many of their business transactions were with people outside their communities that almost one-third of their total cash value of goods and services sold in 1929 were purchased by non-Orientals.[3] Light further argues that the special consumer-demands theory, when applied to the Chinese and Japanese, assumes that "apart from their culturally determined preferences for chop suey or pork chops, there were no culturally-derived differences in the economic behavior of foreign-born Orientals and native-born blacks."[4] Light refuses to accept this assumption. In fact, he believes that Chinese and Japanese immigrants brought with them to America an economic organization indigenous to their cultures which enabled them to become successful shopkeepers. According to Light, this economic organization is the rotating credit association, which may be defined as "an association formed upon a core of participants who agree to make regular contributions to a fund which is given, in whole or in part, to each contributor in rotation."[5]

Light points out that the Chinese and Japanese brought to America their traditional rotating credit systems—*hui*, Chinese, and *tanomoshi*, Japanese—which they have used successfully in creating business capital. Black slaves brought to the land of their captors *ensusu*, a rotating credit association widely used in Africa at that time. Black slaves taken to the West Indies maintained their tradition of business and later used *ensusu* to create business capital. It is argued that the peculiar social and economic life of black slaves in the West Indies enabled them to maintain their tradition. Black slaves outnumbered whites in the Caribbean Islands and were organized into large units. Black slaves in America, however, were not able to keep this valuable tradition. They were forced to live on farms employing no more than twenty slaves. In other words, the group life of black slaves in the South was weakened to the extent that they lost their African culture and adopted the culture of their masters.

Not unlike Chinese and Japanese immigrants, Korean immigrants brought to America their own culture, including *kye*, a traditional rotating credit system which was used widely in Korea prior to their departure. Like the Japanese and Chinese, Koreans have been overrepresented in small business enterprises. Particularly since 1965, Korean communities in America have seen a marked growth of small shops owned and operated by Koreans who market various goods and services demanded by their countrymen. In Los Angeles and its vicinity alone, where there are 80,000 Korean residents, Korean businessmen have established fifty grocery stores, forty restaurants, twenty insurance companies, and ten nightclubs. How does one account for the preponderance of small businesses among Koreans? Could the same lines of reasoning employed by Ivan Light be used to explain the past and present development of ethnic enterprises among Koreans? How plausible is Light's theory of tradition of enterprise in view of the history of Korean enterprise in America? It is hoped that the present study will answer these questions.

The history of Korean ethnic enterprise in America may be divided into three major periods: saving for business capital (1903–1909); business venture (1910–1965); and rapid growth, which began in 1965, when large numbers of Koreans began to be allowed to immigrate to America every year.

During the first period no major entrepreneurial activity was seen among the Korean immigrants in the Hawaiian Islands and the mainland of the United States. A number of factors seem to have been responsible for this total absence of small businesses among Koreans. First, most Koreans, recruited to work on the sugar plantations owned by members of the Hawaiian Sugar Planters' Association, came from the poorer segment of their society. In fact, they were too poor to afford their own steamship fares from Inchon to Kobe, Japan, and from there to Honolulu. Horace N. Allen, American minister to Korea, described the general economic condition of many Koreans in a letter to Sanford B. Dole, governor of Hawaii, dated December 10, 1902:

> The Koreans are so poor that not many of them would have the necessary

funds without borrowing, for the purpose of emigrating with their families, but I am not at all inclined to think that this government has any intention of assisting its people to emigrate by advancing the necessary funds.[6]

The Hawaiian Sugar Planters' Association was well aware of the financial difficulties facing their prospective employees and instructed its agent, David W. Deshler, to set up a bank in Chemulpo, now Inchon. Deshler established the Deshler Bank, which had only one depositor, the Hawaiian Sugar Planters' Association, and made loans available to Koreans immigrating to Hawaii. Previously, Deshler received permission from the Korean government to recruit Koreans with the assistance of Horace N. Allen. Allen had been appointed with the help of George K. Nash, a friend of President McKinley and stepfather of David Deshler.[7]

Second, the wage paid to the Korean worker employed by the sugar planter was so low that the worker was not able to save business capital in a short period of time. Normally, an Oriental under contract received fifteen dollars per month, although his European counterpart received eighteen. The living expenses of one person varied, depending upon the individual's determination to save, but it was generally expected that an Oriental worker would spend from six to ten dollars per month for living expenses.[8] This means that an Oriental worker under a three-year contract could have saved little more than $150 during his entire contract period.

Third, unlike the Chinese and Japanese immigrants, who had access to business capital in their respective homelands, Korean immigrants were not able to depend upon their homeland as a source of business capital, since Korea became a colony of Japan for all practical purposes in 1905. The Korean government was pressured by the Japanese government to discontinue the immigration of Koreans to the Hawaiian Islands, and the immigration came to an end in 1905.[9]

Fourth, a number of patriotic and social organizations were established in the Korean communities in Hawaii and California which solicited contributions from their countrymen. Many Koreans contributed liberally to local churches which were in need of financial support for their religious and educational programs. Local churches established Korean-language schools and taught the language in order to maintain Korean culture and tradition. There were also a number of political organizations in need of funds for the independence movement.[10] These carried on numerous fund raising campaigns and received rather liberal contributions from compatriots. These factors, either singly or collectively, delayed the accumulation of business capital by the Korean immigrants in the Hawaiian Islands and the mainland of the United States.

The period of business venture began with the establishment of three small business firms, two of which were established in California.

First, the Hŭngŏp Chusik Hoesa (Prospering Business Company) was established in February 1910 by local Koreans in Redlands, California, under the leadership of An Sŏk-jung. Sixty $50 stock certificates were issued to create a total of $3,000 in capital to be invested in farming. Second, a group of Korean residents in San Francisco, under the leadership of Ch'oe Yŏng-man, tried to establish a trading company handling merchandise produced in Korea by purchasing stock certificates. A total of $20,000 was to be capitalized by selling 2,000 stock certificates at a price of $10 per certificate, but only 250 certificates had been sold when Ch'oe went to Korea on a business trip and was prohibited from returning by the Japanese colonial administration. Third, on March 1, 1910, the Korean National Association of North America decided to organize the T'aedong Sirŏp Chusik Hoesa (Great Eastern Industrial Company) to finance its political activities. One thousand $50 stock certificates were issued to create business capital of $50,000 to purchase 2,430 acres of farmland in Manchuria. The Korean National Association planned to build a model farm village to accommodate two hundred families, but the agent, sent to Manchuria to purchase the farmland, made a poor decision in selecting the site, and consequently the business venture cost the Korean National Association $3,000.[11]

The most ambitious entrepreneurial scheme of the period was developed by Syngman Rhee and his followers in the Tongji-hoe (Comrade Society). It was said that Rhee always wanted to put into practice the last of the Three Great Principles of the Tongji-hoe, which read: "the economic freedom is the life of a nation; let us promote self-reliance together."[12] When he returned to Hawaii from the Washington Conference on the Limitation of Armament in 1923, Rhee began to talk about developing a business corporation for his followers. The result of this talk was the formation of the Tongji Siksan Hoesa (Tongji Investment Company), which was established sometime in 1924. According to Kingsley K. Lyu, "the corporation was duly organized by selling $100 shares to subscribers, and was incorporated for 25 years under the laws of the Territory of Hawaii."[13] Although the capital stock was limited to $70,000, the corporation was allowed to expand that to $250,000. Several hundred people bought stock certificates issued by the Tongji Siksan Hoesa. Rhee was the company's director, Shin Sung-il and An Yong-ch'an were the president and secretary, respectively.

As its first business venture, the company bought 930 acres of land at Olaa, Hawaii, 18 miles from Hilo, and established an ideal farm village called the Tongji-ch'on, or the Comrade Village. Rhee himself resided in the village and supervised the *koa* tree farm and vegetable farms. A tool shop was established, where the *koa* trees were cut for lumber. Some wooden articles were also manufactured in the village. The company bought a store in Hilo and sold vegetables and other crops raised in the village as well as the wooden articles made of *koa* trees. A store and carpentry shop on Hotel Street, Honolulu, was maintained by the company under the management of Cho Suk-chin and Yi Kyŏng-yong, both of whom were carpenters.

The lack of managerial skills in business brought an end to the dream of members of the Comrade Society of creating economic self-reliance. Kingsley K. Lyu alleged that Rhee had a contract for *koa* lumber with the Pearl Harbor Navy Yard sometime in 1926, but Rhee was unable to deliver the *koa* lumber on time. The result was a great financial loss. Rhee had his men make charcoal from *koa* trees, but when the charcoal was shipped to Honolulu, the freight expenses were so high that the company suffered another financial loss. The village site was sold to a Japanese in 1932, when Rhee left for Geneva to raise Korean objections to the Japanese seizure of Manchuria.[14]

In contrast to the failure of small businesses established and operated by Korean political groups, a few firms established by private individuals succeeded and continued to grow. Included among them are the Kim Brothers' Company in Reedley, California, and Oriental Food Products of California, in Los Angeles. The Kim Brothers' Company was established by the late Kim Ho, also known as Charles Ho Kim, and Kim Hyŏng-sun, who began a truckfarm in 1921. By 1958 their business grew to include a total of 500 acres of farmland in six different locations, a $400,000 packing facility, and a $100,000 nursery.[15] Oriental Food Products of California was established by Peter Hyŏn in 1926. The company succeeded, grew, and employed eighteen Koreans. It produced twenty-seven varieties of canned Oriental foods in 1939, when Helen Lewis Givens undertook a study on Korean residents in Los Angeles County.[16]

Besides the major business firms discussed above, small shops were owned and operated by Korean residents in America. In Los Angeles County there were, in 1939, thirty-three fruit and vegetable stands, nine grocery stores, five wholesale companies, eight pressing and laundry shops, six trucking companies, five restaurants, one employment agency, three herb stores, two hat shops, and one rooming house. Most of these shops were extremely small, employing only a few persons, if any.[17] In Honolulu in the same year, there were a total of twenty-two Korean businessmen, doing business with capital investments ranging from $1,000 to $20,000. They engaged in sixteen different types of business. As well as the usual Oriental restaurants and grocery stores, there were variety goods stores, furniture stores, a ready-to-wear clothing store, and a construction company.[18]

Accurate data on Korean ethnic enterprise from 1958 to 1965 are not readily available. But it seems reasonable that no drastic change in the number and kind of commercial firms occurred until 1965. This assumption is based on three factors. First, there was no major alteration of the pattern of Korean immigration to America until 1965. During the 1959 to 1965 period, a total of 13,406 Koreans were admitted to the United States as immigrants, but of these, 12,044 were housewives and children, who reported no occupation at the time of their arrival. A total of 977 Korean immigrants were classified on their arrival as professional, technical, and kindred workers, and only 2 Koreans were reported as farmers or farm managers. Fifty-five Korean immigrants were classified as managers, officials, and proprietors. Therefore, almost 90 percent of the Korean immigrants arriving between 1959 and 1965 were housewives and children, most of whom were dependents of American citizens.[19] Moreover, the second largest group of Koreans who came to America prior to 1965 were not immigrants in the genuine sense. Most were students and their dependents, who decided to stay in America after completing their educations and wait for a better time to return to their homeland. There were also professionals, who decided to stay in America as they took on positions commensurate with their educations. Most of them were not actively interested in small business enterprise. Finally, the Korean population in America remained relatively small until 1965, and no Korean community had a large population needing special ethnic consumer goods and services.

The period of rapid growth in Korean ethnic enterprise began in 1965, when the United States repealed its national quota system, which had been the base of American immigration policy since 1924. The rapid growth of small businesses among Korean immigrants seems to have been influenced by a number of factors. The change in American immigration policy since 1965 certainly made it possible for many Koreans to come to the United States. During 1974 alone, a total of 28,028 Koreans immigrated to America. Furthermore, the drastic change in policy altered the patterns and characteristics of Korean immigrants. In the past, Koreans entering America for education were a highly select group of people who did not have to engage in business ventures for their livelihood. Students settled in college and university communities, and professionals were able to afford a comfortable living once they completed their educations.

Since 1965 the social characteristics of Koreans immigrating to America have changed as dramatically as the immigration laws. First, Koreans coming to America as immigrants intend to stay and make America their home. Second, most immigrants are less familiar with American society and culture than are students and professionals. Furthermore, almost without exception, they have very little knowledge of English. They are, therefore, handicapped in almost every aspect of daily life. Unfamiliarity with American society, inability to use English, and the need for mutual assistance and collective security in a completely strange land seem to contribute to the heavy concentration of Korean immigrants in such urban centers as Los Angeles, the San Francisco Bay area, Honolulu, Chicago, Washington, D.C., and New York. In addition, more job opportunities, easier access to public transportation, and low rental housing seem responsible for the present trend among Korean immigrants to choose urban centers as their place of residence. As a result of the large numbers of Koreans in these urban centers, various small business firms have rapidly developed in Korean communities to satisfy their special consumer needs.

Table 1 indicates how rapidly small businesses have developed in Korean communities in America.[20] The survey, conducted by the Bureau of the Census in 1972 and published in 1975, reported a total of 1,201 commercial firms owned by Koreans. The state of California led all other states with 540 firms, which constituted approximately 44 percent of the total small business firms. Of the total, there were only 249 firms which employed paid workers. The average number of paid employees per firm was six, while firms in California owned by Koreans employed five persons on the average with a total of 666 paid workers for 141 firms. Naturally, California led in total transactions with $31,981,000. This is approximately 49 percent of the total business transactions made by Korean businessmen in 1972. It is crucial to point out that most of the commercial firms owned by Koreans remained very small. There were 952 firms with no paid workers, bringing in a total of $21,304,000. The average receipts per firm with no paid workers were $22,000, while the average receipts per firm with paid workers were $175,000.

The 141 firms in California with 666 paid workers brought in a total of $21,523,000, which constituted approximately 49 percent of the total gross receipts of firms with paid employees. What is surprising is that the 399 firms in California with no paid workers brought in a total of $10,458,000 or approximately 49 percent of the total gross receipts of the 952 firms with no paid employees. This means that the 399 firms in California, which made up 41 percent of the total firms with no paid employees, did 49 percent of the business transacted by 952 firms.

Although it is difficult in the absence of more detailed data to account for this aspect of Korean ethnic enterprise in California, it seems that the heavier concentration of Korean immigrants in California, particularly in Los Angeles and the San Francisco Bay area, accounts for this peculiar condition.

Table 2 presents the commercial firms owned by Koreans according to kind of business and the Standard Metropolitan Statistical Areas in which they were located in 1972.[21] Table 2 reveals a number

Table 1—Selected Statistics by Geographic Division, State, and Industry Division for Firms Owned by Koreans, 1972

State	All Firms		With Paid Employees					Without Paid Employees		
	Firms (number)	Gross receipts ($1,000)	Firms (number)	Employees (number)	Gross receipts ($1,000)	Average employees per firm (number)	Average receipts per firm ($1,000)	Firms (number)	Gross receipts ($1,000)	Average receipts per firm ($1,000)
N.Y.	136	4,680	8	18	1,503	2	188	128	3,177	25
N.J.	20	306	2	(D)	(D)	(D)	(D)	18	(D)	(D)
Penna.	23	650	2	(D)	(D)	(D)	(D)	21	(D)	(D)
Ark.	10	(D)	1	(D)	(D)	(D)	(D)	9	(D)	(D)
Okla.	3	(D)	1	(D)	(D)	(D)	(D)	7	(D)	(D)
Texas	22	876	4	20	603	5	151	18	273	15
Wash.	24	621	5	21	349	4	70	19	272	14
Oregon	6	(D)	1	(D)	(D)	(D)	(D)	5	(D)	(D)
Calif.	540	31,981	141	666	21,523	5	153	399	10,458	26
Alaska	3	(D)	—	—	—	—	—	3	(D)	(D)
Hawaii	165	15,474	36	(D)	(D)	(D)	(D)	129	(D)	(D)
Others	249	10,251	48	—	—	—	—	193	—	—
U.S.	1,201	64,839	249	1,452	43,535	6	175	952	21,304	22

(D) indicates information withheld to protect the secrecy of individual firms reporting.
— indicates information not available.

Table 2—Selected Statistics by Industry Division in Standard Metropolitan Statistical Area for Firms Owned by Koreans in 1972

Industry	All Firms		With Paid Employees					Without Paid Employees		
	Firms (number)	Gross receipts ($1,000)	Firms (number)	Employees (number)	Gross receipts ($1,000)	Average employees per firm (number)	Average receipts per firm ($1,000)	Firms (number)	Gross receipts ($1,000)	Average receipts per firm ($1,000)
Construction	2[c]	(D)	2	(D)	(D)	(D)	(D)	—	—	—
	5[d]	(D)	1	(D)	(D)	(D)	(D)	4	17	4
Transportation	2[b]	(D)	1	(D)	(D)	(D)	(D)	1	(D)	(D)
	19[c]	117	—	—	—	—	—	19	117	6
	5[d]	(D)	1	(D)	(D)	(D)	(D)	4	131	32
	5[e]	47	—	—	—	—	—	5	47	9
	1[h]	(D)	—	—	—	—	—	1	(D)	(D)
Manufacturing	1[a]	(D)	—	—	—	—	—	1	(D)	(D)
	7[c]	(D)	2	(D)	(D)	(D)	(D)	5	244	49
	18[d]	544	4	(D)	(D)	(D)	(D)	14	(D)	(D)
Retail trade	7[a]	143	—	—	—	—	—	7	143	20
	3[b]	(D)	1	(D)	(D)	(D)	(D)	2	(D)	(D)
	38[c]	2,943	10	133	2,067	13	206	28	876	31
	216[d]	17,857	73	233	11,357	3	155	143	6,500	45
	33[e]	1,421	1	(D)	(D)	(D)	(D)	32	(D)	(D)
	2[f]	(D)	2	(D)	(D)	(D)	(D)	—	—	—
	3[g]	(D)	1	(D)	(D)	(D)	(D)	2	(D)	(D)
	29[h]	1,240	12	(D)	(D)	(D)	(D)	17	(D)	(D)
	4[i]	(D)	2	(D)	(D)	(D)	(D)	2	(D)	(D)
Wholesale trade	5[c]	(D)	2	(D)	(D)	(D)	(D)	3	63	21
	24[d]	2,628	8	20	1,675	2	209	16	953	60
	19[e]	1,779	3	(D)	(D)	(D)	(D)	16	(D)	(D)
	3[h]	(D)	2	(D)	(D)	(D)	(D)	1	(D)	(D)
Finance, insurance, and	1[a]	(D)	—	—	—	—	—	1	(D)	(D)
	25[c]	455	2	(D)	(D)	(D)	(D)	23	(D)	(D)

real estate	12[d]	83	1	(D)	(D)	(D)	(D)	11	(D)	(D)
	1[e]	(D)	—	—	—	—	—	1	(D)	(D)
Selected services	6[a]	(D)	1	(D)	(D)	(D)	(D)	5	3	—
	2[b]	(D)	—	—	—	—	—	2	(D)	(D)
	51[c]	1,631	13	59	1,354	4	104	38	277	7
	80[d]	1,875	12	54	1,028	4	85	68	847	12
	19[e]	175	—	—	—	—	—	19	175	9
	1[f]	(D)	—	—	—	—	—	1	(D)	(D)
	1[g]	(D)	—	—	—	—	—	1	(D)	(D)
	22[h]	510	6	46	404	7	67	16	106	6
	3[i]	(D)	—	—	—	—	—	3	(D)	(D)
Other industries	4[a]	30	2	(D)	(D)	(D)	(D)	4	30	7
	2[c]	(D)	1	(D)	(D)	(D)	(D)	—	—	—
	15[d]	(D)	—	—	—	—	—	14	59	4
	1[f]	(D)	—	—	—	—	—	1	(D)	(D)
Industries not classified	3[a]	(D)	—	—	—	—	—	3	(D)	(D)
	2[b]	(D)	—	—	—	—	—	2	(D)	(D)
	6[c]	(D)	—	—	—	—	—	6	(D)	(D)
	23[d]	(D)	1	(D)	(D)	(D)	(D)	22	253	12
	4[h]	(D)	—	—	—	—	—	4	(D)	(D)
	1[i]	(D)	—	—	—	—	—	1	(D)	(D)

(D) indicates information withheld to protect individual businesses reporting.
— indicates information not available.

[a] indicates firms within the Anaheim-Santa Ana-Garden Grove, Cal., SMSA.
[b] indicates firms within the Fresno, Cal., SMSA.
[c] indicates firms within the Honolulu, Ha., SMSA.
[d] indicates firms within the Los Angeles-Long Beach, Cal., SMSA.
[e] indicates firms within the New York-New Jersey SMSA.
[f] indicates firms within the Riverside-San Bernardino-Ontario, Cal., SMSA.
[g] indicates firms within the San Diego, Cal., SMSA.
[h] indicates firms within the San Francisco, Cal., SMSA.
[i] indicates firms within the San Jose, Cal., SMSA.

of characteristics for examination and discussion. First, a total of 736 firms were reported by the nine Standard Metropolitan Statistical Areas (SMSAs). These comprise 61 percent of the total number of commercial firms owned by Koreans. Of these 736, a total of 335 firms, which constitutes 28 percent of the 1,201 firms reported in 1972, engaged in retail trade. The Los Angeles-Long Beach SMSA alone reported 216 retail stores or 64 percent of the total number of commercial firms engaged in retail business. A glance at the number of paid employees working for the retail stores in the Los Angeles-Long Beach SMSA indicates that 73 retail stores hired an average of three persons per firm, each of which had business transactions in the amount of $155,000, on the average. There were 143 retail stores, each of which brought in an average of $45,000, in the same SMSA with no paid workers. Table 1 indicates that 141 commercial firms in California hired 666 workers (five workers per firm) and transacted an average $153,000. Of the nine types of industry reported, the retail stores in the Los Angeles-Long Beach SMSA hired a total of 233 workers. This constitutes approximately 35 percent of the total personnel for all commercial firms in the state of California.

Second, the Los Angeles-Long Beach and Honolulu SMSAs were the only two areas where all nine kinds of industry were represented. The Los Angeles-Long Beach SMSA had 398 commercial firms, which made up 33 percent of the 1,201 business firms owned by Koreans in 1972. The Honolulu SMSA reported 155 commercial firms. When the commercial firms reported by these two SMSAs are combined, they represent 46 percent of the total business firms owned by Koreans in 1972.

Third, intraindustry comparisons of a number of types of industry reveal different amounts of average receipts according to geographical location. For instance, there were four firms engaged in the transportation business in the Los Angeles-Long Beach SMSA. These firms did business in the total amount of $131,000, an average of $32,000 per firm. In contrast, there were nineteen transportation firms in the Honolulu SMSA, each of which did business in the amount of $6,000, on the average. In the area of retail trade, the firms located within the Los Angeles-Long Beach SMSA also led in the average receipts per firm. The 143 firms with no paid workers in the retail business in the Los Angeles-Long Beach SMSA did business in the total amount of $6,500,000, which meant that each firm brought in an average $45,000. This is a marked contrast to the average $31,000 for twenty-eight retail firms located within the Honolulu SMSA. A wider margin is reported in wholesale trade businesses in the Los Angeles-Long Beach SMSA and those in the Honolulu SMSA. An average of $60,000 per firm for sixteen wholesale trade firms having no paid workers in the Los Angeles-Long Beach

SMSA was reported, while an average of $21,000 per firm for three wholesale trade firms having no paid workers in the Honolulu SMSA was reported. In fact, businesses in the nine types of industry located in the Los Angeles-Long Beach SMSA and having no hired employees led all firms in their respective industries in all other SMSAs in 1972.

The following analysis is based on the results of a survey the author completed in October 1975 of fifty-two Korean businesses in retail trade located in four major metropolitan areas: Chicago, Honolulu, Los Angeles, and the San Francisco Bay area.[22] The present survey is exploratory and strictly limited to the examination of a few salient characteristics of firms owned and operated by Koreans in these four urban areas. It is hoped that a more extensive and comprehensive study can be undertaken in the near future.

Table 3 shows the level of education of Korean entrepreneurs by sex and age. The most distinct characteristic of Korean entrepreneurs is the astonishingly high level of education they received in Korea. No person with less than high school completion was reported in the survey. When persons with college education are added to those with some postgraduate education, they represent 70 percent of the entrepreneurs surveyed. A high percentage of college-educated entrepreneurs were represented in both sexes, although Korean businesswomen were slightly underrepresented. A total of nine businesswomen were reported. Of these nine, three had no college education, and therefore college-educated women comprise approximately 67 percent of the total Korean businesswomen. College-educated businessmen constitute 70 percent of the total businessmen in the survey. Six had some postgraduate education in America, while four men completed American baccalaureate degrees. No Korean businesswoman received any college education in America. The age groupings of the Korean entrepreneurs show a number of characteristics worth mentioning. There were twenty-one entrepreneurs in the thirty-six to forty age group, or 40 percent of the total number reported in the survey. The four women in the thirty-six to forty age group comprise 44 percent of the Korean businesswomen, while seventeen men in the same age group constitute 39 percent of the businessmen. When the thirty-six to forty age group and the forty-one to forty-five age group are combined, they represent 62 percent of the Korean entrepreneurs in the survey. This suggests a rather young population engaged in retail trade in view of the Kerner Commission study, which reported that the typical merchant in urban ghettos is about fifty years old and has a high school education.

Table 3—The Level of Education of Korean Entrepreneurs by Sex and Age

Education in Korea	Age 26–30		31–35		36–40		41–45		46–50		61–65		Subtotal		Total
Sex	M	F	M	F	M	F	M	F	M	F	M	F	M	F	
Postgraduate education			1		1		2						4	0	4
College graduation	3	1	6	1	9	3	5	1	4				27	6	33
Some college education	1		1		1	1							3	1	4
Special school graduation												1	0	1	1
High school education				1	6		3						9	1	10
Total	4	1	8	2	17	4	10	1	4	0	0	1	43	9	52

M = Male.
F = Female.

Table 4 shows the amount of business capital Korean entrepreneurs started with, the type of capitalization, and the number of years of residence in America prior to their beginning business. A number of important characteristics are to be noticed in Table 4. First, it is evident that a majority of Korean business firms began with a small amount of investment capital. For instance, of the fifty firms reporting their initial investment capitals, twenty-three had less than $10,000. These twenty-three firms constitute approximately 46 percent of the firms reported in the survey. When the twenty-three firms are added to the twelve firms reporting their initial capital as $10,000 to $15,000, they represent approximately 68 percent of the total number of firms in the survey. Second, an overwhelming majority (thirty-six) of firms reported as their source of business capital individual savings. These thirty-six firms constitute 72 percent of the firms in the survey. Third, again an overwhelming majority of firms reported fewer than three years of owner residence in America prior to beginning business. Eighteen firms reported less than one year of owner residence, while nineteen reported owner residence in America ranging from one to three years. When these two groups are combined, they represent 72 percent of the total firms reported in the survey. One of the peculiar characteristics revealed by Table 4 is the fact that four firms reported as their source of initial investment capital individual savings of $30,000 per firm. Each owner of the four firms indicated that he started business in less than one year after his arrival in America. Given the fact that the Korean government officially refused to allow Korean immigrants to take large sums of American dollars out of the country, it seems that these people either used unofficial means of bringing their capital out or had their savings accounts outside Korea, which would be considered illegal in Korea. Last, of the fifty firms reporting their sources of capital, only one firm indicated that its initial investment capital came from *kye*, the rotating credit system used for a long time in Korea.

Table 5 presents Korean entrepreneurs in America according to their former professions in Korea. A number of characteristics pertinent to the tradition-of-enterprise hypothesis are to be noticed in Table 5. First, a total of fourteen persons, or 25 percent of the total Korean entrepreneurs reported in the survey, were people who had been unemployed in Korea. Among these fourteen some were college students or college graduates who did not seek work as they prepared to immigrate to America. Second, eight former teachers represent the largest number of people from a single profession. Most were high school teachers and college instructors prior to their coming to America. One of the eight was a college professor who is now a proprietor of a service station. Third, seven persons whose

Table 4—The Amounts of Business Capital, Types of Capital, and the Number of Years of Residence before Business

Amount of capital	Less than 1 year				1–3				3–5				5–7				More than 7 years				Subtotal				Total
Types of capital	B	I	P	K	B	I	P	K	B	I	P	K	B	I	P	K	B	I	P	K	B	I	P	K	
Less than $10,000		6	1		1	6	1	1	1	1			1	3			1				4	16	2	1	23
$10,000–15,000	1	2			1	4				1	1		1	1							3	8	1	0	12
$15,001–20,000	1	2				2								1							1	5	0	0	6
$20,001–25,000						1															0	1	0	0	1
$25,001–30,000		1																			0	1	0	0	1
More than $30,000		4			2									1							2	5	0	0	7
Total	2	15	1	0	4	13	1	1	1	2	1	0	2	6	0	0	1	0	0	0	10	36	3	1	50*

B = bank loans.
I = individual savings.
P = private loans.
K = kye.
*Two firms failed to report the amount of their business capital.

Table 5—Korean Entrepreneurs in America by their Former Professions in Korea

Professions in Korea	Grocery store	Restaurant	Service station	Beauty salon and hair products	Clothing and shoes	Radio and TV sales and repair	Flower and gift shops	Business machines	Transportation	Sewing shop	Business development	Total
Government officials	1	1				1	1					4
Teaching	2		3	2		1						8
Technical and medical	1		1					1				3
Clerical and managerial	2	1	3	1	1							8
Army officers						1	2				1	4
Sales	5		1		1							7
Social workers									1			1
Beauticians				1								1
Journalism					1		1					2
Unemployed	5	2	1	2	2		1			1		14
Total	16	4	9	6	5	3	5	1	1	1	1	52

professions in Korea were in the area of sales are engaged in three areas of retail trade in America. However, it would be incorrect to say that their retail businesses in America are extensions of their businesses in Korea. Most of them had to change their specialized areas of business in order to go into retail trade in America. Last, only one person reported in the survey continued in the same profession. This represents slightly under 2 percent of the total number of Korean entrepreneurs reported in the survey.

Table 6 represents the number of paid workers in Korean firms according to type of business. A number of important characteristics are to be noted in Table 6. First, the total number of people employed by the fifty-two firms was extremely small, 128, or an average of fewer than 3 employees per firm. Second, of the fifty-two firms, twenty had no paid workers. Thus, firms with no paid employees represent almost 40 percent of the total. This finding seems to corroborate the data published by the Department of Commerce, discussed in relation to Tables 1 and 2.

Besides the characteristics mentioned above, the survey revealed other pertinent data. In reporting reasons for starting their business, twelve entrepreneurs indicated that they began their enterprises in order to obtain the permanent visa status which they needed to stay in America. Other reasons varied. When they were asked if they owned or rented their place of business, twelve indicated that they owned their places. When asked to indicate the most difficult problems facing their business, entrepreneurs reported, in order of difficulty, severe competition among the Korean businesses in their respective retail trade, lack of business capital, lack of fluency in the English language, cultural differences between Korea and America, theft and shoplifting, and lack of merchandise.

The data presented here make doubtful the use of Ivan Light's tradition-of-enterprise hypothesis to explain how small business enterprises among Korean immigrants in America developed and how they have continued to exist in their communities. For the hypothesis to be valid, two major conditions must be assumed to have existed among Korean immigrants prior to their immigration to America or immediately after their arrival. First, Korean immigrants must have acquired entrepreneurship either in Korea or in America which they used effectively to develop and manage their ethnic enterprises. Second, Koreans must have brought to America an economic institution or organization which they used to create their business capital.

The available research data do not support the first assumption. Most of the Korean immigrants who came to the Hawaiian Islands

Table 6—Number of Paid Workers by Type of Business

Type of Business	No paid workers	One paid worker	Two paid workers	Three paid workers	Four paid workers	Five paid workers	More than five	Total paid workers	Total firms
Grocery store	8	3		1	2	2		24	16
Restaurant			2		1		1	22	4
Service station	3	1	2	1	1		1	19	9
Beauty salon and hair products	3				3			12	6
Clothing and shoes			2	1			2	24	5
Radio and TV sales and repair	1		1			1		7	3
Flower and gift shops	4	1						1	5
Business machines		1						1	1
Transportation	1							0	1
Sewing shop							1	15	1
Business development				1				3	1
Total	20	6	7	4	7	3	5	128	52

between 1903 and 1905 had no special entrepreneurial skill acquired either through training or practice. According to Kim Wŏn-yong (Warren Kim), 65 percent of the early Korean immigrants were illiterate.[23] There were also many former soldiers of the disbanded Korean army. Others were people faced with famine and starvation who responded to the recruiting efforts of representatives of the Hawaiian Sugar Planters' Association. The second wave of Korean immigration to America, which began in 1965, has brought a large number of highly educated Koreans who are now in retail trade in major American urban centers. However, as illustrated in Table 5, most of these entrepreneurs had other professional, managerial, and technical positions in Korea. As Table 5 indicates, only one businesswoman among the fifty-two shopkeepers who responded to the questionnaire worked at the same occupation in America and Korea. Therefore, it would be incorrect to say that Korean immigrants in America went into retail business because they had acquired entrepreneurial skills conducive to developing and managing small businesses.

The second assumption is also unwarranted according to the data available. Evidence indicates an awareness of the traditional Korean economic system known as *kye* among Korean immigrants in America.[24] However, they did not use *kye* as a means of creating their business capital. Instead, when Korean immigrants decided to start business, they issued stock certificates to capitalize and incorporate their enterprises. Why early Korean immigrants failed to use the rotating credit system indigenous to Korean culture is not clear. What is clear is that when Koreans went into business they used a typically Western method of capitalization. Even among recent Korean immigrants *kye,* as an economic institution, is rarely used. As indicated in Table 4, there was only one business firm among the fifty retail stores which reported that its initial business capital was raised by means of *kye*.

The results of the present study do not necessarily repudiate Ivan Light's contention that the rotating credit system was a vital economic institution which played a major role in creating small business enterprises among Japanese and Chinese immigrants. There are, however, a number of problems with Light's hypothesis which would have to be resolved if the theory is to become a more sound and useful theoretical tool for comparative studies on economic or business development among various minority groups in America. First, Light ignores the fact that Japanese and Chinese immigrants had access to their homelands as a source of business capital.[25] This access was denied blacks and early Korean immigrants in America. In this regard, Korean immigrants and blacks shared the problem of creating business capital. Second, Light does not consider the fact that many blacks in the South had been paid in kind rather than cash for their labor. Third, although Light's hypothesis is mainly built on the idea that a rotating credit system was used by Japanese and Chinese immigrants to create business capital, Light fails to present concrete data concerning how many Japanese and Chinese enterprises were actually established with money capitalized by means of *tanomoshi* or *hui*. It would be extremely difficult to support Light's hypothesis unless or until his belief in the rotating credit system as a means of capitalization has been buttressed by concrete data showing actual numbers of business enterprises established through these systems.

In conclusion, a word of caution. The preponderance of small businesses among Chinese, Japanese, and Koreans in major American urban centers has been mistaken for a symbol of success in American society. These groups have been praised as America's model minorities who have pulled themselves up by their bootstraps. They have been regarded as people too proud to ask for public assistance from local and federal governments. Their social institutions, particularly their family structures, have been considered a stable force behind the maintenance and promotion of mutual assistance in time of crisis. These observations about people of Asian ancestry should be taken with a grain of salt. In the alleys behind the glittering streets of Chinatowns, Little Tokyos, and Little Seouls, there are many residents suffering abject poverty unaided by local and federal government agencies responsible for rendering social services to the poor. According to an official report submitted to the state of California by a local Korean community organization, more than 50 percent of the Korean immigrants in the Los Angeles area have an income below the federal poverty guideline.[26] The data included in the present study also suggest a very low income among Korean shopkeepers, particularly those who do not have paid employees working for them. It is clear that the small enterprises among Korean immigrants in America are more a symbol of disguised poverty than one of marked success. This is not to belittle either the importance of retail trade among Korean immigrants as a means of their survival, or the importance of their struggle to carry out business in an alien culture. Most Korean immigrants have come to America ill-prepared to qualify for professional, managerial, and technical jobs that carry more social prestige and economic stability. Those who come with education and professional training are often denied the opportunity to practice their professions due to discrimination in employment, refusal by local professional accreditation agencies to recognize their education and training, and/or refusal by licensing agencies of various states to issue licenses on the basis of their previous education and training.[27] Because of these obstacles, working together or separately, many of these qualified Korean professionals have moved into retail trade.

It is one of the few available avenues to economic survival, albeit marginal and precarious.[28]

Notes

1. Ivan H. Light, *Ethnic Enterprise in America: Business and Welfare among Chinese, Japanese, and Blacks* (Berkeley: University of California Press, 1972).
2. Light, *Ethnic Enterprise in America*, pp. 11–12.
3. Light, *Ethnic Enterprise in America*, p. 17.
4. Light, *Ethnic Enterprise in America*, p. 18.
5. Shirley Ardener, "The Comparative Study of Rotating Credit Associations," *Journal of the Royal Anthropological Institute*, no. 94, pt. 2 (1964): 201–29.
6. Allen to Dole, December 10, 1902, *Dole-Foreign Officials*, Archives of Hawaii (Honolulu), Governors' Files (Consuls A–M).
7. Wayne Patterson, "Koreans to Hawaii: Failure in 1897 and Success in 1902," manuscript (Columbia University Seminar on Korea, May 17, 1974), pp. 18–28.
8. Wray Taylor, Secretary of the Board of Immigration, to E. A. Mott-Smith, Minister of Foreign Affairs, November 20, 1899, in "Conditions of Hawaiian Labor," Archives of Hawaii, pp. 1–12.
9. Sister Deborah Church, "Korean Emigration to Hawaii: An Aspect of U.S.-Japanese Relations" (paper submitted, University of Hawaii, April 19, 1971), p. 34.
10. Kim Wŏn-yong (Warren Y. Kim), *Chae-Mi Hanin osimnyŏn-sa* [Fifty-year history of the Koreans in America] (Reedley, California: Charles Ho Kim, 1959), p. 283.
11. Kim Wŏn-yong, *Chae-Mi Hanin*, p. 286.
12. *Korean Pacific Weekly*, June 14, 1941.
13. Kingsley K. Lyu, "Korean Nationalist Activities in Hawaii and America, 1901–1945," manuscript in the possession of Professor Donald D. Johnson, Graduate Division, University of Hawaii, 1950, p. 85.
14. Lyu, "Korean Nationalist Activities," pp. 86–87.
15. Kim Wŏn-yong, *Chae-Mi Hanin*, pp. 302–03.
16. Helen Lewis Givens, "The Korean Community in Los Angeles County" (M.A. thesis, University of Southern California, 1939), pp. 48–49.
17. Givens, "Korean Community," p. 49.
18. Ko Sŭng-je, *Han'guk imin-sa yŏn'gu* [A study on the history of Korean emigration] (Seoul: Changmungak, 1973), pp. 218–19.
19. Kim Hyung-chan, "Some Aspects of Social Demography of Korean Americans," in this volume.
20. U.S. Department of Commerce, Bureau of the Census, *Minority Owned Businesses: Asian Americans, American Indians, and Others* (Washington, D.C.: Government Printing Office, 1975).
21. Bureau of the Census, *Minority Owned Businesses*.

22. Three hundred Korean business firms were randomly selected from various telephone directories of the four metropolitan areas, and a questionnaire written in Korean was sent to each during September 1975. Fifty-two questionnaires were returned by the end of October 1975, and the responses have been cross-tabulated for the present study.

23. Kim Wŏn-yong, *Chae-Mi Hanin*, p. 7.

24. Earl K. Paik, *Economic History of Korea* (San Francisco: Korean National Association, 1920), p. 120.

25. L. Ling-chi Wang, "Symposium on Ethnic Enterprise in America," *Journal of Ethnic Studies* 1:4 (Winter 1974): 86–87.

26. *Joong-ang Daily News*, June 18, 1975.

27. It is estimated that there are at least 300 experienced Korean pharmacists in Southern California who are denied the opportunity to practice their profession. They have been prohibited from taking the licensure examination. For a detailed report on the problems facing Korean professionals in the field of health services, see U.S. Civil Rights Commission," A Dream Unfulfilled: Korean and Filipino Health Professionals in California" (Washington, D.C.: Government Printing Office, 1975).

28. According to a study conducted by David S. Kim in March 1975, unemployment is a serious problem for Koreans residing in the Olympic Area of Los Angeles. A report by HEW shows that nearly 60 percent of the adult Korean residents have a college degree or better, but only 25 percent of the professionals are employed as professionals, while 49 percent are employed as operatives, crafts workers, or sales people. Of those with liberal arts degrees, 51 percent are employed as operatives and crafts workers. Only 7 percent are employed as professionals. Underemployment among Korean women with college degrees is more serious. It is estimated that 60 percent of women with liberal arts degrees are employed as operatives or sales-clerical workers. For a detailed study of economic conditions among Korean residents in the Olympic Area, see David S. Kim, "Koreatown to Win: U.S.A." (Los Angeles: University of California, School of Architecture and Urban Planning, March 1975).

Some Aspects of Social Demography
of Korean Americans

Hyung-chan Kim

THIS HISTORICAL SURVEY of the immigration of Korean people to the United States from 1901 to 1971 emphasizes two major aspects of the social demography of the Korean minority in America: an analytical description of Korean immigrants to the United States from 1950 to 1971, and ascribed characteristics of Koreans in America as reported in the 1970 census. Included in the analysis of ascribed characteristics is the composition by age and sex of the native-born Koreans compared with that of the foreign-born Koreans in America. The state of residence is also included to indicate urban and/or rural concentration of Koreans. The analysis of Korean immigrants to the United States during the 1959 to 1971 period includes the following characteristics: age and sex, occupational status at the time of entry, the number who have obtained U.S. citizenship in proportion to the total, and occupational status at the time of naturalization.

The immigration of Korean people to parts of the world outside Asia is a recent development in the long history of Korea. Prior to 1945, Manchuria, Japan, and the Russian Maritime Province were the three principal regions to which Koreans immigrated seeking new political or economic opportunities.

It was reported that there were 1,255,000 Korean residents in Manchuria as of 1961.[1] These immigrants speak Korean and maintain a distinctive Korean culture. Particularly, education for the Korean minority in Manchuria is more advanced than for any other minority nationality in Communist China, a fact that the Chinese Communist government has officially acknowledged. The educational progress among Korean residents in Manchuria may be due to the continuous and systematic attempt by Koreans to build schools even before the Communist takeover of Manchuria.[2]

The second largest group of Koreans living abroad is found in Japan.[3] There are approximately 600,000 Korean residents in Japan. The third largest group of Koreans outside their homeland is found in Soviet Central Asia. A majority of them originally immigrated to the Russian Maritime Province or Siberia. During the Stalin era, however, they were transferred to their present location. According to Walter Kolarz, there are approximately 300,000 Koreans now considered thoroughly Sovietized.[4]

The fourth largest group of Koreans residing abroad is found in the United States. A total of 68,216 Koreans were reported by the 1970 census.[5] The immigration of Korean people to America began in 1899 when Ch'oe Tong-sun, Chang Sŭng-bong, Kang Chae-ch'ŏl, Yi Chae-sil, and Pak Song-gun immigrated to America, but as subjects of the Republic of China, they were regarded as Chinese.[6] The first Korean immigrants reported by the American immigration authorities were Yŏng Paek-hin and Kim I-yu, who arrived in Hawaii on January 15, 1900.[7] Although a small number of Korean students and government officials were dispatched to America proper for their official responsibilities prior to the arrival of Yŏng Paek-hin and Kim I-yu, they were the first to be reported as immigrants from Korea.

The first ship, *S.S. Gaelic,* with 121 immigrants aboard, left Korea on December 22, 1902. In Japan, nineteen of these people failed to pass their physical examination and were sent home. The rest sailed for Hawaii and reached its shores on January 13, 1903. The first group, which included 56 laborers, 21 women, 13 children, and 12 babies, settled on Oahu Island to work at the Waialua plantation. The second and third groups arriving in Hawaii had 63 and 72 people, respectively. A total of 4,567 immigrants went to Hawaii during the following two years: 1,133 in 1903 and 3,434 in 1904.[8] Although 2,659 Koreans went to Hawaii in 1905, 479 of them failed their physical examinations and were sent home.

According to Kim Wŏn-yong (Warren Y. Kim), a total of 7,226 Koreans came to Hawaii before the Korean government put an end to its liberal emigration policy in November 1905. However, there is in his report a discrepancy of 126 persons between the actual number of people who left Korea and those who remained in Hawaii. This discrepancy may be due to the failure on the part of the author to account for the exact number of people who were sent home because of bad health.[9] Among these 7,226 people there were 6,048 men, 637 women, and 541 children, both male and female. Most were farmers by social origin, and consequently there was a high rate of illiteracy among them. It was reported that approximately 65 percent of them were illiterate. According to another source, however, a total of 7,843 Koreans immigrated during the same period. There were 6,701 men, 677 women, and 465 children. A total of 721—653 men, 40 women, 28 children—left Hawaii for either the Orient or the Pacific west coast, leaving 7,122 Koreans behind.[10]

Toward the end of 1905, after learning of the hardships that Korean immigrants had to undergo, the Korean government put an end to all further Korean emigration. Although from 1905 to 1945 several hundred Koreans went to America, by way of China, Europe, and Japan, they were not immigrants in a genuine sense. The emigration of Koreans resumed with the defeat of the Japanese in 1945. The exact number of Koreans who immigrated to America between 1945 and 1947 is not available. The U.S. immigration authorities reported that in 1948 and 1949, 46 and 40 persons born in Korea immigrated to America. But there is no record of the Korean immigrants to America during the 1945 to 1947 period.

As Table 1 indicates, 57,129 Koreans were reported as immi-

Table 1—Korean Residents in America by Immigration Status, 1950–1971

Year	Type Immigrants	Nonimmigrants	Naturalized
1950	10	335	3
1951	32	183	1
1952	127	808	2
1953	115	1,111	46
1954	254	1,270	243
1955	315	2,615	295
1956	703	3,552	155
1957	648	1,798	122
1958	1,604	1,995	168
1959	1,720	1,531	416
1960	1,507	1,504	651
1961	1,534	1,771	1,031
1962	1,538	2,112	1,169
1963	2,580	2,803	1,249
1964	2,362	4,068	1,369
1965	2,165	4,717	1,027
1966	2,492	5,076	1,180
1967	3,956	6,206	1,353
1968	3,811	9,309	1,776
1969	6,045	12,478	1,646
1970	9,314	13,171	1,687
1971	14,297	17,617	2,083
Total	57,129	96,030	17,672

grants during the 1950 to 1971 period. How many of these people had come to America as nonimmigrants and later became permanent residents is not clear. During 1968 a total of 1,098 Korean nonimmigrants adjusted their status of alien residents to that of permanent residents, and in the following year 1,812 nonimmigrants succeeded in changing their status. In 1970 and 1971, 2,079 and 4,049 nonimmigrants adjusted their legal status, but a complete report on the total number of Korean nonimmigrants who have changed their status from alien to permanent is not available.

Table 2 shows the distribution of Korean immigrants by age and sex, according to the year of their entry. Four major characteristics are revealed in the table. First, girls under four years of age constitute the third largest group. This may be due to a larger number of girls than boys who were adopted by American families. More girls than boys are brought to orphanages and foster homes in Korea for adoption at home and abroad. In times of distress, Korean families would rather give up for adoption their girls than their boys. Also, American families seem to prefer girls to boys for adoption. Their choice of girls may be influenced by their concern over the problems of acculturation and assimilation of the adopted into American culture.

Second, the female group of twenty to twenty-nine years of age constitutes the largest group, while women from thirty to thirty-nine years of age is the second largest group. This is mainly due to marriages between Korean women and male American citizens.

As Table 3 indicates, 1,593 out of 1,720 immigrants in 1959 were without gainful employment to report to the U.S. immigration authorities at the time of their entry. During the year, 1,184 females of all age groups came to America. Although this does not necessarily mean that all females were without an occupation, it may be assumed that a majority of them had no significant occupation.

Third, the combined number of males and females of the two age groups, namely, twenty to twenty-nine and thirty to thirty-nine, constitutes approximately 61 percent of the total during the 1959 to 1971 period.

If a person is considered most productive between twenty and forty years of age, a majority of Koreans immigrated to America during their most productive years. Fourth, the total number of male immigrants during the 1959 to 1971 period was 30 percent, whereas the aggregate of the females during the same period made up approximately 70 percent. This is a reversal of the trend established by Korean immigrants during the 1902 to 1905 period.

Table 2—Korean Immigrants to America by Age and Sex, 1959–1971 (%)*

Age	Year	1959	1960	1961	1962	1963	1964	1965	1966	1967	1968	1969	1970	1971
Under 4	M	15.8	9.6	13.3	7.3	3.5	5.5	5.9	3.8	3.2	3.8	3.9	4.2	4.4
	F	27.6	21.9	31.5	19.4	9.2	11.5	11.4	9.5	6.5	8.1	7.5	6.9	7.3
5–9	M	6.1	4.8	5.0	4.1	3.2	3.2	3.7	2.6	3.6	3.1	3.8	3.7	4.2
	F	6.5	5.0	6.5	4.9	3.7	5.5	4.2	4.7	4.4	4.4	4.1	4.8	4.9
10–19	M	2.7	2.4	2.6	2.6	2.6	3.3	2.6	3.2	3.3	3.6	2.7	4.1	4.1
	F	2.6	3.1	3.9	4.0	4.5	6.6	6.5	5.7	6.4	5.8	5.8	5.9	6.0
20–29	M	2.9	3.9	3.4	4.8	7.0	3.3	2.3	4.2	4.9	5.8	5.9	7.4	6.8
	F	26.4	37.1	22.4	38.6	46.4	45.3	45.6	39.6	33.5	35.5	35.2	33.1	29.2
30–39	M	2.3	2.5	2.6	3.7	6.0	2.7	3.2	8.3	13.0	10.1	10.8	10.0	12.7
	F	4.6	7.4	6.1	7.7	10.9	9.9	11.8	14.0	14.8	12.9	12.5	12.3	12.7
40–49	M	0.6	0.1	0.4	0.4	0.7	0.3	0.3	1.1	2.0	1.7	1.9	1.9	2.0
	F	0.5	0.7	0.6	0.7	0.6	1.0	0.6	0.8	1.6	1.6	1.7	2.1	2.1
50–59	M	0.2	0.2	0.1	0.06	0.1	0.2	0.1	0.2	0.3	0.4	0.5	0.7	0.6
	F	—	0.1	0.1	0.5	0.4	0.3	0.3	0.7	0.8	1.1	1.0	1.0	0.9
60–69	M	—	0.1	0.3	0.1	0.1	0.2	0.09	0.1	0.2	0.3	0.2	0.2	0.3
	F	0.05	0.1	0.1	0.2	0.4	0.2	0.5	0.7	0.7	0.5	0.6	0.6	0.5
70–79	M	0.05	0.06	0.1	0.06	—	0.04	0.04	0.1	0.05	—	0.03	0.08	0.1
	F	—	—	—	—	0.1	0.2	0.04	0.08	0.05	0.2	0.1	0.1	0.2
80 and over	M	—	—	—	—	—	—	0.04	—	—	—	—	0.02	0.01
	F	—	—	—	0.06	—	0.08	—	—	0.02	0.07	0.01	0.02	0.02
Total		1,717†	1,507	1,534	1,538	2,580	2,362	2,165	2,492	3,956	3,811	6,045	9,314	14,297

M = Male.
F = Female.
*Due to calculations which include fractions, and omission of values smaller than 0.05, columns may not add up to 100 percent.
†Figure excludes three Koreans who came to the United States from countries other than Korea.

Table 3—Korean Immigrants to America by Occupational Status, 1959–1971 (%)*

Year	1959	1960	1961	1962	1963	1964	1965	1966	1967	1968	1969	1970	1971
Occupation:													
Professional, technical, and kindred workers	5.8	5.3	5.1	7.0	14.3	5.6	4.7	14.0	20.9	18.7	17.8	17.3	21.5
Farmers and farm managers	—	—	—	0.06	—	—	0.04	—	0.05	—	0.01	—	—
Managers, officials, and proprietors	0.2	0.3	0.1	0.3	0.6	0.4	0.3	0.6	0.9	1.1	1.3	1.2	1.6
Clerical and kindred workers	0.5	0.9	0.1	1.1	1.6	1.1	1.4	1.5	1.8	1.6	2.0	1.6	1.3
Sales workers	0.1	0.06	0.1	0.3	0.3	0.2	0.1	0.2	0.2	0.2	0.2	0.2	0.2
Craftsmen, foremen, and kindred workers	0.05	0.3	0.1	0.1	0.01	0.08	0.3	0.2	0.3	0.8	0.8	2.1	2.0
Operatives and kindred workers	0.2	—	—	0.1	0.2	0.1	0.1	0.2	0.6	0.6	0.7	0.7	0.8
Private household workers	0.05	—	0.1	0.1	0.03	—	—	0.08	0.6	1.3	2.0	0.7	0.3
Service workers, except private household	—	0.4	0.2	0.6	1.0	0.6	0.6	0.7	1.3	1.3	1.5	0.9	1.3
Farm laborers and foremen	0.05	—	—	—	—	—	—	—	0.07	0.02	0.09	0.05	—
Laborers except farm and mine	0.1	0.1	0.1	0.06	0.03	0.08	0.09	0.1	0.1	0.2	0.2	0.2	0.1
Housewives, children, and others with no occupation	92.6	92.2	92.8	89.7	81.4	91.5	91.9	82.1	72.8	73.7	72.8	74.6	70.3
Total	1,720	1,507	1,534	1,538	2,580	2,362	2,165	2,492	3,956	3,811	6,045	9,314	14,297

*Due to calculations which include fractions, and omission of values smaller than 0.05, columns may not add up to 100 percent.

Table 3 shows the occupational status of Korean immigrants at the time of their entry, by June 30 of each year from 1959 to 1971. A total of 8,654 persons (approximately 16.2 percent of the total) classified as professional, technical, and kindred workers came to America during the 1959 to 1971 period. The number of housewives, children, and others with no occupational status who managed to come to America during the same period was 77 percent of the total.

What kind of people move from their place of birth to another country, across cultural and/or racial boundaries, is an essential question in research on immigration. The answer to this question is to be found in a critical analysis of the age, sex, marital status, level of education, and occupational status of emigrants at the time of their entry into their new place of residence as well as at the time of their departure from their old place of residence.[11] In the case of Korean immigrants to America, the data pertaining to their educational status are not available for the present study. However, the occupational and marital status, age and sex characteristics of Koreans offer an insight into the kinds of people who have immigrated.

The age and sex characteristics of Korean immigrants have been discussed. There are two major characteristics pertinent to Korean immigrants with regard to their occupational status. First, an overwhelming number of them were housewives and children of American citizens. From 1959 to 1966, more than 80 percent of all Korean immigrants to America had no occupation other than that of housewife, at the time of their entry, to report to the U.S. immigration authorities. Second, the next largest group was composed of professional people. The immigration of professional people was very limited until 1966. During the period of 1959 to 1965, with the exception of 1963, professionals were 7 percent or less of all immigrants. Only after 1966 did the percentage of professional people in proportion to the total number of immigrants go beyond 15 percent. The recent increase in the aggregate of Korean immigrants who are classified as professional, and their increase in proportion to the total, may be a result of changes in U.S. immigration law that have gone into effect since 1965. The act of October 3, 1965, repealed the national origin quota system that had been the legal basis for the immigration policy of the American government since 1924.[12] However, the 1965 act included a three-year phase-out period, which is reflected in the immigration of professional people during the 1969 to 1971 period, as shown in Table 3. In fact, since the expiration of the phase-out period on June 30, 1968, Korean immigrants of all occupational groups increased. During 1969 to 1971, five occupational groups, namely, professional, managerial, clerical, private household workers, and housewives and children, made a gain of about 40 percent per group over the previous year.

The acquisition of citizenship is one of the most important indicators of successful assimilation and integration of immigrants. This seems especially true in the United States, as its laws pertaining to naturalization are less discriminatory than those of other countries.[13] The process of naturalization in America is a relatively simple matter. An applicant for U.S. citizenship must have resided continuously in America and as an immigrant for a period of five years, although there are exceptions to this general rule. Applicants who are wives of American citizens, and members or veterans of the U.S. Armed Forces, may obtain citizenship earlier. The applicant has to renounce his allegiance to his previous country and take an oath of allegiance to the United States. He has to demonstrate that he understands English and that he has a fundamental knowledge of the history and basic principles of the government. Applicants must not have committed any unlawful acts.

Table 4 indicates the number of Koreans who acquired U.S. citizenship by year of entry and year of naturalization, between 1959 and 1971. As shown in Table 4, Koreans naturalized during the 1959 to 1971 period demonstrate a remarkable degree of success in adjusting to American society, when the acquisition of U.S. citizenship is used as the criterion.

How successful a national group of immigrants is in adjusting to their new home is relative to the success or failure of other national groups of immigrants. In an attempt to illustrate the degree of success of Koreans, Table 5 and Table 6 are presented. Table 5 provides information on the number of immigrants and naturalized persons from five countries: Korea, Japan, Mexico, India, and China. The number of immigrants is presented by year of entry, whereas the year of their naturalization is fixed at the year 1971. For instance, 1,720 persons from Korea came to America in 1959, and by 1971 a total of 1,338 had been naturalized. A total of 1,534 Koreans came to America in 1961, and by 1971, 1,269 of them were naturalized.

Table 6 provides information on the number of immigrants from the same five countries by year of entry and the number of naturalized persons at the end of six years of residence, including the year of their entry. For instance, 1,720 Koreans came to America in 1959, and by June 30, 1967, 978 of these people were naturalized. In 1960, 1,507 Koreans immigrated to America and by June 30, 1965, a total of 903 of them were naturalized.

The tables reveal three major characteristics of Koreans who were naturalized during the 1959 to 1971 period. First, as shown in Table

Table 4—Korean Emigrants Naturalized by Entry Year and Naturalization Year, 1959–1971*

Year of Entry	1971	1970	1969	1968	1967	1966	1965	1964	1963	1962	1961	1960	1959
Year of Naturalization:													
1971	64	157	111	208	450	331	274	146	105	79	25	33	16
1970		67	122	73	156	413	243	216	158	93	27	23	15
1969			51	100	61	149	379	234	295	156	36	41	41
1968				53	90	81	188	431	338	279	77	56	49
1967					34	29	43	227	477	180	129	77	58
1966						3	19	11	274	455	113	114	60
1965							24	65	122	204	194	119	121
1964								28	84	143	511	234	135
1963									21	39	103	453	281
1962										7	39	67	465
1961											15	19	66
1960												11	25
1959													6
Total naturalized	64	224	284	434	791	1,006	1,170	1,358	1,874	1,635	1,269	1,247	1,338
Total immigrants	14,297	9,314	6,045	3,811	3,956	2,492	2,165	2,362	2,580	1,538	1,534	1,507	1,720
Rate of naturalization in proportion to the total immigrants (%)	0.4%	2.4%	4.6%	11.3%	19.9%	40.3%	54.0%	57.5%	72.6%	100.6%	82.7%	82.7%	77.7%

*Census and Immigration Service Figures and Statistics have produced discrepancies which become obvious in this table and Table 5.

Table 5—Persons from Five Nations Naturalized up to 1969 by the Year of Their Entry and the Percentages of Persons Naturalized in Proportion to the Immigrants from Their Respective Nations

	Koreans			Japanese			Chinese			Indians			Mexicans		
	Total immig.	Natural-ized	%	Total immig.	Natural-ized	%	Total immig.	Natural-ized	%	Total immig.	Natural-ized	%	Total immig.	Natural-ized	%
1959	1,720	1,338	77.7	5,851	3,059	52.3	5,722	3,262	57.0	506	228	45.0	23,061	1,782	7.7
1960	1,507	1,247	82.7	5,471	2,519	44.2	3,681	1,819	49.5	391	210	53.7	32,684	1,806	5.5
1961	1,534	1,269	82.7	4,313	1,881	43.6	3,213	1,722	53.5	421	236	56.0	41,632	2,108	5.0
1962	1,538	1,635	100.6	3,897	1,648	44.5	4,017	2,187	54.4	545	280	51.3	55,291	1,476	2.6
1963	2,580	1,874	72.6	4,056	1,542	38.0	4,658	3,190	68.4	1,173	410	35.0	55,253	1,037	1.8
1964	2,362	1,358	57.5	3,680	1,007	27.6	5,009	2,036	40.6	634	171	26.9	32,967	686	2.0
1965	2,165	1,127	54.0	3,180	729	22.9	4,057	1,423	35.0	582	177	30.4	37,969	501	1.3
1966	2,492	1,006	40.3	3,394	544	16.0	13,736	1,397	10.1	2,458	226	9.1	45,163	297	0.6
1967	3,956	791	19.9	3,946	388	9.8	19,741	631	3.1	4,642	105	2.2	42,371	142	0.3
1968	3,811	434	11.3	3,613	197	5.4	12,738	186	1.4	4,682	31	0.6	43,563	63	0.1
1969	6,045	284	4.6	3,957	104	2.6	15,440	75	0.4	5,963	12	0.2	44,623	47	0.1
1970	9,314	224	2.4	4,485	72	1.6	14,093	61	0.4	10,114	6	0.05	44,469	12	0.02
1971	14,297	64	0.4	4,457	23	0.5	14,417	13	0.09	14,310	1	0.006	50,103	12	0.02

Table 6—Persons from Five Nations Naturalized at the End of Six Years of Residence by Year of Entry

	Koreans			Japanese			Chinese			Indians			Mexicans		
	Total immig.	Natural-ized	%	Total immig.	Natural-ized	%	Total immig.	Natural-ized	%	Total immig.	Natural-ized	%	Total immig.	Natural-ized	%
1959	1,720	978	56.8	5,851	1,726	29.4	5,722	1,017	17.7	506	86	16.9	23,061	226	0.9
1960	1,507	903	59.9	5,471	1,375	25.1	3,681	731	19.8	391	66	16.8	32,684	232	0.7
1961	1,534	975	63.5	4,313	1,134	26.2	3,213	870	27.0	421	76	18.0	41,632	301	0.7
1962	1,538	1,035	67.2	3,897	1,126	28.8	4,017	1,062	26.4	545	111	20.3	55,291	231	0.4
1963	2,580	1,089	42.2	4,056	1,035	25.5	4,658	1,166	25.0	1,173	148	12.6	55,253	252	0.4
1964	2,362	996	42.1	3,680	701	19.0	5,009	1,048	20.9	634	91	14.3	32,967	202	0.6
1965	2,165	896	41.3	3,180	585	18.3	4,057	918	22.6	582	112	19.2	37,969	237	0.6
1966	2,492	1,006	40.3	3,394	542	15.9	13,736	1,344	9.7	2,458	226	9.1	45,163	283	0.6

4, a majority of naturalized Koreans acquired their citizenship during the year following three years of residence. Since U.S. immigration law does not allow immigrants to obtain U.S. citizenship with less than five years of residence, those naturalized during their fourth and fifth year of residence must be either wives or children of American citizens or members of the U.S. Armed Forces. Second, it seems that from 20 to 23 percent of the Korean immigrants of the 1959 to 1962 period had not been naturalized as of 1971, and if this is used as a prognosticator for the trend in the naturalization of the Korean immigrants, a nearly perfect rate of naturalization within a period of ten years is not to be anticipated. Third, as shown in Tables 5 and 6, Korean immigrants are decisively more successful in acquiring U.S. citizenship than any other nationality group compared. Approximately one-half of the Korean immigrants to America during the 1959 to 1965 period were naturalized at the end of their six years of residence. This is a remarkably high rate of naturalization in comparison with that of immigrants from other nations presented in Table 6.

A number of factors are responsible for such a high rate of naturalization among Koreans. First, there was a relatively high rate of literacy among the females married to American citizens. They were required to take examinations for acquisition of U.S. citizenship. Second, a large number of Korean children were adopted by American families. Also, the high rate of naturalization may have to do with the willingness of Korean immigrants to give up their former citizenship and to adopt the U.S. as their country. In the absence of more reliable and detailed information, a further attempt to interpret the data presented in Tables 4, 5, and 6 is fruitless. For a comprehensive and refined analysis, such data as the level of education of immigrants from these five countries, their professional status at the time of their naturalization, which parallels the year of their entry, their marital status, particularly in the case of women married to or divorced from American citizens, and their psychological propensity for the acquisition of U.S. citizenship are needed.

Table 7 shows the number of naturalized Koreans by occupational status and year of naturalization. Three major characteristics of the naturalized Koreans in America during the 1959 to 1971 period are to be noticed. First, generally speaking, more people in all occupational groups became citizens every year during this period. Particularly, persons classified as professional, clerical, operative, service workers, and housewives and children increased every year during this period.

Second, a steady increase of professional people naturalized in

Table 7—Korean Immigrants Naturalized by their Occupation and Year of Naturalization

Year	1959	1960	1961	1962	1963	1964	1965	1966	1967	1968	1969	1970	1971
Occupation:													
Professional, technical, and kindred workers	16	27	43	63	105	91	79	81	108	217	191	130	168
Farmers and farm managers	1	1	—	1	—	—	—	1	—	—	—	—	—
Managers, officials, and proprietors	5	6	12	7	10	12	7	12	12	29	28	22	29
Clerical and kindred workers	1	9	15	23	23	20	19	26	19	45	40	47	49
Sales workers	—	1	7	5	3	5	3	2	6	7	6	10	16
Craftsmen, foremen, and kindred workers	2	3	4	4	5	6	11	6	10	12	15	10	21
Operatives and kindred workers	10	12	12	14	22	19	31	31	43	61	68	80	71
Private household workers	—	3	2	3	1	3	3	6	—	4	4	1	5
Service workers except private household	7	9	91	21	32	18	35	44	32	63	81	105	136
Farm laborers and foremen	2	—	—	—	—	1	1	1	—	—	—	1	—
Laborers except farm and mine	—	—	3	3	3	3	9	2	2	9	2	10	21
Housewives, children, and others with no occupation	372	580	914	1,025	1,044	1,218	829	969	1,121	1,329	1,211	1,271	1,567
Total	416	651	1,103	1,169	1,248	1,396	1,027	1,181	1,353	1,776	1,646	1,687	2,083

proportion to all naturalized immigrants is apparent. In 1959, only 16 persons classified as professionals were naturalized. This was only 3.8 percent of the total number of naturalized immigrants during that year. In contrast, the housewives, children, and others with no occupation represented 89.4 percent of the total.

Until 1967 the percentage of professional people who were naturalized did not go beyond 9 percent, whereas that of housewives, children, and others with no occupation did not go below 80 percent of the total number of naturalized immigrants. Beginning in 1968, however, the professional people naturalized increased significantly. For instance, the professional people who were naturalized in that year made up 12.2 percent of the total, whereas the housewives, children, and others with no occupation represented 74.8 percent. When the total number of housewives, children, and others with no occupation who were naturalized during the whole 1959 to 1971 period is compared with that of the professional people naturalized during the same period, the former makes up 80.8 percent of all who were naturalized, while the latter represents only 7.9 percent.

Third, three occupational groups—clerical, operative, and service workers—have shown a significant increase in rate of naturalization compared with that of other occupational groups. It is difficult to find how many persons in these three groups came to America with occupational status other than that which they held at the time of their naturalization. It is to be assumed, however, that there were some changes of occupation among these people prior to their naturalization. This applies to people in all occupational groups. How many people of a given occupational status acquired citizenship with the same occupational status is not known.

Consequently, a comparison of an occupational group with others within a nationality group by year of entry, for a better understanding of relative success or failure in acquiring U.S. citizenship, is not possible with the data available to research workers at the present time. Such a comparison requires more refined data including occupational changes from year of entry to year of naturalization.

It was reported that there were 68,216 persons of Korean ancestry in the United States at the time of the 1970 general census. Of these 68,216 a total of 36,681 were foreign born. An analysis of the foreign-born population of Korean ancestry indicates a number of interesting characteristics. First, the most conspicuous characteristic of the Korean minority in America is the large female population of foreign-born Koreans. The female population constitutes approximately 64 percent of the foreign-born Koreans in America. Those between twenty and thirty-nine years of age make up more than

45 percent of all foreign-born Koreans. This age group and the corresponding age group of foreign-born males of Korean ancestry total 24,806 people, which constitutes 67 percent of the total foreign-born Koreans. A further breakdown of this particular population indicates that only 19 percent of 3,797 foreign-born Koreans between twenty and twenty-four years of age are male, while 75 percent of 7,777 foreign-born Koreans between twenty-five and twenty-nine years of age are female. In comparison with the overwhelming size of this potential labor force, the age group of both sexes under 19 years of age constitutes only 17 percent of the total foreign-born Koreans.

In contrast to the foreign-born population of Korean ancestry, the native-born population is extremely young. The total, 18,935, of those under nineteen years of age is approximately 60 percent of all native-born Koreans. This fact alone demonstrates the recency of the immigration of Koreans to America. In comparison with the group under nineteen years of age, the group between twenty and thirty-nine years of age constitutes only 18 percent of the total native-born Koreans.

A total of 30,603 foreign-born as well as native-born Koreans between twenty and thirty-nine years of age were reported in the 1970 census. This is approximately 44 percent of the total Korean population in America. There were reported in the same census 25,515 foreign- and native-born Koreans under nineteen years of age, which make up 37 percent of the Korean minority in America.

Table 8 shows the state of residence of foreign-born and native-born Koreans in America as reported in the 1970 census. The state of California leads all other states with 9,557 foreign-born Koreans residing within its state boundaries. Of these 9,557, Los Angeles claims 4,029 as municipal residents, while San Francisco has 792 foreign-born Koreans. Oakland has the third largest foreign-born Korean population in the state of California with 146. Therefore, a total of 4,967 foreign-born Koreans reside in these three major cities.

California has the second largest native-born Korean population in the U.S. with 7,124, following Hawaii which, with 7,639, has the largest native-born Korean population. It should be pointed out that of 7,124 native-born Koreans in California, only 1,649 reside within the city of Los Angeles. San Diego, with 324, has the second largest native-born Korean population in the state of California. It seems reasonable to conclude from the data that recent Korean immigrants to the U.S. tend to concentrate heavily in major metropolitan centers where employment and other opportunities are more readily available.

Table 8—Koreans in America, 1970

Foreign Born	State	Native Born
190	Alabama	173
177	Alaska	201
208	Arizona	195
20	Arkansas	89
9557	California	7124
512	Colorado	334
543	Connecticut	289
150	Delaware	199
271	District of Columbia	94
420	Florida	357
541	Georgia	228
1986	Hawaii	7619
34	Idaho	55
2506	Illinois	1297
363	Indiana	372
346	Iowa	283
316	Kansas	179
314	Kentucky	137
127	Louisiana	201
57	Maine	37
1415	Maryland	918
863	Massachusetts	542
1239	Michigan	882
597	Minnesota	453
117	Mississippi	63
518	Missouri	317
67	Montana	70
156	Nebraska	183
116	Nevada	114
56	New Hampshire	67
1414	New Jersey	1154
79	New Mexico	70
3855	New York	2254
526	North Carolina	247
57	North Dakota	28
1461	Ohio	918
322	Oklahoma	277
387	Oregon	478
1524	Pennsylvania	1115
119	Rhode Island	43
86	South Carolina	71
46	South Dakota	59
333	Tennessee	191
1151	Texas	866
195	Utah	176
35	Vermont	24
1236	Virginia	569
1042	Washington	651
111	West Virginia	114
459	Wisconsin	384
35	Wyoming	48

The state of New York has the second largest foreign-born Korean population in the U.S. with 3,855, while it has the third largest native-born Korean population with 2,254. Of 3,855 foreign-born Koreans residing in the state of New York, 2,665 live in the city of New York. This constitutes 70 percent of the total foreign-born Korean population in the state of New York. However, the city of New York has 989 native-born Koreans out of the total 2,254 native-born Koreans reported in the state of New York. This means that the city of New York has approximately 43 percent of the total native-born Koreans residing in the state of New York. Illinois has the third largest foreign-born Korean population in the U.S. with 2,506. Of these Chicago has 1,333, while Peoria and Rockford report only 13 and 7 foreign-born Koreans, respectively. In the state of Illinois there were 1,297 native-born Koreans as of 1970. Chicago claims 590 as municipal citizens, which is 45 percent of the total native-born Korean population residing in Illinois.

Of 68,216 Koreans, both foreign and native born, reported in the 1970 census, 15,837 or approximately 23 percent live in five major cities in America. They are Los Angeles with 5,678, New York with 3,654, Honolulu with 3,528, Chicago with 1,923, and San Francisco with 1,084. There are in the United States twenty-seven cities each of which has more than 200 Koreans, both foreign and native born. These twenty-seven cities have a total of 22,183 or approximately 32 percent of the total Korean minority in the United States. The 1970 census shows 143 Standard Metropolitan Statistical Areas (SMSAs) which reported 29,147 Koreans residing within their boundaries. These 143 SMSAs, therefore, have 42 percent of the total Korean population in the United States.

The enactment of the national origin quota system in 1924 restricted the immigration of Koreans to America to fewer than 750 every year until 1956. It was only after 1962 that a significant number of Koreans began to immigrate to the United States. A critical analysis of the Korean immigrants during the 1959 to 1971 period, therefore, reveals some of the major factors that may set the general trend for demographic and socioeconomic characteristics of Korean people immigrating to America.

The following are some of the major findings of the study:

1. An overwhelming majority of the Koreans in America were females. This was a reversal of the trend established by the Korean immigrants who came to America proper during the 1902 to 1905 period.
2. A majority of the Korean immigrants were wives and children of American citizens, and the majority of these did not have gainful employment that they could report at the time of their entry into America.
3. The act of October 3, 1965, has begun to show its impact on the number

and kinds of emigrants from Asia to America. Particularly, more Koreans of all occupational groups as classified by the U.S. immigration authorities are coming to America now as a result of the act.

4. Korean immigrants have shown a remarkable degree of success in adjusting to American society when the acquisition of U.S. citizenship is used as the indicator. When compared with immigrants from Japan, China, India, and Mexico, Koreans show a much higher rate of naturalization than that of any other nationality group.

5. A majority of naturalized Koreans were wives and children of American citizens or members of the U.S. Armed Forces.

6. The 1970 census indicates that Korean immigrants to America tend to concentrate in highly urbanized and industrialized states in America, namely, California, New York, Illinois, Hawaii, Pennsylvania, Ohio, Michigan, and New Jersey.

Notes

1. *China News Analysis* (Hong Kong) 569 (June 18, 1965): 2–3; *Union Research Service* (Hong Kong) 33:14 (November 15, 1965): 218–19.

2. For a thorough historical study of Korean immigrants to Manchuria, see Lee Hoon K., *Manju wa Chosŏn-in* [Manchuria and the Koreans] (Pyongyang: Union Christian College, 1932).

3. For a complete study of the Korean minority problem in Japan, see Richard H. Mitchell, *The Korean Minority in Japan* (Berkeley: University of California Press, 1967).

4. For an interesting study of the Korean minority in Soviet Central Asia, see Walter Kolarz, *The Peoples of the Soviet Far East* (New York: Praeger, 1954).

5. U.S. Department of Commerce, Bureau of the Census, *Detailed Characteristics* (Washington, D.C.: Government Printing Office, 1973).

6. Pak Mun-bŏm, "Nŏlbŏchin Miguk iminŭi mun" [Broad measures for migration to America], *Shintong-a* [New East Asia] 42 (February 1968): 231.

7. *Han'guk Ilbo* [Korean Times], May 5, 1971.

8. Yu Hong-yŏl, "Miguke innŭn Hanin-dŭl" [Koreans in America], *Sasanggye* [Journal of Thought] 6:4 (April 1958): 39–40.

9. According to Yu Hong-yŏl, Korean historian, Koreans who immigrated to Hawaii between December 1902 and November 1905 totaled 6,747. See Yu Hong-yŏl, "Miguke innŭn Hanin-dŭl," p. 39.

10. Hawaii Korean Golden Jubilee Celebration Committee, *Fifty Years of Progress*, n.d., unpaginated.

11. Herbert J. Gans, "Some Comments on the History of Italian Migration and on the Nature of Historical Research," *International Migration Review* 1:2 (Summer 1967): 5.

12. For a more detailed discussion of the act of October 3, 1965, (P.L. 89–236) see Peter Rodino, "New Immigration Law in Retrospect," *International Migration Review* 2:6 (Summer 1968): 56–61.

13. Leo Grebler, "The Naturalization of Mexican Immigrants in the United States," *International Migration Review* 1:1 (Fall 1966): 17.

Part Two

Introduction

THE FOLLOWING ESSAYS, with the exception of the last two, present some of the results of recent research undertaken to study the process of acculturation and its concomitant effect upon the life of the Korean immigrant in America. These studies are more related to the process and product of acculturation or cultural assimilation than to those of structural assimilation. This is understandable in view of the fact that most of the Korean immigrants in America came here after 1965. It is also a realistic approach to Korean immigration because it recognizes that structural assimilation is a longer process than cultural assimilation. Structural assimilation takes place, according to Milton Gordon, when the immigrant or his descendant has made "entrance into cliques, clubs and institutions of host society, on a primary group level"* *and has been accepted by members of the dominant society.* Cultural assimilation, on the other hand, occurs when the immigrant or his descendant has undergone an extrinsic and/or intrinsic change from his own cultural patterns to those of the host society. This is not to suggest that the first generation immigrant is incapable of making a structural entrance, but it seems realistic to expect that cultural assimilation would occur first in his life, as he makes an effort to be accepted into his host society.

In studying the process of cultural assimilation of those Korean immigrants who have come to America since 1965, there are a number of important sociocultural factors that require special attention of students of assimilation. First, the Korean immigrant is essentially different from the Asian and European immigrant of earlier periods in American history. The Korean is well educated, highly skilled in his profession, and expects to succeed in his struggle to attain a better life for himself and his family in America. As indicated in the essay by Ryu, 71.1 percent of all Koreans in America have completed high school, as compared with the U.S.

---

*Milton M. Gordon, *Assimilation in American Life* (New York: Oxford University Press, 1964), p. 71.

129

average of 52.3 percent. More striking is the fact that 36.3 percent of all adult Korean immigrants have college educations, while only 10.7 percent of the American population have. This alone has numerous implications. Unlike most of the immigrants of the earlier period, the post-1965 Korean immigrants are from the urban middle class. They have been exposed through their education—which disseminates information, knowledge, and skills on the basis of objective, rational, and scientific principles—to some of the social and cultural complexities of life which are shared by highly urbanized, industrial, and technological societies regardless of their cultural differences.

Second, no longer in her complex, modern, industrial society has America room as she once did for the unskilled, uneducated, and illiterate. On the other hand, for those immigrants who have acquired basic social and vocational skills required of modern industrial urban dwellers, America seems to make their adjustment easier and faster by means of social agents of acculturation such as education and mass media.

In the first essay, by Chang, communication as a crucial factor determining the process and product of acculturation is discussed. Chang defines acculturation as a process by which original cultural patterns of either or both dissimilar cultures undergo a change as a result of their close contact. He presents two major hypotheses. First, communication is the main vehicle by which acculturation takes place. Second, individual acculturation at a given time may fall within one of the three ideal types into which the cultural patterns are classified: nativistic movement (resistance to change); bicultural movement (recombination of cultural elements into a new whole); and cultural assimilation (acceptance of change). Using thirty Korean residents in Los Angeles as research subjects, Chang tested the hypotheses to find out whether or not communication is the major factor determining the relative degrees of individual acculturation in terms of the three ideal types. His findings indicate that the individuals whose traditional Korean family values had been least affected by their contact with the host society through communication were fearful of American values. On the other hand, the individuals who were opposed to the large family system for its anti-individual values were the most affected by their give and take with American society. Between these two extreme groups falls the third group of individuals, who were unwilling to accept their own individual communication realities in the host society, while at the same time acknowledging the problems which are characteristics of modern industrial urban society.

The essay by Chang focuses its attention on the effect of acculturation on the individual over time, while the second essay, by

Lee, attempts to provide a basic understanding of how the two Korean communities in his study developed historically and how their structural patterns were shaped. Interestingly, Chang seems to imply that there are developmental stages in the process of individual acculturation, while Lee states explicitly that the structural patterns of the two communities are characterized by stages of development. Whether or not these developmental stages can be generally applied to other Korean communities in America is yet to be determined.

Lee hypothesizes that the two Korean communities in Georgia, one in Atlanta and the other in Athens, where the University of Georgia is located, have developed through the period of initiation, the formative period, and the period of institutionalization, and have reached the present period of segmentation. This last period is a natural outcome of the growing number of Koreans in the two communities. Lee maintains that segmentation has been accompanied by the emergence of three networks of social interaction between the members of the community. These networks are low-level networks, medium-level networks, and high-level networks. Low-level networks are founded on common interest, similar personality, age, and/or religion, but no role expectation between individuals sharing these characteristics is involved. Medium-level networks, built on the foundation of similar profession, academic discipline or field of study, length of residence, proximity, and/or native regional origin, involve role expectation between actors. High-level networks are based on alumni and kinship relationships, which are characterized by durability and continuity regardless of time and place.

Lee postulates that a final period of decline will follow the period of segmentation. Some Korean communities, particularly those whose members are Korean students enrolled in various American institutions of higher learning, may experience a period of decline as students graduate and move on to other parts of the country. It is, however, inconceivable at this time that Korean communities established in major metropolitan centers of America will decline in the foreseeable future, unless luck suddenly changes for Koreans in America. It is quite possible that with succeeding generations, more successful Koreans may move out of their communities in order to achieve structural assimilation, but this may have to wait for a number of generations to come.

In the third essay, Yu presents his study of the sociocultural factors associated with degree of cultural assimilation of Korean immigrants in America. He used ten major factors as variables: 1) educational background, 2) occupation in Korea, 3) age at entry into America, 4) number of family members, 5) length of residence in

America, 6) present occupation, 7) income, 8) religion, 9) English proficiency, and 10) intention to stay in America. These ten variables are put into three major groups for the purpose of testing three hypotheses. The first three are called preimmigration factors, while the next five are grouped as postimmigration factors. The last two are called personal factors. The first hypothesis states that assimilation is related to preimmigration factors. This is partially supported by Yu's study. The education variable is found to be most significantly related to assimilation. Second, assimilation is related to postimmigration factors. This hypothesis is not as strongly supported as expected, because no single factor is found to be very significantly related to assimilation. Third, that assimilation is related to other personal factors is partially supported. The English-proficiency variable is most significantly related to assimilation. Yu concludes that only five variables are related to assimilation in any useful degree. They are education, length of residence, occupation, religion, and English proficiency.

In his second essay on acculturation of adult Korean immigrants and their children in America, Yu presents the findings of a study designed to test three hypotheses. First, there is no significant correlation between the degree of parental acculturation of a Korean immigrant and the measured personality adjustment of his child. Second, there is no significant difference in the measured personality adjustment of bicultural Korean children and that of American children. Third, there is no significant relationship between levels of education or the socioeconomic status of the Korean immigrant and his measured degree of acculturation.

Using the California Psychological Inventory as the psychometric instrument for measuring personality adjustment, Yu tested twenty-four children between thirteen and eighteen years of age. The results do not support his first hypothesis. Yu found that there is an inverse relationship between the degree of parental acculturation and the measured personality adjustment of bicultural children. Yu reasons that this phenomenon may be attributable to the fact that highly acculturated immigrants tend to inhibit their native culture, while they are not yet assimilated into the host society. The second hypothesis is partially supported. The research findings do not determine conclusively whether or not bicultural Korean children have more personality maladjustment than their American counterparts. The third hypothesis is not supported. It was found that level of education is related to the degree to which the immigrant becomes acculturated. This phenomenon is also discussed in the first essay by Yu. It seems rather definite that education is a crucial socioeconomic variable in determining the degree of cultural assimilation of the Korean immigrant.

The essay by Professor Cha discusses his findings in a study undertaken to determine the degree of assimilation of Korean immigrants in Los Angeles with regard to five different types of assimilation, i.e., cultural assimilation, structural assimilation, marital assimilation, identificational assimilation, and behavior-reception assimilation. Using these as dependent variables, he investigated how length of residence, education, and income of Korean immigrants in Los Angeles are related to each of them. He concludes that cultural assimilation has begun to take place among Koreans in Los Angeles, although it may vary depending upon their length of residence and the education they have achieved in America. He also concludes that Koreans in Los Angeles cannot be considered either structurally assimilated or identificationally assimilated.

What implications does this study have for the political participation of Korean immigrants in local electoral politics? In the foreseeable future, Koreans in Los Angeles, and perhaps in other parts of America, will remain in their ethnic enclaves with little prospect for achieving structural assimilation. Given this interpretation, it is obvious that the future political orientation of Koreans in America will follow the traditional pattern of ethnic politics: essentially a politics of accommodation which distributes political rewards to the few, and recognizes the ethnic group as a whole.

The essay by Professor Ryu is not a usual study of cultural assimilation. No hypotheses are tested, and no variables are measured to determine the degree of cultural assimilation. The study, however, reports some of the essential data necessary to conduct any basic research on Korean immigrants in America. Also, to the extent that cultural assimilation reflects a change from one socioeconomic and cultural pattern to another, the data presented in Professor Ryu's essay are indispensable to those who are contemplating comparison research on acculturation of Korean immigrants.

The study by David Kim and Charles Wong on Korean businesses in Los Angeles provides students of ethnic enterprise with basic data which have not been made available before. It is extremely difficult to obtain basic data on Korean businesses because their numbers wax and wane depending on the fortune or misfortune of business and the influx of Korean immigrants. Also, Korean entrepreneurs, because of extreme competition among themselves, are highly suspicious of even a well-meaning survey and keep their information discreet.

Much of the data reported in the study corroborate essentially what has been said of Korean ethnic enterprise in a preceding essay by the editor. The Kim and Wong essay, however, offers much detailed information on the types of businesses, the number of employees, total assets, annual sales, and initial source of business capital of a larger number of firms located in Koreatown in Los Angeles. The findings are not conclusive enough to prove that Korean entrepreneurs are more successful than their Chinese or Japanese counterparts or any other small retailer. In fact, there is every reason to believe that most Korean entrepreneurs would not have gone into their business enterprise had there been alternatives for economic survival, and that they would have preferred to enter the professional fields for which they were trained. An evaluation of recent Korean business success is premature, especially since most businesses have been established within the last two or three years. In view of the fact that one out of two new retail businesses in America fails within its first year of operation and two out of three fail within six years, regardless of ethnic membership of entrepreneurs, troublesome days for Korean ethnic enterprise seem not too far ahead.

In the last essay, Professor Gardner presents one of the most comprehensive reviews of literature available both in Korean and English on immigration of Koreans to Hawaii and the mainland, and on their subsequent American experience. In the past, the paucity of information about literature has been a major obstacle to judicious and scholarly studies on the history of Korean immigration. This review, replete with diverse sources of information, used in conjunction with his previous bibliographical work on the Koreans in Hawaii, will serve as an invaluable guide to those interested in serious research.

Communication and Acculturation

Won H. Chang

THIS STUDY CONCERNS the process of acculturation of the Korean immigrants in the United States. The number of Korean immigrants was relatively small until 1965. Since then, as a result of the new immigration law, which permits a larger quota to those of Asian origin, the Korean community has grown rapidly, forming a distinct minority group in several large cities in the United States.

The purpose of this study is to determine the nature of the communications environment within the Korean ethnic group and this environment's relationship to the acculturation process.

Four postulates [1] are fundamental. First, human communication is a constant process within the individual in which he takes something into account for a certain end. It is a self-reflective process at the subconscious and conscious levels through which the individual constructs himself-in-his environment. Second, acculturation is the process by which two groups of individuals with different cultural backgrounds bring about change in the original cultural patterns of either or both groups as a result of their firsthand contact. Such cultural patterns may be classified into three ideal types: nativistic (resistance to change); bicultural (recombination of cultural elements into a new whole); and cultural assimilation (acceptance of change). Third, communication is the main vehicle by which acculturation occurs. Hence this study includes a communication system, which focuses on the reality function, and an interaction system, which focuses on the societal function in a larger system. These systems are interrelated, even though the basic unit of analysis in this study is the communication system. Fourth, therefore communication is the underlying power in acculturation by which an individual accumulates control over change in order to cope with a new environment.

The term "acculturation" has been widely accepted among anthropologists as referring to those changes set in motion by the coming together of societies with different cultural traditions. However, this word, which focuses on the conditions under which change takes place, contains ambiguity concerning the concept of acculturation and its derivatives. Persistent usage has given the concept a meaning resembling that of cultural assimilation or the replacement of one set of cultural traits by another. For example, the term is used in reference to individuals in contact situations who are more or less "acculturated." Also, many anthropological studies have been inconsistent and used the term to apply to both process and product of change.

Most of the acculturation studies have dealt with two groups of individuals who have different cultural traits.[2] This does not exclude acculturation between more than two groups. To identify the difference, the latter is called multiacculturation and the former biacculturation.

Previous studies referred to the contact situation—a given condition—as a causal phenomenon. They ignored the significance of the contact situation in the acculturation process and examined only the acceptance, the rejection, or the mixed culture. However, to deal fully with acculturation one must focus on both extremes of the continuum. Including the contact situation enables the observer to do this. Thus, the present model emphasizes the contact situation as basic to acculturation phenomena.

I believe investigation of the contact situation from the standpoint of communication analysis will provide a better understanding of the acculturation process. The following model is a visual representation of acculturation phenomena.

In the model (Figure 1) group A with culture X and group B with culture Y are identified as separate entities. Since A and B have both giving and receiving functions, they are not labelled as donor group or receiving group. The model is drawn for the two-culture situation, not the multiacculturation situations. Each individual from groups A and B would belong somewhere on the line XY as a consequence of the contact situation. For example, if a person from group B moves toward the Y end, he is interpreted as resisting change (nativistic movement). If he moves in the direction of X, he accepts change (cultural assimilation movement). However,

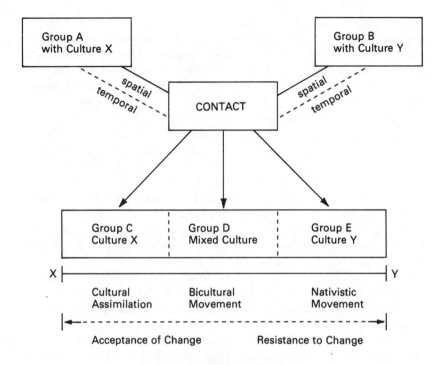

Figure 1. Biacculturation Model

there is no clear border between X and Y. A person who belongs in the central area would be part of bicultural movements.

Acculturation has been defined in the preceding section as the process by which two groups of individuals with different cultural backgrounds bring about change in their original cultural patterns. Communication seems to be the main vehicle by which such change occurs. Communication is the underlying power in acculturation by which an individual accumulates control over change in order to cope with a new environment.

Some earlier communication studies in acculturation are reviewed here in order to provide a background of communication theories. Early in this century, when functional analysis was a prevailing school of sociological theory, Chicago sociologists saw communication as a social mechanism, a function in maintaining cohesive social order. In 1909, Charles Cooley described communication as the means of conveying and preserving the symbols of the mind.[3] He saw no sharp line between the means of communication and other phenomena. Regarding the relationship between society and communication, John Dewey said, "society not only continues to exist by transmission, by communication, but it may be fairly said to exist in transmission, in communication."[4]

Robert Park dealt with communication as the prime medium of interaction in sociology.[5] Communication, he concluded, makes possible consensus which eventually gives a group a specific character. Louis Wirth extended Park's view when he wrote that consensus in mass democracy rests upon a sense of group identification and participation. Consensus is maintained by mass communication, which rests on some sort of society.[6]

The trend of American sociological interest in communication during the early twentieth century coincided with the growing immigration to the United States of people who came primarily from European countries. Implicit in the American attitude toward immigration and subsequent adjustment of immigrants in this country was an attitude that communication, as a mechanism for social cohesion, would facilitate the process of acculturation of incoming settlers. In 1964, Harold Mendelsohn said that mass communication is charged with the task of facilitating the acculturation process.[7]

Communication as a functional process of acculturation needs further study. In 1967 Hugh Duncan said that since the thirties little has been done by American sociologists in the field of communication theory.[8]

Most of the earlier studies regarding communication theory were done by symbolic interactionists. They tended to see communication as an end product without attempting to search for its underlying causes. These studies relegated communication to an incidental role in human affairs. They revealed inadequate understanding of the vital functions of communication in human behavior. Thayer's alternative to this approach explains that communication is a continuous function of human beings.[9] It is vital to human existence.

Clearly, descriptions of communication offered by scholars from almost every academic discipline have missed the heart of the matter. Using "communication" as a catchword, they have camouflaged resistance to our attempts to look into the communication process and comprehend it in a detached way.

The communication system is the smallest, indivisible unit for the systematic study of communication. It includes the individual and that which is being taken into account. The basic unit of analysis here is the communication system, whose functions are exploitation, establishment, confirmation, or alteration of some relationship between the system and some aspects of its environment through the decision of the organism which is informed within that environment, and between some aspects of the environment and the organism. The above two common functions have four operational subfunctions: generating, disseminating, acquiring, and consuming.[10]

While the basic unit of analysis in this study is the communication system (intrapersonal), there are other levels of analysis: interpersonal and organizational (societal function). Ruesch and Bateson divide this context into intrapersonal, interpersonal, groups (one to many and many to one), and cultural (space binding messages of many to many).[11] Levels of communication are divided because of the empirically unavoidable perspective on the basic human process underlying all communication.

Communication and interaction systems function not as a simple composite of independent elements, but coherently and as an inseparable whole. Systems adjust to environmental phenomena and make their adjustments felt by the environment; and in the system, results of change occur by the self-regulating process of the system. If the equifinal behavior of the systems is based on their interdependence of initial conditions, then many different initial conditions not only yield the same final results but also may be produced by the same cause.

A family case study in the field of acculturation has the advantage of bridging the gap between the conceptual extremes of the culture at one pole and the individual at the other. The family thus becomes the middle term in the culture-individual equation. Because the family unit is small and manageable, it can be described without resorting to the abstraction and generalization which one must inevitably use for the culture as a whole. It is in the context of the family that interrelationships between culture and individual communication reality occur in the acculturation process.

Values are general orientations toward basic aspects of life—abstract principles that guide human behavior.[12] When these values are incorporated in generally accepted precise rules of conduct, we call such rules norms. An abstract value such as charity is defined in terms that refer to certain roles we play in society, so as to tell the incumbent of one role how to behave toward the person in the reciprocal role. Thus, we are told to love our neighbors, to honor our parents, and to forgive our enemies.[13]

It is a common value system that holds a society together; the members of a society learn to perceive the world in similar ways and to act toward one another in an understandable fashion through a value system. Sometimes, the press of circumstances causes a man to violate rules, but public opinion finds this behavior threatening and demands punishment through laws or other sanctions. A society without strong common values is unable to reach collective decisions and create viable institutions. And a man without belief in the values of his group is a man confused and distraught.[14]

However, it must be remembered that such value systems are constantly changing. To study the value system, therefore, the observer must restrict the universe of observable phenomena to manageable proportions by placing a limit upon the multivariability of internal and external determinants to be observed, and by specifying some point or some span of time during which to describe the value system or to observe changes occurring in the system. Under these limitations, the observer must listen to what people say, and watch how they behave. From this information, he sifts out the central rules that explain the consistency of words and actions displayed by the people under observation. When these rules are determined in tentative form, the observer can express them to the members of the society under study so that they can comment on them. The more philosophically minded among the society will be able to refine and correct the first impressions of the social scientist.

In this way, we tentatively approach an understanding of the value system of a group, recognizing that it is a distillation from many observations—an abstract set of principles—and that we cannot expect to gain from such principles a high degree of accuracy in predicting what a given man will do in a given situation. But, within manageable limits, we can explain what most men will do in most situations. We may achieve scientific parsimony through a limited set of values describing the core of a culture, rather than a long list of thousands of specific norms.

Some values which are closely related to work and career range from specific norms about how a worker should treat his boss or approach his tasks, through more general ideas about the relationship between education and profession, to even more abstract principles about predictability and orderliness in life.

Under the influence of Confucian teachings and traditions, some values of Korean culture related to marriage and family life, respect for parents, and friendship and seniority are typically distinguishable from those of Western culture.

Following the framework discussed above, I observed and interviewed Koreans in Los Angeles from 1968 to 1970, and again during the month of August 1971. From these observations and interviews, I selected sixty statements.

Each of the statements was printed on a separate two by four inch card in both English and Korean. Each subject was asked to sort the statements into the following quasi-normal forced distribution.[15] Every subject received a new deck of cards which had been shuffled to eliminate possible order effects:

Weight	0	1	2	3	4	5	6	7	8	9	10
Number of Distribution	2	3	4	7	9	10	9	7	4	3	2

Statements are structured according to certain dimensions of evidence and subjects on the basis of certain demographic variables. According to my fundamental postulate, I assumed that there are detectable differences in the ways that different subjects will sort the statements.

The Q-analysis is based upon a correlation matrix, just as R-factor analysis is, but people rather than responses are correlated. Therefore, I attempted to get many different kinds of subjects. The kinds of subjects used in this study are listed below:

Code Name	Sex	Age	Occupation
M37TRADING	Male	37	Foreign trade
F31TRADING	Female	31	Housewife
M40LABTECH	Male	40	Laboratory technician
F36LABTECH	Female	36	Housewife
M48RESTRNT	Male	48	Restaurant owner
F46RESTRNT	Female	46	Restaurant owner
M33ENGINER	Male	33	Electric engineer
F31ENGINER	Female	31	Housewife
M35MERCHNT	Male	35	Grocery shop owner
F34MERCHNT	Female	34	Grocery shop owner
M33LABORER	Male	33	Construction worker
F28LABORER	Female	28	Sewing machine operator
M34ACCNTNT	Male	34	Accounting business
F29ACCNTNT	Female	29	Housewife
M39TEACHER	Male	39	Teacher
F35TEACHER	Female	35	Typist
M39BUSNESS	Male	39	Carwash business
F29BUSNESS	Female	29	Secretary
M29PRGRMER	Male	29	Computer programmer
F26PRGRMER	Female	26	Secretary
M48PREACHR	Male	48	Pastor of Korean church
F46PREACHR	Female	46	Housewife
M38WELFARE	Male	38	Welfare worker
F28WELFARE	Female	28	Housewife
M35ARCHTCT	Male	35	Architect
F31ARCHTCT	Female	31	Housewife
M35FACTORY	Male	35	Factory worker
F32FACTORY	Female	32	Nurse's aide
M38MEDIDOC	Male	38	Medical doctor
F35MEDIDOC	Female	35	Housewife

The data from the Q-factor analysis of the thirty subjects in this study were used to calculate a thirty by thirty matrix of correlations between pairs of subjects.[16] Factor analysis of this matrix reveals that three factors accounted for 57.4 percent of the variance. The three factor solution was chosen to account for as much variance as possible and still allow the isolation of the three acculturation patterns previously discussed. Each subject's loadings on all factors are reported in Table 1. Table 2 shows the reordered list of subjects from the varimax rotated in a simple structure matrix.

The formula $r / 1 - r^2$ was used to find factor weights of each subject within each type. Subject assignments with factor weights by type are given in Table 3. This table shows what kinds of people are

Table 1—Simple Structure Matrix

	Variable	1	2	3
1	M37TRADING	0.84	0.13	0.10
2	F31TRADING	0.91	0.12	0.13
3	M40LABTECH	0.41	0.25	0.50
4	F36LABTECH	0.43	0.23	0.46
5	M48RESTRNT	0.89	0.30	0.04
6	F46RESTRNT	0.88	0.15	0.22
7	M33ENGINER	0.11	0.84	−0.23
8	F31ENGINER	0.05	0.91	0.09
9	M35MERCHNT	0.13	0.46	0.32
10	F34MERCHNT	0.11	0.53	0.25
11	M33LABORER	0.89	0.22	0.24
12	F28LABORER	0.91	0.26	0.19
13	M34ACCNTNT	0.14	−0.04	0.63
14	F29ACCNTNT	0.39	0.02	0.48
15	M39TEACHER	0.20	0.01	0.74
16	F35TEACHER	0.22	0.10	0.72
17	M39BUSNESS	0.37	0.27	0.55
18	F29BUSNESS	−0.02	0.38	0.61
19	M29PRGRMER	0.28	0.45	0.56
20	F26PRGRMER	0.26	0.39	0.58
21	M48PREACHR	0.35	0.05	0.58
22	F46PREACHR	−0.11	0.09	0.75
23	M38WELFARE	0.44	0.18	0.44
24	F28WELFARE	0.14	0.41	0.30
25	M35ARCHTCT	0.21	0.32	0.38
26	F31ARCHTCT	0.32	0.40	0.34
27	M35FACTORY	0.38	0.21	0.28
28	F32FACTORY	0.78	0.08	0.27
29	M38MEDIDOC	0.12	0.82	0.01
30	F35MEDIDOC	0.08	0.84	0.11

in each type, and the relative strength of the weighting of each person in that type—in effect, how close each was to ideal. The higher the factor weighting, the closer the person was to the ideal type.

In order to enhance the interpretation of the findings, the data were also submitted to hierarchical classification by reciprocal pairs, a form of linkage analysis developed by Louis McQuitty.[17] First, respondents were classified at the lowest level of abstraction and then reclassified at successively higher levels. The first level of abstraction above the lowest includes clusters of persons whose Q-sorts are more like each other than they are like any of the other respondents' Q-sorts. Each respondent's Q-sort is correlated with every other respondent's, and the respondents whose highest correlations are with each other are clustered. The pairs clustered in this

Table 2—Reordered Factor Matrix

Seq.		Variable ID	1	2	3	Com.	Pure
Factor	1						
1	1	M37TRADING	0.842	0.128	0.096	0.735	0.965
2	2	F31TRADING	0.906	0.116	0.129	0.850	0.964
3	6	F46RESTRNT	0.883	0.148	0.217	0.849	0.919
4	5	M48RESTRNT	0.892	0.302	0.040	0.888	0.895
5	12	F28LABORER	0.907	0.258	0.191	0.925	0.889
6	28	F32FACTORY	0.782	0.082	0.267	0.689	0.887
7	11	M33LABORER	0.885	0.216	0.241	0.888	0.882
8	27	M35FACTORY	0.383	0.211	0.275	0.267	0.550
9	23	M38WELFARE	0.441	0.117	0.440	0.420	0.464
Factor	2						
10	8	F31ENGINER	0.049	0.907	0.092	0.833	0.987
11	7	M33ENGINER	0.110	0.844	−0.026	0.724	0.982
12	29	M38MEDIDOC	0.119	0.820	0.005	0.686	0.979
13	30	F35MEDIDOC	0.080	0.836	0.109	0.717	0.975
14	10	F34MERCHNT	0.110	0.530	0.254	0.358	0.786
15	9	M35MERCHNT	0.125	0.458	0.316	0.325	0.645
16	24	F28WELFARE	0.141	0.409	0.302	0.278	0.601
17	26	F31ARCHTCT	0.320	0.402	0.340	0.380	0.426
Factor	3						
18	22	F46PREACHR	−0.110	0.087	0.752	0.586	0.966
19	13	M34ACCNTNT	0.140	−0.044	0.628	0.415	0.948
20	15	M39TEACHER	0.203	0.010	0.740	0.591	0.930
21	16	F35TEACHER	0.216	0.097	0.717	0.571	0.902
22	21	M48PREACHR	0.354	0.052	0.584	0.469	0.727
23	18	F29BUSNESS	−0.017	0.375	0.605	0.507	0.722
24	20	F26PRGRMER	0.263	0.386	0.575	0.548	0.603
25	14	F29ACCNTNT	0.388	0.015	0.477	0.378	0.602
26	17	M39BUSNESS	0.366	0.271	0.554	0.514	0.597
27	19	M29PRGRMER	0.283	0.453	0.564	0.602	0.527
28	3	M40LABTECH	0.412	0.246	0.503	0.483	0.523
29	25	M35ARCHTCT	0.208	0.324	0.380	0.292	0.494
30	4	F36LABTECH	0.425	0.231	0.458	0.444	0.472
Total Var.—per factor			0.2307	0.1624	0.1807	0.5738	
		—cumulative	0.2307	0.3931	0.5738		
Com. Var.—per factor			0.4021	0.2830	0.3150	1.0000	
		—cumulative	0.4021	0.6850	1.0000		

way, with respondents yet unclustered, become the types to be examined at the next level of abstraction.

The loadings, weights, and rankings of the statements were used to obtain a profile of the way that the hypothetical ideal person of each type would have sorted the statements. These hypothetical sorts were converted to z-scores to facilitate comparisons among types. A positive z-score indicates that the statement is among those with which a hypothetical person would agree. A negative z-score indicates that the statement is one with which a hypothetical person would disagree.

Table 3—Variable Assignments with Factor Weights by Type

Type		Subject	Weight
Type 1 (N = 9)	1	M37TRADING	2.9012
	2	F31TRADING	5.0349
	5	M48RESTRNT	4.3562
	6	F46RESTRNT	4.0108
	11	M33LABORER	4.0955
	12	F28LABORER	5.0987
	23	M38WELFARE	0.6483
	27	M35FACTORY	0.4493
	28	F32FACTORY	2.0129
Type 2 (N = 8)	7	M33ENGINER	2.9247
	8	F31ENGINER	5.1027
	9	M35MERCHNT	0.5791
	10	F34MERCHNT	0.7379
	24	F28WELFARE	0.4910
	26	F31ARCHTCT	0.4797
	29	M38MEDIDOC	2.4964
	30	F35MEDIDOC	2.7740
Type 3 (N = 13)	3	M40LABTECH	0.6725
	4	F36LABTECH	0.5793
	13	M34ACCNTNT	1.0355
	14	F29ACCNTNT	0.6177
	15	M39TEACHER	1.6463
	16	F35TEACHER	1.4771
	17	M39BUSNESS	0.7989
	18	F29BUSNESS	0.9551
	19	M29PRGRMER	0.8262
	20	F26PRGRMER	0.8581
	21	M48PREACHR	0.8857
	22	F46PREACHR	1.7341
	25	M35ARCHTCT	0.4440

All three types were in relatively high agreement concerning twenty-one of the sixty statements. Consensus statements fail to distinguish between types, but this does not mean that such statements should be ignored when determining patterns of rank for any one type.

The criterion for consensus was a range of z-scores for the statements among the three types of subjects less than 1.0. The fifteen consensus statements are as follows:

Average z-score

a. There is no reason why married women should not work if they want to do so.   0.87

b. There is always something in the human environment that man cannot change.   0.79

c. Sex education for teenagers in American public schools has a high value for their future lives.   0.60

d. Important qualities of a real man are determination and driving ambition.   0.37

e. There is no such thing as "good friends are often better than mother" in America.   −0.36

f. I would be happier if there were more participation by the Caucasian-Americans at our church's regular meetings.   −0.39

g. "I cannot find a real American friend to lean on."   −0.55

h. The best friends are the ones made during grade school.   −0.60

i. Sending an old parent to a nursing home is not too bad.   −0.67

j. Women do not have equal rights and opportunities with men.   −0.68

k. "I prefer an office job with a smaller salary to a factory job with a larger salary."   −0.71

l. It does not make much difference if the people elect one or another candidate, for nothing will change.   −1.16

m. "I always try not to speak first, but let Americans open up."   −1.20

n. When looking for a job, a man ought to find a position in a place located near his parents.   −1.25

o. As things are today, an intelligent person ought to think only about the present, without worrying about what is going to happen tomorrow.   −1.42

Each type was identified in respect to the other types combined. This was done by averaging z-scores of one statement for two types (for example, Type 2 and Type 3) and comparing it (the average z-score) with the third statement's z-score (in this case, Type 1).

The nativistic movement type (Type 3) emphasizes the heritage of the traditional Korean family, building strong boundaries between the family and society in order to keep the family system relatively close-knit.

For traditional Korean society the family is the foundation of all aspects of life. The family is more important than the individual. For example, if an individual becomes a criminal, he does not disgrace himself as much as he disgraces his family. Thus, Type 3 does not see any reason to break away from the relatively closed Korean family system.

Persons in this type believe "obedience and respect from a wife to her husband are the most important things for happy family life." They assert that "a wife should *not* make her own decisions even if she disagrees with her husband." This group opposes the idea that "if husband and wife are unhappy, they should be allowed to divorce." They think "the practice of frequent divorces and remarriage is acceptable among movie stars, but not among ordinary people."

For Koreans, divorce is a disgrace to the family. First, both the husband and the wife are an important part of the family. Even if the husband disregards his wife, she has a function in the family and is important to it. If she divorced, she would be rebelling against the honored and respected family system and would be blamed for everything in the upheaval of the authoritarian family unit. Second, a divorced woman has little chance to remarry. Usually she would have to resort to working as a housemaid.

Moreover, a woman who does not please her husband and who is part of a divorce does not have the opportunity to have children. For a traditional Korean woman, bearing children is the way to status and happiness. Indeed, a married woman lives with her children; she eats with her children rather than with her husband. Clearly, a divorced woman could not return to her own family. She would be a disgrace to them. This emphasis against divorce is not surprising in light of Type 3's commitment to the Korean family tradition. Obviously, the wife's submission to her husband is basic to this system.

Elderly parents are the center of authority in the traditional Korean family and community. Their care is not an option, but a moral responsibility. The family which does not revere its elderly parents actually is rebelling against the unwritten law and order and traditional values of the community.

Traditional Koreans teach their children to adopt established family-centered values. They want their children to respect their parents and grandparents before anyone or anything else. Even the introduction in Korea of a new educational system which compelled children to go into the community for their education and which taught independence from parental control and caused a conflict in values within families, did not deter the traditionalists, as represented by Type 3, in their determination to keep the family as the keystone of life.

This type strongly agrees with the statement, "I have to live with my old parents and be responsible for their care," and "elderly parents bring family members closer to each other." Even though they agree that "the social security system for old people in America is not too bad," they believe that "sending old parents to a nursing home is very bad."

Looking at their children's future, this group believes "teenagers dating without their parents' control will bring an unhappy life." Moreover, they agree that the "children's future should be based on the parents' desire." Children in the traditional Korean home are trained to respect their parents and older persons. If this is true in trivial matters, it is not surprising that in important matters such as dating and marriage, parental control is expected. Clearly, the parents, as centers of authority within the family, have an obligation to direct their children's futures in a manner that will enhance the family.

Regarding their relatives, Type 3 agrees that "if I have the chance to hire an assistant in my work, it is always better to hire a relative than a stranger." Type 3 strongly objects to the notion that "I do not care about my neighbors. I do not even know their names." But members of this group agree that "I would be happier if there were more participation by the Caucasian-Americans at our church's regular meetings."

Relatives in the traditional Korean system are an extension of the immediate family unit. As a result, relatives are well loved. In fact, relatives tend to live close to one another and form communities. These communities form *kye* (rotating credit associations) which provide banking, wedding, funeral, and other services for everyone in the community. These mandatory services plus the close relations within a community result in close-knit neighborhoods within traditional Korean society. Type 3 people are accustomed to this kind of community, but in the United States community life is not close-knit. Neighbors may even be strangers. Persons in Type 3 obviously would like to have more interaction with their neighbors.

Participation in social activities tends to widen the family boundary. Such involvement makes persons of this type feel uneasy. They don't believe "Western dance parties make good social activity," nor "should one enjoy his life in America because everything is so convenient." They do not believe "making plans only brings unhappiness because the plans are hard to fulfill."

For Koreans, social life can occur only with those whom one knows well. One does not have social activity with persons who are strangers, as Americans commonly do at cocktail parties and dance parties. Moreover, American life includes so many conveniences that a person of Type 3 feels an obligation to save money for his future life. These conveniences do not mean that life is more enjoyable. Indeed, without intimate social interaction with the community, life is filled with alienation.

Type 3's occupational expectations are lower than any other type. They do not think "engineering and medicine are the best jobs for Korean-Americans because of Korean racial origins." They also object to the idea that "one ought to seek some prestigious 'public offices' even if it is financially risky." Furthermore, they do not "prefer an office job with a smaller salary to a factory job with a larger salary."

Type 3 basically includes persons who are not treated as professional people. They have a language problem and an Oriental appearance which cause them to build distance between themselves and Caucasian Americans. As a result, money is more important than prestige.

Basically this is because persons of this group feel alien. They do not believe they can achieve a status where they will be treated as professionals. However, money has utility and can be obtained.

Contrary to the nativistic type, the cultural assimilation group (Type 2) is characterized by social activity. For this group the family boundary is wider than it is for the nativistic type, and there is no strong indication of how this type feels about the relationship between husband and wife, or interaction with neighbors.

Members of a nuclear type family strongly oppose keeping old parents with them. They affirm that "looking after my old parents demands too much of me," and "it is often difficult to keep one's temper with old parents." This group does not think that "when things are difficult, old parents are often a great source of courage and inspiration." They think problems of old people should be dealt with by the social system rather than by the family and they object to the statement "the social security system for old people in America is not too bad."

They acknowledge that "parents' influence on their children's future should not be based on the parents' desire to make them what they (the parents) want," and that "sex education for teenagers in American public schools has little value for their future lives." They do not tend to get help from relatives and oppose the statement, "when you are in trouble, only a relative can be depended upon to help you out." For persons in this group it is not important to build lasting family relationships. The tendency is to ease out of family ties because they feel comfortable with American social banter. The trivialities of American conversation do not puzzle them. They do not need deep personal relationships as persons in Type 3 do.

Participation in social activities is common for Type 2. These people strongly agree with the statements—"Western dance parties make good social activity," "it is easier to get along with people in America," and "I can be friendly in a light manner in America." This type is against the Oriental tradition of seniority. Its members object to these statements—"I hate to see a boy of 20 talk to a man of 45 as an equal," and "I always use polite language with elderly people."

They feel comfortable with their occupational environment and strongly affirm their "equal opportunity to be as successful in the occupational world as is the Caucasian-American." They object to loyalty in an occupation, by agreeing that "a man ought to move out of his present job without considering loyalty whenever he finds a better salary or position" and that "the boss on the job is the boss only when he is on the job." They believe in the prestige of a job and not in the statement that "to work with tools is as good as to work with papers." For them, "a person needs good connections to get ahead in the occupational world." However, they object to the statement, "the son of a laboring man does not have a very good chance of rising into a professional job." They also disagree with the idea that "even if one works hard on his job, when he works overtime he should be paid overtime wages."

For the traditional Korean, an employer is more than a company that pays a salary. The boss becomes actively involved in his employees' lives. He provides financial assistance for employees' children to attend college. He helps settle financial difficulties. He helps with any personal emergency of employees. In such a system, salaries generally are low, but company benefits are high. The company is humanized in the person of the boss. Therefore, an employee feels a loyalty—even an obligation—not to betray the trust or refuse responsibility to the boss who cares for him. Thus, the personal relationship has high value. However, Type 2 does not feel this traditional loyalty toward the boss.

Type 2 people are satisfied with what is happening around them and object to the statement that "it is important to make plans for the future." They agree that "making plans only brings unhappiness because the plans are hard to fulfill."

Nonetheless, they maintain Korean ties by not agreeing that "knowledge of English is much more important than the knowledge of the Korean language in a Korean-American community." Perhaps this is because Type 2 persons do not have difficulty learning English and, thus, English is not as important for them as it is for those in Type 3.

The bicultural movement type (Type 1) is a combination of the previous types, but closer to Type 3. The correlation between Type 1 and Type 3 is 0.511 and between Type 1 and Type 2 is 0.335. Persons in Type 1 and Type 3 are quite similar. They agree on the authority of the family and on the impossibility of achieving recognition in America. Nonetheless, in contrast to Type 3, they somewhat enjoy their life in America. They also differ with Type 2 on friendship. For them, friendship with Americans is not easily made. They wait for Caucasian Americans to initiate the relationship. Type 1, like Type 3, retains many Korean life values. However, they, like Type 2, are somewhat motivated toward the American life-style.

Type 1 people widen the boundaries of the family system. Persons in this group object to the idea that "parents have the right to reject the choice of their children's marriage partners." They are convinced that "selection of a marriage partner should be by a prospective bride and bridegroom," and "a wife should make her own decisions even if she disagrees with her husband." They disagree that "one of the most important things for parents to do is to help their children get further ahead in the world than they did." In other words, parents should not play a dominant role in their children's future. Moreover, they seem to prefer a state of independence in relation to their relatives. Members of Type 1 disagree that "if I have the chance to hire an assistant in my work, it is always better to hire a relative than a stranger." Nevertheless, Type 1 people don't feel comfortable in their relationship with Americans. They say they cannot "be friendly in a light manner in America," and agree that "I always try not to speak first, but let Americans open up."

Type 1 people have a low opinion of their opportunities in the occupational world. They don't believe "they have an equal opportunity to be as successful in the occupational world as is the Caucasian-American." Therefore, "engineering or medicine are the best jobs for Korean-Americans because of Korean racial origins." Although they disagree that "a person needs good connections to get ahead in the occupational world," members of this type do not believe "promotion in a job should be based on one's ability and hard work rather than on his connection with 'big wheels.'" They think "jobs that make their hands dirty are bad jobs." Therefore, "one ought to seek some prestigious 'public offices' even if it is financially risky." They disagree that "the boss on the job is the boss only when he is on the job."

In summation, Type 3 maintains that family relations are of the highest value; Type 2 holds to social participation as its most important value; and Type 1 is a compromising group. While not accepting American values, this last type goes along with the prevailing social system.

Indeed, communicational realities for traditional Koreans are premised on family values. However, as Koreans become more acculturated to America, they begin to perceive reality according to more individualistic values.

In acculturation the same events are viewed from the perspective of two or more systems—for example, the American culture system and the Korean system. These systems have specific foci and limited ranges of convenience. Such constructs enable the individual to develop a course of behavior explicitly or implicitly, stated or unstated, consistent or inconsistent, rational or intuitive. In acculturation these systems enable the individual to accumulate control over change in order to cope with a new environment.

Constructs in acculturation are used for prediction of things to come, and the world keeps moving and revealing these predictions to be either correct or misleading. Thus, constructs and whole systems are revised. Everyday experience calls for consolidation of some aspects of our outlook, revision of some, and outright abandonment of others. For example, suppose a person's constructs of reality mislead him, he misses his cues. In other words, his communication system presents him with many rude surprises. Obviously he must reclassify his role within his personal constructs. When a person tries to readjust to life within the framework of his personal construct system, the dimensions, of course, tend to remain the same. Therefore, his freedom is possible only along the axis which he has established for himself.

Because such trial and error involves the man plus the mind plus the environment, all parts of the system are involved. Thus, the organism which destroys its environment destroys itself. However, the individual must cope with his environment—for example, learn consciously or unconsciously how to be acculturated. This activity is at the heart of communication.

Persons in Type 3 are anxious about and fearful of American values. They feel insecure among Americans. They emphasize the heritage of the traditional Korean family, building strong boundaries between the family and society in order to keep the family system relatively close-knit. The wife's submission to her husband is basic to this system and elderly parents are the center of authority. Persons who do not revere their elderly parents are rebels against the unwritten law and traditional values of the community. Moreover, in the Korean family system, children are taught to adopt family-centered values. Children are trained to respect their parents and older persons. Social activity can occur only with those whom one knows well.

Persons in Type 2 feel more capable of moving with the give and take of American society. They are characterized by social activity. For this type, the family is a part of a wider society. Involved in a nuclear family, this type opposes the large family system with its anti-individual value system. For this group the large family system does not allow for the rights of various subsystems such as the husband and wife dyad and sibling cliques. Clearly, individual values form the perspective of judgment of Type 2. For this group the problems of old people are dealt with through the social system rather than through the traditional family system. In other words, the authoritarian values of the Korean society are rejected. For example, this group does not accept the absolute authority of parents, the seniority system, and absolute hierarchical structures.

Persons in Type 1 are located somewhere between Type 2 and Type 3. The directions of this group seem ambivalent. They do not seem so anxious about American society that they retreat entirely into the Korean-oriented family structure. Nor do they seem willing to accept freely their own individual communication realities. Nonetheless, persons in this type admit to problems which are characteristic of industrial society as it attempts to cope with an urban environment.

In general, the individual becomes acculturated by widening his constructs to provide better fits. Going through this process he repeatedly is halted by the damage to the system that will result from the alteration of a subordinate personal construct. Frequently his personal investment in the larger system, or his personal dependence upon it, is so great that he will avoid the adoption of a more precise construct in the subculture.

This is a relatively open system, a structure which maintains itself in a stream of "through-put." It is the continuous giving and taking of the structure from its environment to maintain its structure as well as its environment. In the growth of all living systems the structure must take into account its environment and adapt to required forms.

In communication we are talking about a system in which the increase in information is not the difference between what has been taken in and what has been given out (equifinality phenomena). When a system is informed, the added information is not subtracted from the source. In fact, the source informs itself at the same time that it informs another. Communication is never ceasing. In other words, threats to man and his ecological system are the results of error in thought—conscious or unconscious. So when the mind is separated from the structure in which it has developed, the circuits and balances of nature are askew.

Findings in the present study exhibit a continuous lessening of control over change from the Korean value to the American value systems. The nativistic movement group (Type 3) demonstrates a belief pattern with more Korean values, while the cultural assimilation group (Type 2) shows more American values. The bicultural movement group (Type 1) was somewhere between these two groups in the process of acculturation. Clearly, communication realities for the traditional Korean are premised on family values. However, as he or she becomes more acculturated to American culture, the Korean begins to evaluate reality according to more individualistic values.

A significant aspect of the acculturation process among the Korean ethnic group in this country is the paradox of the individual communication system. This results from the continuing conflict between the authoritarian values of Korean culture and the values related to individual freedom which characterize American culture. For example, a Korean American wife could not or would not hold her husband's hand in front of the rest of the family, but when she goes out to a social activity, she shakes hands with everybody. She may even dance with Americans. Her husband often may advocate individual rights, freedom, and democracy outside the family. But when he comes home, he assumes an authoritarian role. Neither his children nor his wife may argue with him about anything. They are his subordinates.

Obviously, there are many illustrations of this type of personal value conflict within individual Korean Americans. It is part of their new situation. It is something they cannot escape and it may have tragic consequences.

Notes

1. "Postulate," in this study, is an assumption that an essential prerequisite to carrying out some operation or line of thinking exists which is so basic that it antecedes everything said in the logical system it supports. Therefore its value is in utility and not in truth. When we question the truth of a statement proposed as a postulate, we must recognize that we are arguing other postulates either explicitly or implicitly. See Fred N. Kerlinger, *Foundations of Behavioral Research* (New York: Holt, Rinehart and Winston, 1964), p. 420; George A. Kelly, *Psychology of Personal Construct,* vol. 1 (New York: W.W. Norton, 1955), p. 46.

2. For general discussions of the concept of acculturation, see W.J. McGee, "Piratical Acculturation," *American Anthropologists* 11 (August 1898):243; Franz Boas, *Race, Language and Culture* (New York: Macmillan, 1948), pp. 426–36; Margaret Mead, *The Changing Culture of an Indian Tribe,* Columbia University Contribution to Anthropology, vol. 15 (New York: Columbia University Press, 1932); Monica Wilson, *Reaction to Conquest: Effects of Contact With Europeans on the Pondo of South Africa* (London: Oxford University Press, 1961); Robert Refield, Ralph Linton, and M.J. Herskovits, "Memorandum for Study of Acculturation," *American Anthropologists* 38 (January–March 1936):149–50; M.J. Herskovits, "African Gods and Catholic Saints in New World Negro Belief," in William A. Lessa and Evon J. Vogt, eds., *Reader in Comparative Religion: An Anthropological Approach* (New York: Harper, 1965), pp. 541–47; Ralph Linton, *Acculturation in Seven American Indian Tribes* (New York: D. Appleton-Century, 1940), pp. 463–520; Ralph Beales, "Acculturation," in A. L. Kroeber, ed., *Anthropology Today: An Encyclopedic Inventory* (Chicago: University of Chicago Press, 1953), p. 622; Social Science Research Council Summer Seminar on Acculturation, 1953, "Acculturation: An Exploratory Formulation," *American Anthropologists* 56 (December 1954):973–1002.

3. Charles H. Cooley, *Social Organization: A Study of Larger Mind* (New York: Charles Scribner's, 1909), p. 61.

4. John Dewey, *Democracy and Education* (New York: Macmillan, 1916), p. 5.

5. Robert E. Park, "Reflections on Communication and Culture," *American Journal of Sociology* 44 (September 1938):191.

6. Louis Wirth, "Consensus and Mass Communication," *American Sociological Review* 13 (February 1948):9–10.

7. Harold Mendelsohn, "Sociological Perspective on the Study of Mass Communication," in Louis A. Dexter and David White, eds., *People, Society, and Mass Communication* (New York: Free Press of Glencoe, 1964), p. 31.

8. Hugh D. Duncan, "The Search for a Social Theory of Communication in American Sociology," in Frank E.K. Dance, ed., *Human Communication Theory: Original Essays* (New York: Holt, Rinehart and Winston, 1967), p. 236.

9. Lee Thayer, *Communication and Communication System* (Homewood, Ill.: Richard D. Irwin, 1968), pp. 15–16.

10. Lee Thayer, "Communication: *Sine Qua Non* of the Behavior Science," paper presented at the Air Force Office of Scientific Research 13th Science Seminar, Albuquerque, New Mexico, June 13–14, 1968.

11. Jurgen Ruesch and Gregory Bateson, *Communication: The Social Matrix of Psychiatry* (New York: W.W. Norton, 1968), pp. 273–89.

12. Clyde Kluckhohn, "Values and Value Orientations in the Theory of Action," in Talcott Parsons and Edward A. Shils, eds., *Toward a General Theory of Action* (Cambridge: Harvard University Press, 1951), pp. 388–433; M. Brewster Smith, "Personal Values in the Study of Lives," in Robert W. White, ed., *The Study of Lives* (New York: Atherton Press, 1963), pp. 324–47.

13. Judith Blake and Kingsley Davis, "Norms, Values and Sanctions," in Robert E.L. Faris, ed., *Handbook of Modern Sociology* (Chicago: Rand McNally, 1964), pp. 456–84.

14. Emile Durkheim, *The Division of Labor in Society,* trans. George Simpson (New York: Free Press, 1966). Durkheim discussed the function of the value system and abnormal forms of adjustment in a society.

15. The Q-sort distribution was taken from Kerlinger, *Foundations of Behavioral Research*, p. 583.

16. The computer programs used for this study are "Quanal" and "Hirak," developed by G. Norman Van Tubergen, School of Journalism, University of Iowa.

17. Louis L. McQuitty, "Single and Multiple Hierarchical Classification by Reciprocal Pairs and Rank Order Types," *Educational and Psychological Measurement* 26:2 (1966):253–65.

A Study of Social Networks within Two Korean Communities in America

Don-chang Lee

THE PURPOSE OF this study is to analyze the historical development and structural patterns of two Korean communities in Georgia—an academic community, Athens, and an urban community, Atlanta. An attempt has also been made to compare these communities in terms of developmental stages and social relations. This study covers the period 1960 to 1972. In general, this study is both diachronic and synchronic. The analysis is based on the theory that the Korean community will develop on a continuum and that the structure will change. The methodology is based on the assumption that these approaches are interdependent. One approach without the other is meaningless.[1]

An effort was made to analyze the structure of the two Korean communities in terms of social interaction (network linkage). This involved gathering data from twenty families within each community. Interviews, informants, and researcher participation and observation were the chief sources of information utilized.

The sociogram was constructed by asking personal questions about interaction. When the responses were summarized, a certain pattern of network linkage emerged and the reasons for such linkage were revealed.

One purpose of this study is a cross-structural comparison of the two Korean communities. This approach seems worthwhile considering their distinctive development and structure. Thus, a cross-cultural study was not undertaken.

The Korean community in the United States is generally dispersed. It is different from communities like the Chinatown or Japanese-town in a large city where the communities have proximity and fixed geographic boundaries. Some Koreans have attempted to establish a Koreatown in Los Angeles but it is not yet fully developed. Nevertheless, a variety of Korean communities do exist in the United States and the size and structure of each community vary according to environmental factors. The community may be simple or complex, homogeneous or heterogeneous, academic or business centered. Regardless of the size and nature of the community, each has its own history and structural pattern. The community system is complex and a variety of social relations are maintained in order to meet the sociopsychological needs of Korean residents.

The two communities used in this study are separated by a distance of about seventy miles. In the academic community, there are about 75 Koreans, and they are all affiliated with the university as students or professionals or families of such. Virtually none is engaged in business. On the other hand, in the urban community, there are more than 300 Koreans and most of them are either engaged in business or service work.

The urban community and academic community are different in the following aspects. The urban community is growing fast and within it the number of Koreans has been increasing rapidly over the past few years. In contrast, Koreans in the academic community have been decreasing since 1970. This trend will continue for the foreseeable future as students complete their schooling.

It is difficult to discover how many Koreans lived in the areas prior to and in the early 1960s. It is assumed that there were only a few Koreans, most of whom were students. Between 1960 and 1970, Koreans in both communities increased rapidly, and when this study was completed in 1970, there were more than 300 Koreans, including children and adults, in the two communities.

In the early 1960s, Koreans in both communities were mainly students. There were a few professionals but no businessmen in either community. Therefore groups in both areas were homogeneous. Although the number of Koreans has increased, the academic community still maintains homogeneity. Its residents are either students or university employees. There are no Koreans in Athens who are not affiliated with the university. The situation in Atlanta is quite different: there are students, businessmen engaged in many kinds of occupations, and the interracially married—mainly Korean women married to American men.

The increase in Koreans with different backgrounds and occupations has produced a heterogeneous and complex structure. As a result, many institutions and subgroups have emerged to meet sociopsychological needs.

The change in structure follows a pattern analogous to the folk-urban continuum.[2] The structure has changed from a simple and cooperative atmosphere in which there was little conflict, to an individualistic pattern characterized by conflict. The main cause for such a structural change is that more institutions such as the Korean Association, the Korean Church, and alumni clubs have been formed so that the individual's sphere of interaction has been broadened.

Out of the total process of change in both communities, the following developmental stages have been formulated: initiative period (prior to 1960); formative period (1960–1965); period of institutionalization (1966–1970); period of segmentation (1970–); and period of decline (hypothetical). The stages apply to both communities and the distinctiveness of each community is presented in the following discussion. The five stages are formulated on the basis of the characteristics of structure.

During the initiative period, both communities had few Koreans. They were all students and no complex networks existed. All were familistic and had a strong sense of togetherness. Status concept was meager and the common nationality was the main source of network. During this time, they wanted to live together by renting a house or sharing a dormitory room. They had limited access to the material wealth of American culture and the situation did not allow them to appreciate the new culture fully. The main problems for Koreans at this time were transportation, communication, and finances.

This period can be characterized by the general term "nationality network." In this network, mutual interdependency was great and an informal face-to-face interaction was a means of overcoming cultural loneliness. The informal interaction included cooking Korean food and eating together, drinking beer, and spending leisure time at sports such as ping-pong and tennis that are popular in Korea. There were few Korean families, and most married Koreans did not bring their families to the United States. Therefore, most of them had to learn how to cook rice and other Korean dishes. The new environment forced males to play a new role as cook. From a traditional viewpoint, cooking by males has been taboo in Korea. Cooking by a male is an indication of a value change which is one of the significant aspects of the struggle for survival, and at the same time suggests that diet has been one of the largest problems for Korean residents in the United States.

During the formative period, more Koreans came to the two communities as students and professional workers. Meantime, some Koreans left the communities. There were no businessmen, and the professional workers were mainly engaged in teaching or office work. These

Koreans were very few and students were the majority group within the communities. They tended to maintain familistic relationships and were often willing to help newcomers. The interaction pattern was simple but the growing Korean population spawned a variety of subgroups. Conflict arose between the newcomers and the early arrivers, and between the married and unmarried persons. Some students got married or brought their families from Korea. Thus, family organization necessitated ownership of automobiles and some students began to drive cars.

Adaptation to technological devices increased, and the expanded interaction area of Koreans led to more dependency on the Koreans who owned cars. Economy was a main factor but initiative exerted by one Korean to drive a car encouraged other Koreans to attempt to get their driver's licenses. However, during this period, not many Koreans owned automobiles. Having a car contributed to an easier life and at the same time it accelerated conflict among Koreans. Since car owners felt an obligation to help other Koreans, they were bound to every Korean without a car in the community. Automobile-centered activities include shopping, rides to school, taking children to the hospital, and carrying Koreans to picnics, a major form of recreation and an opportunity for unmarried Koreans to eat Korean dishes cooked by Korean women.

When this type of interaction is repeated, gossip starts to develop and a different set of networks begins to emerge.[3] The gossip of Koreans is mainly confined to economic matters, status, and personality. Economic gossip focuses on both the poor and the rich. Status gossip, which is mainly normative, revolves around differences in age, education, and student-teacher status. Personality gossip covers lack of politeness, conflict in personality, money handling, and other behavior patterns. Other miscellaneous gossip relates to food preferences, family background, and mode of dress. The main source of gossip is the wife rather than the husband. Gossip spreads with exaggeration and becomes a main cause of conflict, since the Korean community is a closed and limited system as far as its interaction sphere is concerned.

The period of institutionalization is characterized by the rapid increase of Korean residents in the communities. More students and professionals have come to the community because of the rapid expansion of the university and the industrial development in the urban community. The university has offered scholarships to more foreign students, and industrialization has provided more opportunities for employment in the urban community. Korean residents have gained wealth, most Koreans own cars, and even some Korean wives have learned how to drive. During this period, more families were established, and unmarried students began to be a minority group within the Korean community.

The increase in the Korean population brought a desire to meet together at community picnics, and Christmas and New Year parties. These social gatherings provided opportunities for the newcomers to meet and chat with other Koreans. In general, the community picnic is held twice a year, usually during vacation times (quarter breaks) when students are not busy with their studies. The event normally includes games such as soccer, volleyball, and baseball. The games may be important psychologically for releasing the tensions accumulated during a period of intensive study at school. An arbitrary team is organized either by age group or field of study. Sometimes the losers have to pay for beer or other drinks.

A big Korean dinner prepared by the Korean wives is served after the game. There is no clear assignment as to which family provides what kind of Korean dishes. However, each family brings enough rice and other Korean dishes like *kimch'i* and *pul-goki*, so that they can provide for a few extra persons. One function of the gathering is to share Korean food with single Koreans who miss their native foods. The gathering involves all participants in contributing food preparation, games, or fellowship. Thus, the gathering is aimed at meeting many needs.[4]

An organization through which more systematic programs could be carried out became necessary, and the Korean Association was formed and its officers elected. The person elected president of the organization is required to meet certain criteria. He (women are never chosen) must be married and must own a car. He is typically older and more affluent than the majority. And, of course, he must have some leadership characteristics which make him popular. The marriage requirement exists so that the wife will be able to manage food problems in cooperation with other wives. A fairly good income is necessary because there are many situations requiring that he fulfill relatively expensive social obligations. The president must be likable and respected by the majority of Koreans in the community. Car ownership is fundamental if a variety of services are to be rendered for the organization and for residents who need occasional transportation. According to Oriental ethics, an older person has priority in becoming a leader in most situations. Korean cultural concepts require that external problems be solved by the male, and the male is usually more fluent in the use of English and plays a more active role than the female.

The Korean Association became involved in politics due to its connection with the Korean diplomatic agency. It registered as a formal organization with the Korean diplomatic agency and provided services to the agency such as submitting lists of Koreans, and reporting Koreans who were employed or engaged in special fields of study. Thus, the Korean community has expanded its function to include extracommunity affairs.

The term for the presidency is only one year and the new president is elected at the Christmas gathering or at the New Year's Eve party. With time, competition to become president has emerged and political campaigns have become necessary to win the election. This political rivalry has brought conflicts and generated distinct subgroups.

Another characteristic of this period is the emergence of religious institutions in the urban community. Christians in the community began holding services on Sunday afternoons at two o'clock and named the institution the Korean Church. It was possible to have the church in the community because there were Korean ministers who attended divinity school. The Korean Church functions mainly as a social institution for Koreans, and many non-Christian Koreans attend. Thus Koreans maintain their solidarity as an ethnic group, while the church provides opportunity for social interaction. In this aspect the Korean Church is a social fact and arose out of the nature of social life itself.[5]

One of the strongest ties among Koreans is between alumni groups. Most Koreans are linked by the schools they attended in Korea, primarily high school and college. Some college graduates organized an alumni club of alumni living in both communities. The main activities of these institutions are visiting, eating and drinking together, and providing mutual support. The senior and junior class of alumni comprise a kind of fictive kinship system and if one attended a college earlier than the other, he is regarded as an elder brother and he exercises authority over junior alumni. A senior class member is called a *sŏnbae,* and a junior class member a *hupae.* This relationship is an important one in both communities.

Due to the institutionalization and increase of Koreans in the community, total interaction of Korean residents in both communities began to disappear during the period of segmentation. Instead, diverse subgroups have emerged and interaction is largely confined to these. Typical subgroups are based on common interests, personality, religion, occupation, proximity, field of study, length of residence, Korean regional origin, age, alumni relationships, and kinship.

The above categories of networks are shared by both males and females, and they usually follow both husband and wife's linkage. Husband and wife always follow the same pattern of interaction according to the above set of categories. One may belong to more than one network and this constitutes a complex structure of interaction. At this stage there is no longer a familistic atmosphere among Korean residents and many subgroups interact independently. Groupwide activities are discouraged by the same diversity of interests and backgrounds which generate the subgroups. For example, the community picnic carried out up to the period of institutionalization is seldom practiced in the academic community. The Korean community as a system seems to be under stress and those who are not linked with each other become apathetic toward relationships. This apathy is especially obvious in the urban community where competition in business is increasing.

On the other hand, even though the academic community is in a period of segmentation, the Koreans in the community believe in the neighborhood concept and feel obligated to help Koreans faced with problems. Koreans share the feeling that they are all connected to the university either as students or professionals. The relationship within the academic community is comparable to the neighborhood relationship in a rural community, and the relationship within the urban community is comparable to the neighborhood concept prevalent in towns and cities which have larger membership and space than the former community.[6]

The given networks could be classified in a hierarchy according to the strength and durability of linkage: low-level networks, medium-level networks, and high-level networks.

Low-level networks may be defined as situational, and no expectation between actors is involved. Examples of low-level networks are the common interest network, the personality network, the religious network, and the similar age group network. Interest in the same sports, movies, and beer drinking would be characteristic of a common interest network. Interaction with an amiable person or one of similar personality is an example of personality network. A religious network occurs mainly at church, and no expectation is involved. The same age group interacts freely, but there is no specific role involvement.

Medium-level networks may be defined as those in which role expectation is involved. They are generally more durable than the first level of networks. Medium-level networks are identified by similarities in proximity, profession, academic discipline or field of study, length of residency, and native regionalism.

Through proximity of residence those living in the same local area are accessible to one another and are more likely to know one another than if they were scattered.[7] In this type of neighborhood relationship, one develops expectations of those who live near him and senses their expectations of him. In case of emergency, one naturally feels more comfortable asking for help from a Korean neighbor. When a ceremony is observed (mainly a birthday), one feels an obligation to invite Korean neighbors to share food and drink. Because of easier accessibility, more reciprocity is involved. Frequent visits and exchanges of food result. In general, the members of the network have the same social status. Those who live in the university housing area are all students and those in suburban residential areas are professionals. A Korean proverb about the neighborhood seems relevant: "Neighbors are better than cousins living far away."

In the network formed by those in the same field of study, the members interact by exchanging ideas about their subject, asking questions, and helping to solve problems. This network has mutual expectations and when this stage is over, it may be merged into a higher level, the alumnus network.

The newcomers usually interact among themselves and sometimes create conflict between themselves and older residents. If conflict arises due to variables such as social status or leadership in the community, it is difficult to make close connections with old residents. This may be due to the traditional concept of seniority in Korea that can be easily distressing when one moves into a new community. It is customary for newcomers to pay a visit to old residents and sometimes the old residents invite the newcomers to dinner. In this way, new and old residents may develop a bond, but this is not always true. If newcomers share less linkage of the given network with the old residents, the relationship becomes weak and the newcomers tend to establish their own groups. The personal pride and traditional concepts of Koreans decline in the new setting. The new and old resident relationship is not everlasting; it usually operates only so long as the individuals live in the same community.

Native regionalism is another form of network. There are several traditional regions in Korea: first, South and North, and in the South, the Seoul area, the Kangwŏn province area, the Ch'ungch'ŏng province area, the Kyŏngsang province area, and the Chŏlla province area. The Kyongsang region (Southeast) and Chŏlla region (South-west) have the strongest antagonism toward each other. Therefore, networks are most easily formed between those living in the same region. Koreans try not to manifest regionalism in public but it is a factor of interaction. One expects closer ties with those who are from the same region and feels comfortable communicating with them. In this relationship, region of birth and former residence are fundamental.

High-level networks consist of alumni relationship and kin relationship. These relationships are characterized by durability and continuity regardless of time and place. Alumni relationships unite those who attended the same high school or college in Korea. This relationship exists potentially, whether or not they knew each other before coming to the United States. A *hupae* always treats a *sŏnbae* respectfully, and this brotherhood relationship, which is somewhat like a fictive kin relationship, is maintained. Kin relationships are most durable and involve least conflict. If one shares the same blood stock genealogically, one is considered kin. In both relationships the senior and junior concept is very strong and the feeling of obligation, mutual aid, and courtesy, to meet an ethical standard, is always manifested.

The period of decline may arise from Koreans leaving the community to seek better livings and educations. In the academic community, when Korean students finish their education, or when they are not able to continue their schooling due to financial or academic problems, they are forced to leave the community. Even when they want to stay, there is no opportunity for a better living in the academic community. On the other hand, fewer newcomers have arrived since 1971 and more people have left and will continue to leave. An important factor for the newcomer is that the university does not offer as many scholarships as it once did. Thus, the structure of the academic community may become the same as in the first period. From this fact, it is assumed that the main factor in the complexity of the structure is the size of the population. The urban community is experiencing a continuous increase in Korean residents and is still maintaining the period of segmentation.

According to the above diachronic and synchronic analysis of the Korean communities, structure seems to become complex as the stage of development changes.

The survey revealed a number of main causes of conflict among Koreans. These, most often mentioned by both men and women, included lack of courtesy, lack of respect for elders, gossip, jealousy, arrogance, differences in backgrounds, and differences in personalities. Men were more likely than women to mention problems of prejudice, differences in interest, length of residence, and problems of status.

Koreans do not accuse each other face to face, and accusations are seldom made to a known intimate of a person. However, gossip tends to travel very rapidly in the community and it creates friction. Other conflicts arise over status, education, economic matters, and age. Conflicts between one who has a doctoral degree and one who does not, between the rich and the poor, and between the young and the old belong to this category.

Psychological problems are obviously important in triggering conflict. A wide range of conflicts seem to arise from the fact that

Koreans as a minority group have a limited sphere of interaction
and so daily living becomes tedious. They find few opportunities
to relieve tedium and tension. Jealousy and gossip create few conflicts
when people are able to interact broadly: business and professional
competition do not seem to engender a great deal of animosity;
women do not seem to be concerned with status or new and old
residentship, and they seem to lack interest in social activities. Korean
women participate socially much less than men, and they do not
become involved directly in competition because their main work
is the care of the household. However, men are directly involved
in gaining status and in social relationships and so feel more conflict
than women.

Conflicts occasionally become more pronounced when stimulated
by the situation, but usually animosity is latent. It is clear that those
who have less contact with other Koreans seem to have fewer conflicts,
but they may feel isolation. However, to meet sociopsychological
needs, one must have opportunities to establish social relations with
other Koreans. The degree of conflict seems to be related to the
level of the network. A high-level network such as alumni or kin
creates less conflict than other networks. When conflicts arise, networks break down, social relations are reduced, and isolation increases.

It may be hypothesized that those who share more networks will
feel less isolation, and those who share more networks with the same
person will have more linkage or closeness. As far as durability is
concerned, if a high-level network is shared, more analysis of
qualitative and quantitative aspects is required. The following provides
some examples of such cases.

Qualitative Aspect The following represents kin relationship. It is
assumed that two persons share no other relations. This relationship
is quantitatively low, but its quality produces a strong tie.

Diagram 1.   High-Level Network

$$Yi \; \rightarrow \; \boxed{Kin} \; \leftarrow \; Yi$$

In the case below, although two persons interact through plural
networks, their relationship may be less durable because the quality
of the networks is less than that of kin.

Diagram 2.   Plural Networks of Low Level

$$Kim \; \rightarrow \; \boxed{\begin{array}{c} Common\ Interest \\ Religion \\ Similar\ Age \end{array}} \; \leftarrow \; Pak$$

Quantitative Aspect The following examples are given on the basis of a hypothesis that those who share plural networks are likely to have a closer relationship than those who share a single network, provided that the quality of networks is similar. The following diagrams indicate both situations.

Diagram 3. Simple Network

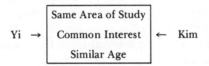

Diagram 4. Plural Network

$$
\text{Yi} \;\rightarrow\; \boxed{\begin{array}{c}\text{Same Area of Study}\\ \text{Common Interest}\\ \text{Similar Age}\end{array}} \;\leftarrow\; \text{Kim}
$$

According to Diagrams 3 and 4, Yi shares a single network with Pak, whereas he shares a plural network with Kim. Therefore, the relationship of Yi and Kim is stronger than that of Yi and Pak. According to the above analysis, it is hypothesized that quality precedes quantity, and within the same category of quality more connections provide a stronger tie than fewer connections.

In this study, an attempt has been made to formulate a model of Korean community development in America as demonstrated by the Koreans in the Atlanta and Athens areas. The study does not imply that every Korean community, either small or large, will follow the same developmental cycle. Some communities may be in one of the stages and maintain that same stage indefinitely. An attempt has been made to analyze each stage structurally by means of network. The nature of the network is presented under each stage and each network belongs to a certain level having a different degree of durability. The structure of relationships between Korean residents in the Atlanta and Athens areas seems to develop from simple to complex as the population increases. The population increase brings a multinetwork pattern by way of institutionalization and segmentation.

The relationship among Koreans may be measured in terms of quantity and quality of networks shared. A stronger tie seems to result from sharing a high-level network than from sharing any number of low-level networks. However, among the low-level networks, sharing more connections seems to establish a stronger tie than sharing fewer connections.

Analyzing Korean residents as a group or system with regard to structural change through and at a given time may allow formulation of a theory of relationships between Koreans in America. According to this analysis, relationships between Korean residents are complex, and may be continuations of relations that first existed in Korea. However, the relationships, except for the high-level networks such as kin and alumni, seem temporal. It has also been found that isolation motivates Koreans to interact in order to overcome loneliness. Lack of socialization impels individuals to strategically broaden their interaction spheres and, as a result, conflicts arise.

It is assumed that components of system or structure do not function for the maintenance of the system, but rather for the sake of meeting sociopsychological needs. However, it is observed that Koreans as a group manifest little enthusiasm for the unity of that group, but for the sake of external or interethnic relations, they exhibit a strong sense of togetherness.

Notes

1. Pertti J. Pelto, *Anthropological Research: The Structure of Inquiry* (New York: Harper & Row, 1970), pp. 24–25.

2. Robert Redfield, *The Folk Culture of Yucatán* (Chicago: University of Chicago Press, 1941), pp. 338–69.

3. J. Clyde Mitchell, ed., *Social Networks in Urban Situations: Analysis of Personal Relationships in Central African Towns* (London: Manchester University Press, 1969), pp. 119–27.

4. Bronislaw Malinowski, *A Scientific Theory of Culture and Other Essays* (London: Oxford University Press, 1960), pp. 155–61.

5. E.E. Evans-Pritchard, *Theories of Primitive Religion* (Oxford: Clarendon Press, 1965), pp. 55–56.

6. Rudolf Herberle, "The Normative Element in Neighborhood Relations," *Pacific Sociological Review* 3:2 (1960): 3–11.

7. Elizabeth Bott, *Family and Social Network: Roles, Norms, and External Relationships in Ordinary Urban Families* (London: Tavistock Publications, 1957), p. 103.

The Correlates of Cultural Assimilation of
Korean Immigrants in the United States

Chae-kŭn Yu

THE PRESENT INVESTIGATION, concerned with a search for factors associated with the degree of assimilation of Koreans in the United States, attempts to analyze certain background factors which may be related to variations in the degree of assimilation achieved.

Assimilation, for the purpose of this study, is defined as integration of the members of an ethnic minority into a majority culture group. The concept of assimilation as a process rather than a product involves establishing criteria for measuring the dynamic aspect of such social interaction. It is possible, however, to measure the degree of assimilation in terms of objective acculturation factors, at least operationally, by defining certain variables as indices of assimilation.

This study attempts to measure the degree of assimilation of Koreans by means of the variables which have been thought to be indices of assimilation and to determine the relationship between the degree of assimilation and certain background variables that may constitute variations in the achievement of assimilation. By testing the practicability of the background factors, it may be possible to determine the usefulness of these variables as correlates of cultural assimilation and to predict with some confidence the probability that a given group of individuals will become assimilated into the general culture within a specific period of time.

The term "assimilation" in this study shall refer to "the gradual process whereby cultural differences tend to disappear." [1] The best

167

French dictionary, Paul Robert's *Dictionnaire alphabétique et analogique de la langue française,* defines assimilation as "the act of making alike." Applied to an individual, "alike" is similarity between his manner of living and that of another person. The notion of assimilation is thus opposed to that of differentiation or of separation. When we speak of assimilation, we mean the process of constant interaction of cultural elements of divergent groups. Hannibal Duncan declares that "assimilation is fundamentally a cultural process"[2] which implies, according to Kimball Young, "the fusion of divergent habits, attitudes, and ideas of two or more groups and societies into a common set of habits, attitudes, and ideas."[3] Charles Marden interprets the term "common" as the sense of group identity and considers it essential to any adequate definition of assimilation.[4] Bunle makes explicit this sense of being one people, of belonging together:

> When we speak of an assimilated person (immigrants here), we refer to someone who has become part of the receiving community and who resembles its inhabitants, as closely as can be, in certain essential points. . . . An immigrant is assimilated only when he speaks the language of his new country by preference, has adopted its customs, and when his general conduct and way of life become those of his new compatriots and his original outlook gives way to that of his new surroundings.[5]

Theoretically, assimilation involves change in the basic structure of any two or more cultures that come into contact. These differing structures must act reciprocally as supplementing and symbolic elements to create a new cultural milieu in which a cultural fusion occurs. Therefore, assimilation is in process only during a constant interaction of cultural elements of divergent groups, and finally common beliefs, folkways, attitudes, memories, sentiments, and values develop. This interaction itself cannot, however, be called assimilation unless one cultural pattern displaces another or a third pattern emerges as a blend of the two. But the restriction of the concept of assimilation to that phase of social interaction which absorbs a person or minority group into a dominant group does not seem inappropriate, especially in the case of immigrants. As Brewton Berry suggests, assimilation is rarely, if ever a completed process.[6]

The fact that adoption of tangible features from a foreign culture reflects and expresses, rather than causes, a changed life orientation in a new cultural environment must not be overlooked. When the immigrants become assimilated, they share the culture of their adopted society with the dominant group, and they express themselves through the behavior system that characterizes the dominant group.

For this investigation, a number of variables thought to be indices of assimilation and operationally defined as such were selected. The questionnaire design and the construction of the assimilation scale will be discussed in the following section. The preimmigration and postimmigration factors will be tested to establish the relationship between these predictor variables and the degree of assimilation.

From the concept of assimilation defined above, the following propositions are formulated. Various specific hypotheses can be derived from these propositions.

1. The degree of assimilation will vary with preimmigration factors, such as educational background, personal occupation in Korea, and age at entry into the United States.
2. The degree of assimilation will vary with postimmigration factors, such as family size, present occupation, length of residence, and religious preference.
3. The degree of assimilation will vary with other personal factors, such as length of residence in America and English proficiency.

The Sample Ideally, a random sample of all Korean families in the United States is desirable. However, there is nowhere available a complete list of all Korean residents in the United States as would be necessary for drawing a random sample. The sample here was drawn by the area cluster sampling technique. Washington State was selected as an area sample. Although the sample of 450 Korean families was not randomly selected from all Koreans in the United States, the sample is fairly representative of all Koreans in terms of its number and homogeneity.[7]

The final sample used for this study consisted of 238 Korean families. The median age of heads of households was 35 years. The median length of residence in America was 4 years; the median number of family members 4.1; the median income per family $4,200; the median years of schooling was 16 years.

Two principal methods of data collection were the questionnaire and interviews. In the questionnaire, the variables were divided into several classifications:

Section A (demographic variables) consists of questions about general and social characteristics such as age, country of birth, length of residence, educational background, income, occupation, family size, and religion.

Section B (sociopsychological variables) consists of questions or items, some of which are to be combined to form an assimilation index, chiefly concerned with the adaptation to external or more easily measured aspects of American culture, such as English competence and language spoken in the home, social contact, recreational behavior, and assimilation index.

The questionnaire was constructed after a pretest of twenty randomly selected respondents. The interview schedule closely followed the format of the questionnaire.

Nineteen items constitute the assimilation scale used to measure the degree to which immigrants are assimilated or Americanized. These items are arranged in a modified Likert-type scale. The scale has construct validity and is highly weighted concerning verbal preference. The underlying assumption is that "language is the symbol of one's culture."[8] Therefore, although each item may be described as having more than a single dimension, there are twelve items which primarily measure verbal facility, three items measuring reference group behavior, and four items measuring identification with America versus identification with Korea. The scale is, as previously mentioned, of the modified Likert variety, the primary difference being that the scale is a measure of behavior rather than attitude, as in the orthodox Likert scale. The researcher has also taken the liberty to deviate from the basic rule of equal-appearing interval scale construction by including two items which are not of equal interval measure. Another modification is the varying of the number of categories from as few as four to as many as six.

The split-half reliability corrected with the Spearman-Brown formula is .89. A main contributing factor to such high reliability is the fact that overt behavior can be much more reliably related than covert traits or attitudes.[9]

Each item was placed on a five or six point continuum ranging from one (high assimilation) to five or six (low assimilation). For a given individual, the responses on these items were assigned and weighted. These nineteen weights were then added. It is recognized that such an arbitrary assignment of weights to various categories of indices results in a scale which has an unknown error emphasis.[10] However, unless there are some definite reasons for assigning specific weights to particular variables the only recourse is an arbitrary system. It should be recognized that the statistical validity of the present assimilation scale is an unknown factor. For these reasons it was necessary to develop a means of correlational analysis which would not require such a refined measurement of the statistical validity and reliability of the scale. Therefore, all of the individual assimilation scores were dichotomized into either high or low. Though such a dichotomy is a cruder measurement, it is probably more reliable and therefore equally as useful as a more refined scale.

In general, the preimmigration, postimmigration, and personal and cultural factors (variables) were dichotomized for the purpose of determining the relationship between each factor and the degree of assimilation as measured by the dichotomized assimilation index scores.

1. Preimmigration factors:
    a. Educational background: (1) college education; (2) all others.
    b. Occupation in Korea: (1) white collar; (2) blue collar.
    c. Age at entry into the United States: (1) 15–32; (2) 33 and over.

2. Postimmigration factors:
    a. Number of family members: (1) 0–3; (2) 4 and more.
    b. Length of residence in U.S.A.: (1) 0–3; (2) 4 and more.
    c. Present occupation: (1) white collar; (2) blue collar.
    d. Income: (1) less than $6,000; (2) above $6,000.
    e. Religion: (1) Christian; (2) all others.

3. Personal and Cultural factors:
    a. English proficiency: (1) high; (2) low.
    b. Intention to stay: (1) high; (2) low.

The relationship between the above factors and the degree of assimilation was determined by the simple procedure of computing the contingency coefficients between the dichotomized assimilation scores and the dichotomized classifications of the variables.[11]

The significance of the relationship can be determined by examining the table for 1 degree of freedom. The test is for the null hypotheses of no associations, and the hypotheses will be rejected at the .01 level of significance. That is, if the value has less than 1 chance in 100 of occurring by sampling fluctuations alone, the association is regarded as statistically significant. The Chi-square value, contingency coefficients, significance level, and decision to reject or accept will be presented in Table 1.

The educational background proved to be a better than average index of assimilation, but not among the best. A point worthy of note here is that the intercorrelation between educational background and previous occupation was substantially high $(C = .71)$. A later study may utilize the multiple correlation method in order to interpret these relationships more academically. Such a study is beyond the scope of the present research.

The occupation of the individual in Korea gives some insight into the self-concept and role of the individual in relation to society as a whole. It was therefore thought likely that the person in white collar work would become more quickly adapted to the new culture. However, the relationship $C = .16$ was too small to be of any real value. More adequate measurement procedures might yield a significant relationship.

A young age at the time of entering the United States was expected to contribute to greater assimilation, since the young are thought to adapt more quickly to a new culture. However, the present evidence, which may stem from the fact that most Korean immigrants came to this country when over twenty years of age, does not support this assumption.

Table 1—Summary of the Statistical Associations between the Degree of Assimilation and Correlates*

Variables	X^2	C	Prob.	Significance
Education	6.82	.52	p < .01	Significant
Previous occupation	2.05	.16	p < .01	Not significant
Age at entry	.97	.11	p > .01	Not significant
Number in family	1.80	.15	p > 0.1	Not significant
Length of residence	9.25	.54	p < .01	Significant
Present occupation	3.01	.28	p < .01	Significant
Income	1.02	.14	p > .01	Not significant
Religion	2.91	.45	p < .01	Significant
English	12.30	.63	p < .01	Significant
Intention to stay	.98	.11	p > .01	Not significant

*Since this is for the relationship between two or more nominal scales, the Chi-square test is a very general test that can be used whenever we wish to evaluate whether or not frequencies which have been empirically obtained differ significantly from those which would have been expected to produce a certain set of theoretical assumptions. Pearson's contingency coefficient, C for the strength of relationship between two nominal variables, is assumed to be appropriate and is given by

$$C = \sqrt{\frac{X^2}{X^2 - N}}$$

Source: Hubert M. Blalock, *Social Statistics,* 2d ed. (New York: McGraw-Hill, 1972), pp. 276–98.

Size of family again shows little relationship to the degree of assimilation. The assumption was that since most Korean immigrants have extended families and the size of family depends on number of children, the more children in a family the greater degree of exposure to American culture on the part of parents; this factor may therefore be expected to influence the degree of assimilation the parents have attained. The low relationship found can be explained by the fact that the number of children per family itself might not have influenced the degree of assimilation the family attained. What should have been taken into account are the age of children, the process of socialization, sending the child to school, etc. Older children in a family may provide more chance for parents to be exposed to American culture.

The relationship between the number of years a person has been in the United States and his degree of assimilation was significant at the 0.01 level. The length of residence definitely influenced a person's degree of assimilation.

Employment outside the home may be a factor promoting assimilation in that at work a person is more likely to be involved in secondary interaction with American co-workers as well as with the larger American social system. The result of such interaction, apart from influencing the individual's immediate family, especially in more prestigious occupations, is a broadening of the person's understanding and concept of the new culture, and an increase in the chance of a high degree of assimilation. The relationship between present occupation and degree of assimilation shows significant intensity but not as much as expected.

There is no significant relationship between income and the degree of assimilation. These data should be analyzed by multiple correlation techniques with the data on education, occupation, and income in order to observe direct and indirect relationships. Another point that should be noted is that the arbitrary dichotomy of the income variable probably causes a negative relationship.

The fact of membership in a Christian church suggests conformity to prevailing American mores. Conversely, Buddhism is a sign of nonconformity and nonassimilation. The present evidence shows some relationship between religious affiliations and the degree of assimilation but not a high relationship (C = .45). While not particularly high, such a relationship indicates that under conditions of more adequate sampling and measurement (in this analysis, religion was dichotomized into Christian and all other religions) a significant relationship might be found (see Table 2).

Because language is the symbol of culture and a medium through which culture is transmitted, language proficiency is absolutely essential for assimilation into a host society. Language is a means by which an alien can understand American culture. The present findings show a significant relationship between language and the degree of assimilation. That is to say, the person with a better knowledge of English will be highly assimilated.

There is no association between the person's intention to settle in this country and his degree of assimilation. It was assumed that a highly assimilated person might not want to return to Korea and might want to settle in this country. However, the findings show a negative relationship.

The hypothesis that assimilation is related to certain preimmigration factors such as education, previous occupation, age at entry into America, was partially supported. Only the education variable was found to be significantly related to assimilation. The remaining variables relate less significantly.

The second hypothesis, that assimilation is related to certain postimmigration factors, such as number in the family, length of residence, present occupation, income, and religious affiliation, was also partially supported. In spite of the fact that the correlation between the postimmigration factors was positive, the evidence does not fully support the hypothesis since only one coefficient was

Table 2—Coefficient of Contingency Value Derived from Chi-Square in Cross-Tabulation Between Variables*

Variables	Yb	X1	X2	X3	X4	X5	X6	X7	X8	X9	X10
Y (Assimilation)	—	.52	.16	.11	.15	.54	.28	.14	.45	.63	.11
X1 (Education)			.55	**	.12	.11	.36	.25	.17	.61	.23
X2 (Previous occupation)				**	.18	**	.36	.19	.15	.47	.21
X3 (Age at entry)					**	.13	.15	.12	**	.24	.31
X4 (Number in family)						**	.21	.11	.14	**	.21
X5 (Length of residence)							.24	.25	.12	.36	.33
X6 (Present occupation)								.63	.21	.47	.25
X7 (Income)									.18	.46	**
X8 (Religion)										.12	.21
X9 (English)											.22
X10 (Intention to stay)											—

*The matrix is symmetrical; therefore the values in the upper half of the table duplicate those in the lower half.
**These Chi-square values were not significant; therefore no C values were computed.

significant. Such a situation points to a need to make reliable and valid measurement of these factors since, if there were actually no relationship between these factors and assimilation, one would not expect to find consistently positive relationships.

That assimilation is related to other personal factors, such as English proficiency and length of residence, was also partially supported. English proficiency is the strongest predictor in this measure.

Thus, only five variables are related in any useful degree to the assimilation score. These five variables are education, length of residence, occupation, religion, and English proficiency.

With more refined measurements of the educational backgrounds and socioeconomic statuses of immigrants it may be possible to predict with some degree of confidence the probability that a given group of individuals will become assimilated into the general culture in a specified period of time. We can conclude that there is considerable evidence from the present study that the other variables are related, but should be retained for further study, with other factors being examined for their influence on assimilation.

In conclusion, the more assimilated individual tends to be the person who has a relatively prestigious occupation and whose educational level in Korea was high.

Notes

1. John F. Cuber, *Sociology: A Synopsis of Principle* (New York: Appleton-Century-Crofts, 1955), p. 609.

2. Hannibal G. Duncan, *Immigration and Assimilation* (New York: D.C. Heath and Company, 1933), p. 520.

3. Kimball Young, *Sociology: A Study of Society and Culture* (New York: American Book Company, 1949), p. 615.

4. Charles F. Marden, *Minorities in American Society* (New York: American Book Company, 1952), p. 32.

5. Henry Bunle, *Cultural Assimilation of Immigrants* (London: Cambridge University Press, 1949), pp. 5–6.

6. Brewton Berry, *Race and Ethnic Relations*, 3d ed. (Boston: Houghton Mifflin, 1965), pp. 253–63.

7. Washington has a large Korean population, the third largest Korean community

in the United States. See Training Project for the Asian Elderly, "On the Feasibility of Training Asians to Work with Asian Elderly: A Preliminary Assessment of Needs and Resources Available to Asian Elderly in Seattle, Washington," Seattle, Washington, March 1973, p. 12. (Mimeographed report in the possession of the author.)

8.   E. Des Brunner, *Immigrant Farmers and Their Children* (New York: Doubleday, Doran, 1929), p. 239.

9.   Frank S. Freeman, *Theory and Practice of Psychological Testing,* 3d ed. (New York: Holt, Rinehart and Winston, 1962), p. 524.

10.   For example, perhaps the frequency of reading American papers and magazines is far more important a factor of assimilation than the frequency of watching television. If they both receive the same weight, the result is an incorrect emphasis resulting in a loss of validity.

11.   Detailed discussions about statistical techniques may be found in many social statistics textbooks. Of all these textbooks, Hubert M. Blalock, *Social Statistics,* 2d ed. (New York: McGraw-Hill, 1972), is assumed to be the best and most widely used.

Personality Adjustment of Korean Children in the United States

Chae-kŭn Yu

IN SPITE OF the number of studies on ethnic acculturation, assimilation, and personality adjustment in the present body of research, no research concerning assimilation and acculturation and their relationship to the personality adjustment of individual Korean immigrants has been conducted. [1]

Much literature reveals a significant relationship between biculturalism and personality adjustment of immigrant children. Dorothy Spoerl concluded, in a study of bilingual students, that cases of emotional maladjustment among certain students were indeed a reaction against social frustration, family disharmony, and cultural conflict, and reflected a lack of identification with the present American environment or with the parental cultural background. [2]

Mike Prpich, in a significant study of Greek American children, concluded that as compared with subjects of American descent, the subjects of Greek extraction in general felt less accepted by others, had a greater tendency to withdraw within themselves, and showed less understanding of American social standards than did the American-born control group. [3] The Greek American children also had a greater tendency toward aggressiveness of an undefined sort, and were less well adjusted in terms of interpersonal relationships.

Since the mid-nineteenth century, when Chinese laborers were brought to the northwestern region of the United States, voluminous work has been done on both Chinese and Japanese immigrants, since they came in large numbers and were the first to settle. However, the presence in America of the Korean minority as a "minority within minorities" has either been ignored or neglected. Very few writers have been aware of the presence of Koreans, and there has been little or no attempt to study their lives in the United States systematically. An attempt will be made here to investigate the sociopsychological conditions of Korean immigrants in the United States.

The purpose of this study is to determine the relationship between the degree of acculturation of Korean immigrants and the personality adjustment of their children and to determine the relationship of certain variables such as socioeconomic status and level of education with the degree to which an immigrant has become acculturated.

The history of America is the story of merging cultures, to a greater degree than that of any other nation in the world in any given period of time. The founding of America is unlike the merging of European tribes into city-states and eventually into nations. America's growth has been largely due to the influx of immigrants from nearly every culture and subculture throughout the world, rather than from a confined geographical area. Hence, the meeting of cultures has been very intense and characterized by a great deal of diversity, and in each case, language has played an important part.

Because language is the symbol of culture and the medium through which it is transmitted, it is absolutely essential to gain a sociopsychological understanding of bilingualism and cultural pluralism.[4]

Robert Park has appropriately emphasized the pertinence of focusing upon this area of research:

> It is in the mind of the marginal man that the moral turmoil which new cultural contacts occasion manifests itself in the most obvious forms. It is in the mind of the marginal man . . . where the changes and fusions of culture are going on . . . that we can best study the processes of civilization and of progress.[5]

The marginal man was viewed as straddling two cultures simultaneously, without a definite feeling of belonging to either of two groups. The life of the marginal or bicultural man may be segmented into three general phases.[6] First, the period of preparation, when the individual is first introduced into the two diverse cultures, e.g., in childhood. During the second phase, the individual becomes aware of the cultural conflict which involves his own career. This awareness may well arise from a crisis experience and express itself as a response to a given situation. The third stage involves the adjustment of the individual to an enduring situation.

Enrique Vargas has described this phenomenon of marginality in terms of "culture shock." According to Vargas:

> Culture shock is precipitated by the distressing feeling of uncertainty and anxiety that result from not finding all the familiar symbols, signs, and cues that guide a person through his own culture. He finds himself having to use a different design for living.[7]

This design for living or mode of adjustment is characterized by Vargas as occurring in three phases: the spectator in the new society; personal involvement in the new situation; mastery of the new environment or withdrawal and reliance upon the old culture.[8] These three phases are synonymous with the three stages of marginality previously cited.

In this study, the latter two stages, namely, awareness of the differences between the cultures concerned and the immigrant's adjustment to an enduring situation, will be emphasized. Particular attention will be paid to the personality adjustment of bilingual and bicultural children.

In the case of the bicultural child, the conflict of adolescence may be magnified by a lack of identification with either his immigrant parents or his American peers. Of particular interest here is determining how this conflict is affected by the degrees to which the adolescent's parents have become Americanized or acculturated.

Acculturation and assimilation may assume several forms. There is no set procedure or definite process through which acculturation occurs. Milton Gordon has credibly analyzed this phenomenon and treats acculturation as merely a type of assimilation rather than as a separate entity.[9]

There are several basic phases through which assimilation may pass, according to Gordon's analysis, although they occur in no definite sequence. These are shown in Table 1.

Acculturation is seen as a process actively involving the immigrant, and is a matter dependent upon his own course of action. Assimilation is considered to be a process involving the host society's decision to accept a member of another culture. Acculturation is perhaps most likely to be the first type of assimilation to occur, upon a minority group member's introduction into a new host culture. In fact, acculturation of the minority group may take place even when one of the other types of assimilation occurs simultaneously or later, and this condition of acculturation only may continue indefinitely.[10] According to Ralph Linton, an anthropologist, acculturation is "the establishment, in the two cultures involved, of mutual modification and adaptations which will enable the two groups to live together rather than a mere change of the cultural patterns of the minority group to those of the host society," as proposed by Gordon.[11]

Table 1.—The Assimilation Variables

Subprocess or Condition	Type of Stage of Assimilation	Special Term
Change of cultural patterns to those of host country	Cultural or behavioral assimilation	Acculturation
Large-scale entrance into cliques, clubs, and institutions of host society on primary group level	Structural assimilation	None
Large-scale intermarriage	Marital assimilation	Amalgamation
Development of sense of people-hood based exclusively on the host society	Identificational assimilation	None
Absence of prejudice	Attitude receptional assimilation	None
Absence of value and power conflict	Civic assimilation	None

Source: Milton M. Gordon, *Assimilation in American Life* (New York: Oxford University Press, 1964), p. 71.

In order for acculturation to occur, several factors must be operative:

1. The dissemination and acquisition of cultural elements are strongly influenced by their utility and by the desire of the receiving group for a novel experience.[12]

2. Acculturation is also largely affected by the compatibility of "new" cultural elements or customs with the pre-existing culture. Even when considerable economic gains can be made, innovations may be rejected because they are different from the familiar and expected.[13] It can be said that no element of a given culture will be eliminated until its substitute has proved itself superior.[14]

3. Another factor affecting acculturation is the desire of the receiving group for prestige, or the degree of prestige which the host country is perceived to have.[15]

4. Acculturation is also affected to a large degree by spatial isolation from the host country, which eliminates many cultural contacts and prevents dissemination of cultural elements.

Spicer has categorized the primary problems involved in cultural change in the following manner:

1) Problems of cultural linkage—which arise because of failure to understand the connection between certain beliefs and customs.

2) Problems of social structure resulting from a failure to work through existing social organizations, or from miscalculation of the functions of certain social units.

3) Problems of the role of the innovator—arising from poor relations between people of the different cultures involved, or from misunderstanding or poor definition of the role of the innovator.

4) Problems of cultural bias—characterized by ethnocentricity and the interpreting of behavior in one culture in terms of another culture.

5) Problems of participation—arising from the failure to bring people into the planning and carrying out of a program for change.

6) Problems of buffer organizations—which may develop from any or all of the previously mentioned problems and result in the organizing of groups resistant to change.[16]

On the basis of a review of literature and the theoretical framework, the following null hypotheses have been formulated: there is no significant correlation between the degree of acculturation of a Korean parent and the measured personality adjustment of his child; there is no significant difference in the measured personality adjustment norms of Korean bicultural children and the norms of American children; no significant relationship exists between level of education or the socioeconomic status of the Korean immigrant and his measured degree of acculturation.

Subjects in this study are Korean families living in Seattle, Washington.[17] It would have been desirable in our sampling procedure to obtain the names of all Koreans in the area and randomly select from this population a sufficient number of cases for study. However, there is nowhere available a complete list of all Koreans residing in this area such as would be necessary for drawing a random sample. It was decided, under the circumstances, that an availability sample based on lists of Koreans inclusively, would be most advantageous.

The final sample used for intensive examination consisted of seventeen families with a combined total of thirty-four parents and twenty-four children between thirteen and eighteen years of age, a total of fifty-eight individuals directly involved in the study. Since the bicultural children were the primary object of the research, as mentioned previously, only those families with children in this age range were selected for final analysis.

Such a judgmental sample has the advantage of introducing some stratification effect. However, such a sample also requires strong assumptions or considerable knowledge of the population and the subgroup selected.[18] This foreknowledge of the sample became the rationale for selecting the sample. As the researcher has lived and worked with the people in this particular locality, he is confident that he has sufficient and intimate knowledge of the subjects to present a balanced picture. In addition, the researcher's ability to speak the Korean language facilitates a bilingual approach to interviewing, which was necessary in most cases.

The sample frame was quite homogeneous in nature. The median age for household heads was thirty-nine years. The median length of time in America was 4.8 years per family. The median age of the children in the sample was fifteen.

The interview schedule consisted of thirty-one items, twelve of which constitute the acculturation scale used to measure the degree to which immigrants are acculturated or Americanized. These items are arranged in a modified Likert-type scale and were derived from previous scales.

The scale has construct validity and is highly weighted concerning verbal or speech preference, the underlying assumption being that language is a symbol of one's culture. [19]

The interview schedule was pretested and revised three times. In addition to the acculturation scale, the interview schedule contains ten questions aimed primarily at determining the respondent's demographic background.

Persons scoring high on the acculturation scale tended to be those with high proficiency in English who read as much (or more) in English as in Korean. They had more contacts with American friends and seldom thought of returning to Korea.

A person scoring low on the acculturation scale tends to have problems speaking English. He is quite ethnocentric about his homeland and may show little or no interest in becoming an American citizen. He tends to live in a neighborhood where several other Koreans live, and has strong ties, through correspondence, with friends and relatives in Korea.

The California Psychological Inventory (CPI)[20] was used as the psychometric instrument for measuring personality adjustment. The CPI consists of 480 items with 18 subtests grouped into 4 clusters of scales. The scales in Class 1 emphasize feelings of interpersonal and intrapersonal adequacy in such matters as ascendancy and self-assurance. These personality traits are measured by the following scales: dominance, capacity for status, sociability, social presence, self-acceptance, and sense of well-being.

Class 2 is comprised of scales principally concerned with social norms and values and dispositions to observe or reject such values. The three main characteristics, socialization, maturity, and responsibility, are measured by the following scales: responsibility, socialization, self-control, tolerance, good impression, and communality.

The scale in Class 3 is aimed at measuring achievement potential and intellectual efficiency as expressed in terms of achievement via conformance, achievement via independence, and intellectual efficiency.

Class 4 scales include psychological state of mind, flexibility, and femininity, all of which are focused at the gross measurement of intellectual and interest modes.

In order to detect dissimulation, three scales have been devised for the CPI which detect subjects who deliberately exaggerate or distort their responses to the inventory. The scores on the CPI lend themselves to the construction of a very useful and revealing personality profile which, when interpreted correctly, reveals conformity or deviation from the overall testing norms. Each subscale becomes the basis for a corollary hypothesis, inasmuch as each subtest measures a different dimension or personality trait.

Table 2 shows the findings obtained from the following scales of interpersonal and intrapersonal adequacy: dominance, capacity for status, sociability, social presence, self-acceptance, and well-being.

The inverse direction of the correlations, together with their magnitude, greatly surprised the researcher, who had expected positive correlations. The question arising from this finding was why do bicultural children from a relatively highly acculturated home tend to have lower personality adjustment than bicultural children coming from homes of low acculturation? Linton maintains that ill effects are as easily derived from the blocking of pre-existing cultural patterns as from the introduction of new ones. He adds:

> The only elements of culture which can be forced upon another society are certain forms of behavior. The attitudes and values of the dominant group cannot be transferred in this way. The receiving group can usually modify and re-interpret the new enforced behavior in terms of its own value system and finally assimilate it successfully. The inhibition of pre-existing patterns, on the other hand, inevitably leaves some of the society's needs unsatisfied, with resulting hardship. [21]

Vargas describes the futility of the immigrant's forced adoption of the new culture:

> Another system a person suffering from culture shock may have is the tendency to "go native." In an attempt to cure his discomfort he may take an overdose of the foreign culture. He tries to talk and dress like a native, and he may become a furious "anti-" whatever country he comes from. . . . Such a person is very likely to end up more frustrated and unhappy than when he started. [22]

We may reasonably infer that in a highly acculturated immigrant home, although the culture of the family is very similar to that of the host society, the family culture is very unlike the pre-existing culture, thus leaving the family in a state of quandary. The family has, in effect, inhibited their former culture, but they are not fully assimilated into the host society. Their mere acquiring of certain cultural elements does not necessarily constitute final acculturation. Perception of cultural elements by the immigrant is the first step in their dissemination. However, most cultural elements are transferred in terms of objective form stripped of the meaning which is an integral part of them in their original context.

Inasmuch as all findings relate in the same inverse direction, the researcher will not analyze each scale separately. Table 2 is comprehensive.

It may be concluded that if a child's parents are supportive and understanding rather than rejective and ethnocentric regarding their

Table 2—Rank Order Correlation between Parental Acculturation and Personality Adjustment of Bicultural Children

Subject	Do	Cs	Sy	Sp	Sa	Wb	AI	Parental Acculturation
1	11	12	14.5	12	17	3	12	4.5
2	8.5	1	2	4.5	3	1.5	7	4.5
3	6	3.5	3	3	7	5	5	4.5
4	1.5	7	1	6	7	1.5	5	4.5
5	12	9	8	1	4.5	9	12	14
6	8.5	8	9	10	7	7	10	14
7	6	3.5	7	9	11	4	5	14
8	13	17	11	16	12	13	15	9.5
9	15.5	10	13	8	16	16	15	9.5
10	15.5	11	12	13.5	13	7	3	16.5
11	6	15	10	13.5	4.5	10.5	1.5	16.5
12	10	13	14.5	15	9	17	17	1
13	4	5.5	5.5	7	1	12	9	11.5
14	17	15	17	11	14	14	12	11.5
15	1.5	2	4	4.5	2	7	8	2
16	3	5.5	5.5	2	10	10.5	1.5	7.5
17	14	15	16	17	15	15	15	7.5
18	10	11	13	11	16	4	8	4.5
19	7	7	9	8.5	10.5	3	9	13
20	16	9	12.5	8.5	15.5	16	14	10.5
21	9	11	13	14.5	8.5	17.5	16	2
22	2	3	5	5.5	3	8	11.5	3
23	8	4.5	5.5	3	10	9	2.5	6
24	4	6	3	5	6	2	6	5.5
(r_s) 23	-.068	-.139	-.041	-.294	-.410	-.399	-.975	

former culture, the child may reach better personality adjustment than a bicultural child from an anti-fatherland home.

The second hypothesis tested was that there is no significant difference in the measured personality adjustment norms of bicultural Korean children and the norms of American children.

These comparative findings are merely tentative, since norms differ greatly among various ethnic groups, socioeconomic strata, rural and urban areas, religious groups, etc. The norms, though not tested statistically for significance, are illustrated in Figure 1. The sample norms for Korean boys fall below those for American boys on sense of well-being, socialization, self-control, and good impressions, and the sample norms for Korean girls are above the CPI norms, except on the self-control scale.

In determining whether an individual has adjusted successfully, or in probing for signs of maladjustment, one must take all subtests into account and examine the entire profile for personality discrepancies. It is, therefore, nearly impossible to compare statistically a sample group of such small size with the norms of the CPI, which are based on thousands of individuals. The comparison of profiles indicates areas which may be probed further with a large N.[23] Certain individual profiles indicated areas of maladjustment, whereas group profiles tended to regress toward the norms.

The last hypothesis is that there is no relationship between level of education or socioeconomic status and the degree to which an immigrant parent is acculturated. As it is assumed that socioeconomic status is highly dependent upon one's level of education, and because the sample is small, this theory will be treated descriptively and analytically rather than statistically. For most immigrants, immigration means a loss of prestige and socioeconomic status. They may earn more money in America, but the immigrant stigma and higher cost of living decrease relative prestige. Those studied were lower-middle-class people who came to America primarily to seek economic and educational opportunities.

One might conclude that the higher the level of education, the greater the degree of acculturation. Because Koreans emphasize learning English, the educated are likely to have had exposure to American customs. The data revealed that socioeconomic status and the degree to which an immigrant is acculturated are closely related, inasmuch as higher prestige occupations tend to require a high degree of acculturation.

The immigrant's bicultural child may be seen as a marginal individual in many instances. His parents cling to the culture of their homeland and his peers are ethnocentric about their American heritage.

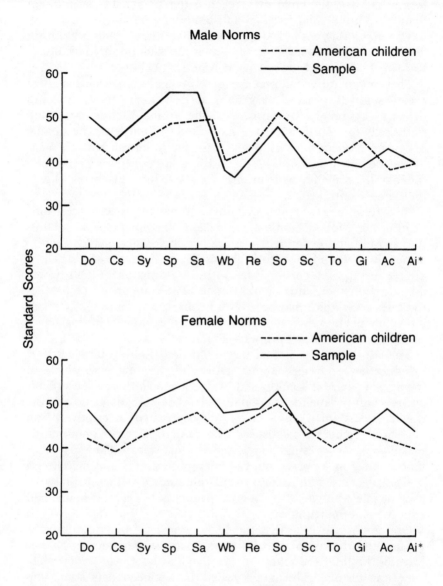

* Do = Dominance, Cs = Capacity for status, Sy = Sociability, Sp = Social presence, Sa = Self-acceptance, Wb = Well-being, Re = Responsibility, So = Socialization, Sc = Self-control, To = Tolerance, Gi = Good impress, Ac = Achievement via conformity, Ai = Achievement via independence.

Figure 1. Mean Profiles for American Children and Korean Sample

However, the immigrant child need not remain permanently caught in this dilemma. He is not merely in the in-group and excluded from the out-group. The out-group assimilates him into its schools and churches and gradually into its primary groups. He is, as mentioned above, becoming structurally pluralistic in his behavior, as well as bicultural. He is literally "going out of one culture" and "coming into another."

As the bilingual child loses all vestiges of the language handicap, he leaves the in-group environment of family and immigrant friends and gradually gains status in the out-group. Thus to merely treat the whole process as either in or out is to ignore the dynamics of the entire phenomenon. Hence the expressions "out-ofs," representing significant others within the immigrant culture from which the bicultural child is emerging, and "in-tos," the generalized others within the secondary groups and potential primary groups into which the child will become assimilated.

The role of the bicultural family has often been seen as agent of resistance to the immigrant child's becoming fully assimilated. However, a shared perception of the foreign environment as unfriendly often makes the bicultural family very mutually supportive. A young immigrant child may suffer few adjustment problems if his family buttresses him against the impact of the strange culture.

Another significant finding of interviews with immigrant families was that although the parents were the primary agents of socialization, bicultural children played a reciprocal role as agents of acculturation for the parents, especially in cases where the parental command of English was uncertain. In other words, the bicultural child "brings up his parents in the American way." Through attending American schools, Korean children observe that Americans hold their forks in their right hands. Through visiting school friends, they observe that American women do not shine their husband's or children's shoes. The children further learn correct pronunciations of English words, and proper word order in a sentence. These American values and ways are transmitted to parents by children.

The Korean immigrant father is often pictured as an overbearing figure in the family, supported by a submissive wife and obedient, overly conforming children. This may be true of earlier generations, but the researcher observed that the image no longer represents reality. Just as Cooley speaks of the "looking glass self," the family here reflects its social context. If a family exists in the framework of a totalitarian society, it tends to be authoritarian or patriarchal. However, in a democratic environment, the family tends to be autonomous and democratic. This point is borne out by Dorothy Blitsten in her comparative treatment of several forms of the family in various countries.[24]

The extremely high negative correlation between parental acculturation and scores on the achievement via independence scale seems to be linked to this matter of a democratic home environment, especially in cases where the child becomes the agent of acculturation for the family. The transmission of American culture by the child to his immigrant parents may well endow him with considerable feelings of responsibility and independence which are absent when the parents become acculturated on their own.

Three final conclusions may be drawn from this study. First, there is an inverse relationship between the degree to which immigrant parents become acculturated and the measured personality adjustment of bicultural children. This phenomenon appears to be a result of the fact that highly acculturated immigrants tend to inhibit their pre-existing culture while not yet assimilated into the host society. This condition may well change over an extended period of time.

Second, although certain individuals in the study showed definite patterns of personality maladjustment, the group norms for boys were only slightly below the test norms. The group norms for girls in the study tended to be above the CPI norms. These findings may be susceptible to serious sampling error because of the small size of the sample, and also because of the variation in norms in different areas.

Third, the level of education attained is related to the degree of acculturation. Socioeconomic status is related to the degree to which one becomes acculturated, inasmuch as the more prestigious occupations tend to require a high degree of acculturation.

Notes

1. Between 1900 and 1972, approximately 100,000 Korean immigrants arrived in the United States. This figure is based on U.S. Department of Justice, Immigration and Naturalization Service, *Annual Reports*, 1950–1972, tables 14, 15. However, there is no sociopsychological study on Korean immigrants except several historical studies such as No Chae-yŏn, *Chae-Mi Hanin saryak* [A concise history of Koreans in America], 2 vols. (Los Angeles: American Publisher, 1951, 1963); and Kim Wŏn-yong (Warren

Y. Kim), *Chae-Mi Hanin osimnyŏn-sa* [Fifty-year history of the Koreans in America] (Reedley, California: Charles Ho Kim, 1959).

2.   Dorothy T. Spoerl, "Bilinguality and Emotional Adjustment," *Journal of Abnormal and Social Psychology* 38 (January 1943): 37–57.

3.   Mike Prpich, "A Comparative Study of Personal and Social Adjustment of American-born Descendants of Greek Immigrants and of Native Americans in Salt Lake City, Utah, 1950" (M.A. thesis, University of Utah, 1953).

4.   See Seth Arsenian, "Bilingualism in the Post-war World," *Psychological Bulletin* (February 1945): 78–79. Since the "melting-pot" philosophy was much too idealistic to fit reality and the "Anglo-Saxon conformity" philosophy too lacking in understanding, a more realistic approach to assimilation is that of cultural pluralism. See Isaac B. Berkson, *Theories of Americanization* (New York: Teachers College, Columbia University, 1920). Perhaps even more fitting than cultural pluralism would be the term "structural pluralism." Structural pluralism refers to an immigrant's dual membership in the secondary groups of the host society and the primary groups of his own ethnic origin. See Milton M. Gordon, *Assimilation in American Life* (New York: Oxford University Press, 1964), pp. 158–59.

5.   Robert E. Park, "Human Migration and the Marginal Man," *American Journal of Sociology* 33 (May 1928): 883.

6.   Everett V. Stonequest, "The Problem of the Marginal Man," *American Journal of Sociology* 41 (July 1935): 10.

7.   Enrique Vargas, "The Jet-age Malady," *Saturday Review* (May 29, 1965): 18–19.

8.   Vargas, "Jet-age Malady," pp. 18–19.

9.   Gordon, *Assimilation in American Life.*

10.   Gordon, *Assimilation in American Life.*

11.   Ralph Linton, *Acculturation in Seven American Indian Tribes* (New York: D. Appleton Century, 1940), p. 519.

12.   Linton, *Acculturation in Seven Tribes,* p. 519.

13.   Anacleto Apodaca, "Corn and Custom," in Edward H. Spicer, ed., *Human Problems in Technological Change* (New York: Russell Sage Foundation, 1952), pp. 35–39. A case in point is the introduction of improved farming methods among Spanish American farmers of New Mexico. The innovation was simply not compatible with the existing culture, and it was therefore rejected.

14.   Linton, *Acculturation in Seven Tribes,* p. 481.

15.   Linton, *Acculturation in Seven Tribes,* p. 474. The U.S. government has tried to better the status quo of the Navaho Indians on several occasions through a variety of agricultural innovations, e.g., the Fruitland Irrigation Project. The Navahos, however, are psychologically a defeated people. Their distrust of whites flares up during periods of tension, and the Navaho Service (Bureau of Indian Affairs) becomes the scapegoat for all the wrongs of the past. See Tom Sasaki and John Adair, "New Land to Farm," in Spicer, ed., *Human Problems in Technological Change,* pp. 97–111.

16.   Spicer, "Suggestions for Study: Recurrent Groups of Problems," in Spicer, ed., *Human Problems in Technological Change,* p. 281.

17.   Lists of Korean community organizations in the Seattle area were reviewed and the sample was drawn from these lists. While the availability of a listing from which to draw a random sample restricts our possibility of generalization, it seemed preferable to interview a small sample in depth rather than to mail self-administered questionnaires or tests to a large population. The study is exploratory with a relatively focused area of concentration.

18.   Russell L. Ackoff, *The Design of Social Research* (Chicago: University of Chicago Press, 1953), p. 125.

19.   E. Des Brunner, *Immigrant Farmers and Their Children* (New York: Doubleday, Doran, 1929), p. 239.

20.   Harrison G. Gough, *California Psychological Inventory Manual* (Palo Alto, Cali-

fornia: Consulting Psychologists Press, 1957), p. 5.

21.   Linton, *Acculturation in Seven Tribes,* p. 507.

22.   Vargas, "Jet-age Malady," p. 18.

23.   The formula for Spearman's rank-order correlation is:

$$r_s = \frac{6 \sum_{i=1}^{N} Di^2}{N(N^2 - 1)}$$

This formula for r_s is derived by taking the formula for a product-moment correlation and applying it to ranks, and thus Spearman's measure can be interpreted as the product-moment correlation between the ranks X and the ranks on Y. Hubert M. Blalock, *Social Statistics,* 2d ed. (New York: McGraw-Hill, 1972), pp. 416–17.

24.   Dorothy R. Blitsten, *The World of the Family* (New York: Random House, 1963), pp. 251–63.

An Ethnic Political Orientation as a Function of Assimilation: With Reference to Koreans in Los Angeles

Marn J. Cha

THE CONCEPT OF immigration evokes from immigrants hope as well as despair. It promises a new and richer life but also brings anxiety and uncertainty in a new environment. The history of immigrants to America is replete with unfulfilled promises and disappointments as well as with the realization of dreams. Whether Irish, Italian, Greek, Polish, or Chinese, the problems immigrants faced were real—economic survival, cultural conflict, social discrimination, competition, and the erosion of identity.

Korean immigrants in the United States are increasingly faced with unemployment and underemployment, family disintegration, cultural adjustments, and various psychological strains. There is a real need for organized effort to solve these problems, which are already widespread in major urban areas where Korean immigrants are concentrated. How these problems are resolved will determine much of the individual as well as collective well-being of the rapidly growing Korean population in the United States. [1]

However, no less important than socioeconomic and cultural problems is, or perhaps should be, the relationship of Koreans, as a growing ethnic minority, to the American political system. How are they likely to exercise their franchise? What pattern will it take? Will their political participation follow the same pattern as that of other ethnic groups? Given time to grow, will they become politically mature and sophisticated enough to demand and obtain a fair share of benefits from the American political system?

These are questions this study explores through analysis of the assimilation pattern of a sample of Korean immigrants in Los Angeles. The socioeconomic and educational variables often employed to explain the electoral behavior of the general population are not important factors in studies of ethnic groups. What emerges as the single most important variable relating to political behavior in American politics is ethnic identification, as reflected in the tendency of ethnic groups to vote alike and to show a rather consistent preference for a particular party.

This study attempts to investigate the degree to which Koreans in Los Angeles are assimilated with respect to each of five types of assimilation: cultural, structural, marital, identificational, and behavior-receptional. For the purpose of investigation, the five types of assimilation are treated as dependent variables whose occurrence is a function of certain independent variables. Any group of Koreans, although distinct from other ethnic groups, is itself a conglomerate of individuals with varying backgrounds and life experiences, and thus it is likely that the degree of assimilation will vary among the individuals. It is assumed that variations in assimilation may be determined by examining three individual characteristics: time— length of exposure to the American experience; education—the number of years of education completed in the United States, and income. The rationale for considering these characteristics as independent variables rests on a series of assumptions and hypotheses.[2]

The longer one has lived in the United States, the more affinity and appreciation may be felt for American values and culture. This may lead to favoring the adoption of American cultural practice, i.e., the beginning of acculturation. Since developing a close primary relationship is a time-consuming process, the longer one has lived in the United States, the more likely it is that one will have entered into a variety of social relationships with host culture members. These indicate some structural assimilation and may include the attainment of some measure of identificational assimilation. The better one comes to know host members and institutions, the more balanced his perception regarding problems in behavior reception in the United States.

Educational experience in the United States may also be an important variable. It is plausible that a person who completed some college education in the United States possesses a better command of English and a more systematic knowledge of American institutions and society than one whose understanding is entirely dependent upon education in Korea. Better command of English and more systematic knowledge of American society increase social relationships with the majority group members and result in more exposure to the American life-style. Systematic knowledge of American society may also lead to better appreciation of American values and norms, which in turn may lead to a measure of identificational assimilation and a reduced feeling of discrimination.

Income is another determinant of assimilation. The higher the level of income, the more resources are available to aid the sort of assimilation represented by a move to suburbia and acquisition of the amenities of the middle class. Physical proximity and middle-class status may lead to primary relationships with the majority, possibly with a concomitant increase in the sense of identification with the host society and acceptability by host members. The overall assumption is that life experience, education, and income will have a combined effect on the degree of assimilation. High levels of these independent variables augur that the dependent variables will be realized. This hypothetical relationship is shown in Table 1.

Data in this study were derived from a questionnaire administered in 1971 to an audience gathered for a Korean Association of Southern California meeting, where a broad cross-section of the community was represented.[3] Operationalization of dependent and independent variables was attempted.

Cultural assimilation (dependent) was determined on the basis of the reading and entertainment habits of Koreans in Los Angeles. Obtaining a complete set of data on a broad and complex concept of acculturation was beyond the scope of this study.

Table 1—An Hypothesized Relationship between Time, Education, Income, and Four Types of Assimilation

Independent Variables		Types of Assimilation			
		Cultural	Structural	Identity	Behavior Reception
Time	Long	H	H	H	H
	Short	L	L	L	L
U.S. Education	Some	H	H	H	H
	None	L	L	L	L
Income	High	H	H	H	H
	Low	L	L	L	L

H = High degree of assimilation.
L = Low degree of assimilation.

Koreans in Los Angeles live in a bicultural environment. More than 80,000 Koreans are now concentrated in Los Angeles. As a result, there are various services and other facilities catering exclusively to Koreans: a number of Korean newspapers and magazines; a Korean bookstore; radio and television hours in Korean; a couple of movie theaters showing Korean films; over a dozen Korean entertainment centers complete with bands, bars, and dance floors; and more than two dozen Korean restaurants. There are also seventy-two Korean churches and ninety-eight nonprofit alumni, social, and fraternal organizations.[4] All these provide such varied social activities as sports, bazaars, group tours, and recreational events. A rudimentary Koreatown is emerging in downtown Los Angeles and is cluttered with Korean-owned shops with their signs and advertisements in Korean.

Convenient, and perhaps even admirable, as these achievements may be, they are not necessarily a boon to the Koreans' assimilation into American culture and society. Korean services and facilities are so plentiful and readily available that a Korean in Los Angeles can, if he chooses, live in a miniature Korea virtually isolated from the mainstream of American society.

Yet, Los Angeles is a megalopolis where a variety of modern American entertainment and cultural events are as easily accessible to Koreans as to Americans. Los Angeles also affords Koreans ample opportunity to learn the modern American way of living and adopt majority life-styles. Viewed this way, Los Angeles offers an ideal setting in which a Korean immigrant can have a real choice of going either Korean or American.

In an attempt to examine how this kind of bicultural setting affects acculturation, subjects were asked whether they read American or Korean publications most frequently to inform themselves of new and current events, and whether they prefer American or Korean entertainment (movies, bars, sports events). Data on individual behavior in these two areas should reveal some aspects of cultural assimilation. The more acculturated one is, the more likely he is to choose American entertainment and publications in English; conversely, the less acculturated, the more likely he is to choose Korean publications and entertainment.

Structural assimilation (dependent), according to Milton Gordon, is "a large-scale entrance of an immigrant group into cliques, clubs, and institutions of host society, on a primary group level."[5] It was impossible to investigate all kinds of clubs and institutions, composed predominantly of Americans, where Koreans may have obtained individual entry. However, American religious institutions are relatively open to all aliens, including Koreans, and in them one should be able to develop a close primary and secondary relationship with host members. Thus, patterns of church membership are used as an indication of some structural assimilation. Subjects were asked whether they are regular churchgoers. If so, they were asked to state whether they attended a Korean or American church.

No effort was made to obtain data on marital assimilation (dependent) because fewer than 1 percent of Koreans registered with the consulate office have intermarried. Marital assimilation of Koreans in Los Angeles is insignificant at this point.

Identificational assimilation (dependent) was measured by a question asking whether the subject considered himself primarily Korean or American, regardless of current legal status.

Behavior reception assimilation (dependent) was measured by asking subjects if they felt discriminated against on or off their job in America. This is a perceived discrimination as opposed to an objective measure of discrimination.

Time (independent) was measured by asking subjects to indicate the number of years lived in the United States. However, there was a need to establish a threshold at which those less assimilated, due to a relatively short time spent in the United States, could be distinguished from those more likely to be assimilated because of a longer period spent in the United States. Five years was selected as a benchmark.

Korean news media in Los Angeles report an increasing number of cases of divorce suits, spouse's disappearances, family brawls requiring police intervention, and child battery among Koreans.[6] Informal interviews with those familiar with these cases disclose that families in difficulty usually have fewer than five years of experience in the United States. Cultural conflict, financial difficulty, and confusion about their new life seem to underlie the strain and stress in new immigrant families. It seems to take at least five years to complete the transition from initial insecurity to relatively stable settlement.

This five-year benchmark provides at least a rough guide, in the absence of a better alternative, for grouping respondents into those having relatively long experience with American life and those of relatively short experience.

Education (independent) indicates command of English and general knowledge of American society. Subjects were asked to indicate the number of years of college education completed in the United States. Those who indicated more than two years of college completed are held to be "United States college-educated."

An income (independent) level had to be selected to distinguish those more assimilated because of a relatively high income from those less assimilated and of a relatively low income. An annual income of $7,000 was selected as a benchmark.

Table 2—The Pattern of Reading and Entertainment Habits of Koreans in Los Angeles

	Cultural Assimilation									
	Reading Habits					Entertainment				
	K-Pub.	E-Pub.		N	X^2	K	A		N	X^2
	(percentage)					(percentage)				
(Time)										
Fewer than 5 yrs.	56.04	43.96	100	91	6.126*	62.00	38.00	100	100	2.571
More than 5 yrs.	36.84	63.16	100	76		50.00	50.00	100	78	
(Education)										
Some U.S. college	36.46	63.54	100	96	23.880*	29.81	70.19	100	104	18.439*
No U.S. college	74.65	25.35	100	71		62.16	37.84	100	74	
(Income)										
Less than $7,000	52.78	47.22	100	72	1.521	46.58	53.42	100	73	5.211*
More than $7,000	43.16	56.84	100	95		63.81	36.19	100	105	

K-Pub. = Korean publications.
E-Pub. = English publications.
K = Korean entertainment.
A = American entertainment.
df (degree of freedom) = 1; $p < .05$; *indicates significant relationship; N's vary due to missing information and nonresponse of interviewees to certain variables.

Data in Table 2 relate to reading and entertainment habits of Koreans in Los Angeles. For those whose life experience in the United States is fewer than five years, the percentage difference between readers of Korean and those reading English publications most frequently is not significant (56.04 percent and 43.96 percent respectively). However, of those who have been in the United States for more than five years, readers of Korean publications are far fewer (36.84 percent) than those who read English publications most frequently (63.16 percent).

With respect to entertainment habits, time spent in the United States does not seem to have a significant effect. It appears that a majority of Koreans in Los Angeles participate primarily in Korean rather than American entertainment activities and events, although the percentage of those attending Korean entertainment is much higher (62 percent) than the percentage seeking American entertainment (38 percent) among those whose life experience in the United States is fewer than five years. However, half of those whose life experience in the United States is more than five years indicate that their source of entertainment is also Korean activities.

Education emerges as the most important variable. Of those who completed some (more than two years in this case) college education in the United States, a significant majority are oriented in their reading and entertainment habits toward English publications and American entertainment (63.54 percent and 70.19 percent respectively). Conversely, a majority of those who had no college education in the United States tend to read primarily Korean publications and favor Korean entertainment (74.65 percent and 62.16 percent respectively).

Income seems to have little to do with reading habits (Table 2), but it does seem to affect entertainment habits. However, this effect appears in a manner contrary to what was assumed in this study. The assumption was that the higher the level of income, the higher the degree of assimilation, i.e., more American entertainment, and the lower the level of income, the lower the degree of assimilation, i.e., more Korean entertainment. Data show an opposite pattern; the high income group prefers Korean to American entertainment (63.81 percent and 36.19 percent respectively) and the low income group chooses American rather than Korean entertainment (53.42 percent and 46.58 percent respectively).

This finding warrants some observations. First, it may be that Korean entertainment is no cheaper than its American counterpart, which would reflect a function of economics in entertainment habits. Second, education does not seem to be a close correlate of income of Koreans in Los Angeles in this sample. It should be recalled that a majority of those with some American college education (70.19

percent) indicated that they choose American entertainment. If a high correlation between education and income existed, those with some U.S. college education should appear in the high income group. This should have yielded data showing the high income group favoring American entertainment. A possible explanation is that a large number of Korean immigrants come from the upper strata of Korean society and recent arrivals seem to come to the United States with considerable personal wealth. Thus it is likely that those with personal wealth brought from Korea, not achieved as a result of education received in the United States, are represented in the sample. This may have distorted an otherwise logical relationship between education, income, and entertainment habits.

Data in Table 3 relate to structural assimilation. An overwhelming majority of Korean churchgoers in Los Angeles (77 percent–91 percent) are affiliated with Korean churches, regardless of differences in length of time in America, education, and income. If this is an indication of structural assimilation, Koreans in Los Angeles are structurally assimilated to a low degree. Data on identificational assimilation show about the same pattern as that of church affiliation. A large majority of Koreans in Los Angeles consider themselves basically Koreans whether they are American citizens or permanent U.S. residents (70 percent–86 percent, see Table 3). This sense of being Korean is firm across all three variables.

Data on behavior receptional assimilation are shown in Table 4. The longer one lives in the United States and the more he knows about American society (presumably as a result of some formal education in the United States), the more acute is the feeling that he is discriminated against because of his color and ethnic origin.

In contrast, it appears that a person whose life experience in the United States is relatively short, and who consequently knows little about American society, does not feel discrimination—at least not as acutely as one whose experience and knowledge are more extensive. A person new to the United States is likely to be overwhelmed by the apparent egalitarian quality of American life, especially when he compares the relative freedom of the United States with his experiences in Korea. This may prevent him from sensing the subtleties of discriminatory practices.

Differences in the sense of discrimination of those making more than $7,000 and those earning less are insignificant (see Table 4).

It appears that acculturation or cultural assimilation, posited by Gordon's model as the first stage of assimilation, is beginning to take place among Koreans in Los Angeles. This may vary, however, with length of American life experience and education. Koreans can hardly be considered structurally assimilated. Nor are they identificationally assimilated; their sense of being Korean appears

Table 3—Church Affiliation and Self-Perception

	Structural					Identificational				
	Church affiliation					Self-perception				
Variables	KC	AC		N	X²	K	A		N	X²
(Time)	(percentage)					(percentage)				
Fewer than 5 yrs.	91.25	8.75	100	80	5.275*	86.41	13.59	100	103	6.650*
More than 5 yrs.	77.19	22.81	100	57		70.89	29.11	100	79	
(Education)										
Some U.S. college	87.14	12.86	100	70	.348	84.11	15.89	100	107	3.163
No U.S. college	83.56	16.44	100	67		73.33	26.67	100	75	
(Income)										
Less than $7,000	86.05	13.95	100	86	.007	75.34	24.66	100	73	.685
More than $7,000	84.31	15.69	100	51		80.61	19.39	100	98	

KC = Korean church.
AC = American church.
K = Korean.
A = American.
* indicates significant relationship.

Table 4—Feeling of Discrimination
Behavior Receptional
Sense of Discrimination

Variables	Feel little discrim- ination	Feel discrim- ination		N	X^2
(Time)	(percentage)				
Fewer than 5 yrs.	70.59	29.41	100	102	31.063*
More than 5 yrs.	28.57	71.43	100	77	
(Education)					
Some U.S. college	36.42	63.58	100	104	16.489*
No U.S. college	65.33	34.67	100	75	
(Income)					
Less than $7,000	47.22	52.78	100	72	1.353
More than $7,000	56.03	43.97	100	107	

*indicates significant relationship.

to be the ultimate frame of reference for identification. It is evident that Koreans in Los Angeles live mostly within their own ethnic subsociety, notwithstanding some evidence of cultural assimilation.

This absence or lack of structural assimilation in the midst of at least some acculturation lends support to Gordon's proposition that structural assimilation does not necessarily follow acculturation, and also supports Michael Parenti's argument that a social or structural assimilation has never occurred among American ethnic minorities despite a high degree of acculturation.

Further analysis of data on behavior receptional assimilation offers some insights into why Koreans are less assimilated in a social and identificational sense and form their own substructure. The new-comers, whose American life experience is fewer than five years and whose educations are at low levels or were obtained in Korea, have little sense of discrimination. Logically, this should help them relate to host culture members and institutions because they sense that acceptance by the host society is likely, however false or correct that sense might be. However, the pattern of their church affiliation shows that they stay well within the substructure of the Korean community. This may be caused by a sense of insecurity stemming from the language barrier and lack of experience in American life, which may prevent them from venturing into relationships with members of the host society. Consequently, newcomers test out their new life within the substructure of the Korean community until they feel that they have overcome these handicaps.

While the newcomers feel little discrimination, long-term residents are aware of discrimination. The longer immigrants live in the United States and the more they know of the country, the more acute is their feeling of being discriminated against in American society. As this sense of discrimination increases, long-term residents may also retreat into the substructure of the Korean community for comfort and defense against the discriminatory majority society. The newcomers may find staying within the substructure a desirable alternative to venturing into the unknown society, at least until they master the language and know more about the new society.

However, if the way long-term residents feel about discrimination is any indication, the newcomers will experience an increased sense of discrimination as they remain in the society longer. They will find themselves remaining within the substructure even after some of them have overcome the handicaps. The result is maintenance of the substructure and little structural assimilation.

Given that Koreans in Los Angeles, and perhaps in other parts of the United States, are likely to remain in their subsociety, with little prospect of structural assimilation, it may be that their political orientation will follow the traditional ethnic voting pattern. They will differ little in their political behavior from other ethnic groups and will be merely another addition to ethnicity in American politics. They will support the candidate and party that awards "recognition" to Koreans in the form of rewarding a few Koreans with appointments to local commissions and boards. Koreans rewarded in this way will be those viewed by candidates and parties as those who delivered the votes of their ethnic group. It seems highly unlikely that Koreans will be able to make inroads into the inner circle of majority power.

There may be one or two mavericks among first-generation Koreans who will try for an elective office. Desire to support the party of fellow Koreans will cause occasional party-crossing. There will also be a shift in party affiliation as candidates of other minority groups such as Japanese or Chinese Americans appeal to Koreans to support their candidacy on the basis that all share an Asian background. This remains political behavior based on ethnic identification, although more broadly defined than that based exclusively on a nationality group.

It appears that Koreans in Los Angeles are beginning to culturally assimilate. It can hardly be said, however, that they evince any measure of structural or identificational assimilation. A concomitant of this absence of structural and identificational assimilation is the existence and development of a social substructure, a Korean community largely independent of American majority society. Granted that this substructure will not only endure but will be further solidified as the population grows, it may be surmised that the political orientation of Koreans will be toward ethnic voting like that of other ethnic groups in the United States. Some basic normative questions remain. Should Koreans in the United States remain unassimilated? Is it healthy to live within an ethnic enclave largely insulated from the majority society? Whatever the reasons Koreans choose to lead a largely unassimilated life, does it necessarily follow that their political orientation should be a replication of past practice in American politics? Are there no alternatives? If Koreans as an emerging ethnic minority are to develop a different pattern, what should it be? From a theoretical standpoint, does Parenti's thesis fully explain ethnic politics? Where should future theoretical research on ethnic politics be directed? Some preliminary observations on these questions follow.

The American folklore of "melting pot" or "Anglo-conformity" has not been an accurate description of the behavior of large numbers of immigrants, other than those of Anglo-Saxon descent. Assimilation should perhaps ultimately be a function of a natural configuration of desires and wishes of each ethnic group. Assuming a need for preservation of the pluralistic character of American society, ethnics, living "as ethnics," will do little violence to the concept of a pluralistic society where tolerance for varying social patterns is valued. As an alternative to traditional ethnic political behavior, Korean immigrants might consider two approaches. It may be desirable to trade symbolic recognition and a political brokerage role for active participation in more significant socioeconomic issues and policies in American politics. Another approach is the cultivation, as issues warrant, of close alliances with other minority groups and issue-oriented organizations of the white majority to increase the potential political leverage of Koreans in the United States.

With respect to an alternative to Parenti's thesis, there is suspicion that the persistence of ethnicity in American politics may not be entirely attributable to the existence of an ethnic substructure. Rather, the American political system itself may be an important independent variable. Campaigns often invoke ethnic consciousness as a strategy for gaining support. Parenti himself did not overlook the role of the political system itself; however, it is raised in passing, not as the major thrust of his argument:

> Part of the reason for the persistence of ethnic voting may rest in the political system itself . . . the political system, i.e., party, precinct workers, candidates, elections, patronage, etc., continues to rely upon ethnic strategies such as those extended to accommodate the claims of newly arrived ethnic middle-class leadership; as a mediator and mobilizer of minority symbols and interests, the political system must be taken into account.[7]

Although correct, Parenti says little further about the role of the political system, which is probably a more important variable than the substructure as an alternative explanation for saliency of ethnicity in American politics. More productive theories of American ethnic politics might be obtained by focusing future research on how the American political system itself contributes to the persistence of ethnicity in American politics.

Notes

1. The Korean population, according to the 1970 census, was 70,598. See U.S. Department of Commerce, Bureau of the Census, 1970 Census of Population, PC(2)-1G, *Subject Reports: Japanese, Chinese and Filipinos in the United States* (Washington, D.C.: Government Printing Office, July 1973), pp. 180–81. However, the study conducted by Yu Ŭi-yŏng, Department of Sociology, California State University, Los Angeles, indicates that the census may have grossly underestimated, and the actual number of Koreans in the United States may have been close to 120,000 in 1970. During the 1972 to 1973 fiscal year alone, 23,000 Koreans immigrated to the United States. If this increase in a single year is an indication, there may have been close to 200,000 Koreans in the United States by 1974. See, for a detailed report of Yu's study, *Miju Tong-a* [Tong-a Daily in America], May 21, 1974; the English section of *Shinhan Minbo* [New Korea], December 5, 1974.

2. For evidence that these three are important factors in the assimilation process see George Kagiwada, "Assimilation of Nisei in Los Angeles," and Stanford Lyman, "Generation and Character," in Hilary Conroy and T. Scott Miyakawa, eds., *East Across the Pacific: Historical and Sociological Studies of Japanese Immigration and Assimilation* (Santa Barbara: ABC-Clio, 1972), pp. 268–78, 279–314; Herbert Gans, *The Urban Villagers* (New York: Free Press, 1962); Oscar Handlin, *Boston's Immigrants: A Study in Acculturation* (Cambridge: Harvard University Press, 1959); Judith Schuval, *Immigrants on the Threshold* (New York: Atherton Press, 1963); Reinhard Bendix et al., eds., *Class, Status, and Power* (New York: Free Press, 1953); Reynold Frarley, "The Changing Distribution of Negroes Within Metropolitan Areas: The Emergence of Black Suburbs," *American Journal of Sociology* 75 (January 1970): 512–27.

3. Nevertheless, the sampling cannot be considered random, and the method seriously limits this study.

4. Data were obtained from a statistical survey of Koreans in Los Angeles reported in *Shinhan Minbo*, December 5, 1974. It is reported that the survey was conducted by Key's Printing under contract with the Korean Association of Southern California.

5. Milton M. Gordon, *Assimilation in American Life* (New York: Oxford University Press, 1964), p. 71.

6. No specific statistics are available. No systematic study has been done; some information was gathered through informal conversations with pastors and community leaders. For recent news items on this subject, see *Miju Tong-a*, May–July 1974.

7. Michael Parenti, "Ethnic Politics and the Persistence of Ethnic Identification," *American Political Science Review* 61 (September 1967): 717–26.

Koreans in America: A Demographic Analysis

Jai P. Ryu

AS PHILIP HAUSER and Otis Duncan characterized the field of population studies, it is concerned with "determinants and consequences of population trends." [1] Serious study of the determinants and consequences of population trends of Koreans in America, however, has been—and continues to be—severely limited by the unavailability of certain essential data and by the limited nature of available data. It is important to note these limitations, as they qualify the claims of validity and reliability of research and suggest a need for data and illustrate the problems of research.

Unlike structural analysis, which speaks to demographic characteristics at a given point in time, process analysis identifies demographic patterns over a period of time. This kind of study of Korean Americans has been limited for a number of reasons. First, the 1970 census included the first count of Koreans as a distinct ethnic group. Although Korean immigration began at the turn of the century, reliable descriptions of detailed characteristics of Koreans up to 1970 are rare if they exist at all. [2] Second, statistics concerning Koreans since 1970 are too general to allow meaningful process analysis. [3] Although this is obviously true of all other ethnic groups, the problem is exacerbated in the case of Korean Americans because of the rapid increase in Korean immigration since 1970. [4] This means that even the available 1970 data on Koreans are becoming outdated more quickly than those on other ethnic minorities that are growing less rapidly.

Next, lack of published vital statistics on Koreans severely limits process analysis study. Of course, this is true of studies of other ethnic groups in the United States. However, in most other cases, derivations of birth and death figures are available from two or more censuses. In the case of Koreans, for whom only one set of census figures is available, estimates of births and deaths are almost impossible to obtain. As a result, computations based on even crude measures of birth and death are impossible.

Fortunately, however, the 1980 census is not far away, and it promises to be of greater value for students of Korean demographics.[5] In the early 1980s, a meaningful process analysis, identifying key demographic trends among Koreans, will be possible.

From the above, it is obvious that analysis of the causes and consequences of population trends among Korean Americans is virtually impossible at present without an adequate process analysis. Another constraint on causal analysis in the case of Korean Americans is that, in spite of the fact that the Korean population is growing very rapidly, its overall size has not been of great demographic significance. Consequently, there has been little demand for the publication of even the available census data on Koreans. For this reason, much of the data on Koreans, as of 1970, remains in the form of microfilm or computerized tape in the Census Bureau. The use of films or tapes for a demographic study is possible, but it is expensive and time consuming for such a limited study.

Published census reports on Koreans in the nation, regions, some selected states, Standard Metropolitan Statistical Areas (SMSAs), and cities are available. Population characteristics of Koreans by wards, counties, tracts, and blocks are unavailable. For such units, Koreans are lumped into the "other races" category, and reliance on such figures can mislead more often than clarify. Data by small demographic units are, however, essential for the identification of explanatory variables and for the establishment of causal statements related to the population trends of Korean Americans. There is urgent need for a greater number of publications on Koreans and easier accessibility to microfilm for individual and institutional researchers to come from the 1980 census.

Even for the structural analysis that will establish a demographic pattern at a given point in time, the 1970 census data on Koreans is decidedly lacking. In terms of completeness and accuracy of the data, the 1970 census was a great improvement over previous counts.[6] Even with this improvement, however, admitted errors are many. The Bureau estimates that the nonwhite population was underenumerated by 6.9 percent, while whites were underenumerated by only 1.9 percent.[7] Reasons for this underenumeration are several.

The groups most likely to be undercounted are racial and ethnic minorities living in major urban centers. Koreans belong to this category. According to the 1970 housing estimate, 67 percent, 58.9 percent, and 33.3 percent of all Korean Americans resided in urban areas, in SMSAs, and in central cities, respectively. It is highly probable that the 33.3 percent city figure is the result of an undercount. The undercounted populations tend to reside in low-socioeconomic and high-density areas. In such areas, households may be missed in address registers, mail delivery tends to be poor, and census forms might have missed a large number of households.

In 1970, 76 percent of Koreans reported their mother tongue as Korean. Furthermore, it is reasonable to assume that nearly all Korean immigrants since 1970 have Korean as their mother tongue. The resultant linguistic difficulties for Koreans in this country have been amply documented.[8] Given such difficulties in English comprehension, it is likely that many Koreans had trouble completing the census forms. The only Asian language into which census questionnaires were translated was Chinese and this was used only in two cities—San Francisco and New York.

The tabulation of 1970 census data on Koreans was based on those who reported their race as Korean. When the birthplace of a parent was used as the criterion, the census established the existence of an additional 16,000 Koreans. For these additional Koreans, however, detailed data were not presented.

According to the 1970 census definition, when the race of a person was not clearly defined on the census form, the person was enumerated by the race of his/her father, and if a person's parents were each of different ethnic origins, the origin of the father was assigned. If the mother's race was also used as the defining criterion, Koreans would have numbered far more than those reported. In the case of Koreans as well as Japanese, at least one-third of all women married non-Asian husbands.

Given these difficulties, which impede effective demographic analysis of the Koreans in America, the present study will attempt a limited structural analysis, utilizing various 1970 census reports and several scattered publications about the subject.

This study will include the basic components of any structural analysis of populations—compositional and distributional descriptions. It will be divided into five sections: growth of the Korean population in the United States; distribution of Korean Americans; age, sex, and marital status of Korean Americans; socioeconomic characteristics of Korean Americans; and housing and household characteristics of Korean Americans. These are divided only for analytic and descriptive purposes. Statements of interrelationship will be presented in the most appropriate section.

For each section we will try to identify two general areas of inquiry:

what descriptive statements can be made on the basis of available data, and how additional research and service in different areas can increase the understanding of this minority group.

Korean immigration to America had its known beginning with the arrival of two Koreans in Hawaii on January 15, 1900. The beginning of Korean immigration, however, coincided with the growing resentment of white Americans toward the Chinese and Japanese, who were beginning to grow in number on the West Coast. Koreans became incidental victims of the 1924 act establishing the national origin quota system, which was designed primarily to restrict Southern and Eastern Europeans and the other two Asian groups.

The 1965 act (P.L. 89–236) increased the number and growth rate of Koreans to an unprecedented level. This act opened the doors for immigration of especially those Koreans with occupations classified by the United States Department of Labor.

In response to the growing size of the Korean American population, the 1970 census counted Koreans as a distinct ethnic group for the first time. The census enumerated 70,598 Koreans, recognizing them as the fifth largest Asian group following the Japanese, Chinese, Filipinos, and Hawaiians. The majority of these Koreans were recent immigrants, as indicated by the fact that 54 percent of them were born outside the United States (see Table 1).

In 1970, foreign-born Koreans accounted for 0.4 percent of all foreign born in the United States and 6 percent of all foreign born who were neither white nor black. The 1970 census also reveals an interesting sex ratio among Koreans, which will be discussed later.

The flow of migration that began in significant numbers in the 1960s accelerated in the 1970s. From 1970 to 1974, 84,131 Korean immigrants were added to the 1970 figure, representing a 119.2 percent increase over the 1970 estimate.[9] This increase in the 1970s makes Korean Americans the fastest growing Asian group in the United States, except for the South Vietnamese, who increased rapidly during the latter half of 1975. This rapid rate of increase of Koreans, however, has been due in part to the relatively small number of Korean residents in the early days. The total number of immigrants in the ten year period 1965 to 1974 indicates that the volume of Korean immigration is smaller than that of the Filipinos and Chinese (Table 2).

Although there exists no valid method by which to ascertain the exact number of Koreans in the United States at present, the actual number should be far more than census and immigration figures indicate.[10]

As of 1974, therefore, the actual number of Koreans was estimated

Table 1—Increase in Asian Population in the United States, 1970 and 1971–1974

	Koreans	Japanese	Chinese	Filipinos	Total
1970 Estimates					
Total	70,598	588,324	431,583	336,731	1,427,236
Male	28,491	271,453	226,733	183,175	709,852
Female	42,107	316,871	204,850	153,556	717,384
Foreign-born	38,145	122,500	204,232	178,970	543,847
% Foreign-born	54.0	20.8	47.3	53.1	38.1
Immigrants since 1970					
FY1971[a]	14,297	4,457	17,622*	28,471	64,847
FY1972	18,876	4,757	21,730	29,376	74,739
FY1973	22,930	5,461	21,656	30,799	80,846
FY1974	28,028	4,860	22,685	32,857	88,430
Total: 1971–1974	84,131	19,535	83,693	121,503	308,862
% Increase over 1970	119.2	3.3	19.4	36.1	21.6

Source: U.S. Department of Commerce, Bureau of the Census, PC(1)–D1; U.S. Department of Justice, Immigration and Naturalization Service, *Annual Reports*, 1971–1974.

[a]Fiscal years ending on June 30 of the stated year.

* Figure includes 14,417 from Taiwan and 3,205 from Hong Kong.

Table 2—Total Number of Immigrants from Asia and all other Countries, Fiscal Years 1965–1974

Country	Immigrants	Percent
Koreans	111,914	3.0
Japanese	42,110	1.0
Chinese	146,914	4.0
Filipinos	210,269	6.0
All Asia	821,888	22.0
All Countries	3,718,149	100.0

Source: U.S. Department of Justice, Immigration and Naturalization Service, *Annual Reports*, 1965–1974.

at around 217,000. This represents a 151 percent increase since 1970. With more significant information from the Bureau of the Census, the Immigration and Naturalization Service, and the Department of Health, Education and Welfare, future estimates will be more accurate (see Table 3).

Another interesting demographic feature related to immigration is the naturalization of Koreans. As Table 4 indicates, the number of Koreans who have become naturalized citizens of the United States has increased steadily since 1965. For the ten year period alone, it amounted to 21,698 individuals. Although the ratio of naturalized to the annual total of immigrants has been declining, the decline is mainly due to the recent vast increase in the number of immigrants. It is presently anticipated that, assuming a more or less constant rate of immigration for the next five or six years, naturalization of Koreans will probably increase at a greater rate.

Several interesting facts emerge upon close examination of Table 4 and related figures. Of all naturalized Korean Americans, almost

Table 3—Estimate of Actual Number of Koreans in the United States, 1974

1970 census figure	70,598
Additional census figure [a]	16,000
1970 undercount	—
Immigrants, FY1971–FY1974	84,131
Nonimmigrants, FY1974	30,377
25% of Nonimmigrants FY1971–FY1973 [b]	16,041
Natural increase since 1970 census	—
Total [c]	217,147

Source: U.S. Department of Justice, Immigration and Naturalization Service, *Annual Reports*, 1971–1974.

[a] For this figure of 16,000, see the introductory section of the present paper on the limits on structural analysis.

[b] 25% is somewhat arbitrary. This is based on the assumption that approximately 75% of nonimmigrant Koreans in the United States obtain the status of permanent resident in one to three years after entry into the country.

[c] The total figure obviously does not take into account the natural increase (births-deaths) or the 1970 census undercount beyond the 16,000 recognized by the Bureau of the Census.

Table 4—Naturalization of Koreans by Age, Sex, and Naturalization Provisions

Year	Total	% Immigrants	% Female	% 18 Years and Over	Provisions % Wife of U.S. Citizen	Provisions % Children of U.S. Citizen
FY 1965	1,027	47.4	79.0	68.3	51.9	32.0
FY 1966	1,180	47.3	78.6	67.1	52.7	32.9
FY 1967	1,353	34.2	78.7	69.3	54.2	31.0
FY 1968	1,776	46.6	76.7	74.8	49.0	25.0
FY 1969	1,646	27.2	77.0	76.6	49.0	24.8
FY 1970	1,687	18.1	80.9	76.7	52.8	23.2
FY 1971	2,083	14.6	81.3	78.7	52.5	17.2
FY 1972	2,933	15.5	74.0	84.0	43.2	16.5
FY 1973	3,562	15.5	76.4	82.5	43.6	18.2
FY 1974	4,451	15.9	75.2	79.1	39.9	21.5

Source: U.S. Department of Justice, Immigration and Naturalization Service, *Annual Reports, 1965–1974.*

78 percent, or 16,843, are eighteen years old and over. All of these individuals are potential voters, and some of them may become candidates for public offices.

The annual growth rate of naturalized persons eighteen and older from 1965 to 1974 was 20.8 percent. If this rate continues (and we are using the 1974 naturalization figure to make this projection), there will likely be 60,000 eligible voters of Korean origin in the 1980 election. In a democratic pluralistic society, there may be many ways to utilize this political power for the betterment of this ethnic minority group.

Another fact of interest is that for the last ten years or so the total annual naturalization volume made up by wives and children of United States citizens constituted the majority of all those naturalized. However, the combined proportion of these groups steadily declined from 84 percent in 1965 to 61 percent in 1974. Naturalization based on other circumstances has been rising proportionally. So long as the American military presence in South Korea continues, however, the number of wives and children of United States citizens will remain significant. [11]

There presently exists a great need for extensive research on and service for these groups, especially for Asian wives of U.S. servicemen. From a study of 137 (108 of them Koreans) randomly selected Asian wives of U.S. servicemen in Seattle, Kim Sil-tong concludes that this is "the most isolated group, both culturally and socially, in the United States." [12] This group has been noted for its severe culture shock, lack of education, impoverishment, isolation, malcommunication in the family, lack of occupational skills, high divorce rate, and general alienation. It was also noted that the magnitude of problems was much greater among Korean wives than among Japanese wives.

Distributional analysis of Korean Americans will be divided into two sections: urban-rural distribution and regional-state distribution. It is generally true that Korean Americans tend to concentrate heavily in major metropolitan centers where most other Asian minority immigrants have settled for employment, service facilities, business activities, education, and the like. Based on a 15 percent sample analysis, census publications maintain that in 1970, 67 percent and 62 percent of Korean Americans resided in urban areas and metropolitan areas, respectively. In spite of the data, the tendency to settle in these areas seems less apparent than among the Japanese, Chinese, and Filipinos (see Table 5).

Curiously, Korean Americans are more dispersed than fellow Asian groups. This atypical feature holds true even among Koreans inside SMSAs. Although the percentage of Korean Americans living in

Table 5—Urban-Rural Distribution of Asian Americans, 1970

	Korean %	Japanese %	Chinese %	Filipino %
Total Population	100	100	100	100
Urban	67.0	89.2	96.6	85.5
Rural	33.0	10.8	3.4	14.5
Inside SMSAs	61.8	86.3	93.7	85.0
Outside SMSAs	38.2	13.7	6.3	15.0
In central cities	33.3	48.4	68.8	48.1
In suburbs	28.5	39.9	25.0	37.0

Source: U.S. Department of Commerce, Bureau of the Census, HC(7)–9, 1973.

suburban settings is lower than that of Japanese and Filipinos; of all Asians, fewer Koreans in proportion to their numbers in the SMSA as a whole live in central cities. A significant 46.2 percent of Korean Americans in SMSAs live in suburbs, compared to 28.6 percent of Filipinos, 44.0 percent of Japanese, and 26.6 percent of Chinese. All in all, the general tendency among minority immigrants to concentrate in urban-metropolitan-central-city areas is considerably less for Koreans than for their fellow Asians.

The regional distribution of Korean Americans also displays the atypical feature of the urban-rural distribution (see Table 6). In the western region, where only 16 percent of the total United States population resides, all Asian groups showed a heavy concentration both for the 1970 census year and thereafter. Forty-four percent of Korean Americans resided in the West in 1970. Since then, however, the pattern has changed considerably. Among Koreans immigrating between 1971 and 1974, fewer than one-third went to states in the West. The remaining immigrants settled in more or less equal proportions in three other major regions of the United States. This pattern is quite unlike those of the other three Asian groups. Although the other groups have shown some decline in their concentration in the West since the 1970 census, the proportion of each of these groups in the West remains significantly higher than that of Koreans. Koreans in the United States seem more dispersed than other Asian groups in regional as well as urban-rural distribution, as noted above.

Distribution by state, however, shows a bit more concentration. Although Koreans show a more suburban, less urban, and more regionally dispersed pattern than other Asians, they seem to aggregate in highly urbanized and industrialized states, namely, California, Hawaii, Illinois, Michigan, Maryland, Virginia, New York, New Jersey, Pennsylvania, Ohio, and Washington, D.C. Of the 70,382 Korean nationals who reported under the alien address program in 1973, 75 percent or 52,924 lived in these ten states and the District of Columbia.

Table 6—Regional Distribution of Asian Americans in 1970 and Region of Intended Residence in other Periods

		Northeast %	North Central %	South %	West %	Total %
Koreans:	1970 census	20	19	17	44	100
	1971–1974	24	20	24	32	100
Japanese:	1970 census	8	7	5	80	100
	1965–1967	16	14	17	53	100
Chinese:	1970 census	27	9	8	56	100
	1965–1973	34	12	10	44	100
Filipinos:	1970 census	9	8	9	74	100
	1965–1973	15	15	9	61	100
U.S.:	1970 census	25	29	30	16	100

Source: U.S. Department of Commerce, Bureau of the Census, HC(7)–9; U.S. Department of Justice, Immigration and Naturalization Service, *Annual Reports*, 1965–1974.

Because of the close interrelationships between age, sex, and marital status, these variables are being treated in the same section. For the sake of clarity, however, each will be dealt with separately as far as possible.

For the period 1970 to 1974, the sex ratio of Korean immigrants was 61 males per 100 females (Table 7). Females also outnumbered males among foreign-born Korean Americans in 1970, when, according to the census, the ratio was 56 males per 100 females, an even more uneven ratio than that for later immigrants.

The greatest unevenness was in the 20–29 years of age category, with the sex ratio (number of males per 100 females) of 29. This can largely be explained by the great number of Korean women married to U.S. servicemen. Their number has been four-digit figures ranging from 1,225 in 1966 to 3,033 in 1971. Even when we discount these women, however, the sex ratio remains uneven in favor of females, as will be shown later in the marital status section.

Other unevenness was found in the under five years of age bracket with a sex ratio of 65, the 50–59 category with a sex ratio of 65, and the 60 and over category with a sex ratio of 48. The unevenness among children might be the result of the great numbers of Korean children adopted by U.S. citizens, who tend to prefer female children over males.[13] The smaller number of male elderly may be due to the differential in life expectancy, which tends to be longer for females.[14] Another explanation is that mothers are more likely than fathers, who may have occupational or other obligations, to visit their children in the United States.

In 1970, the median age of Korean Americans was 26.1, younger than that for all U.S. citizens, 28.1, and older than black Americans

Table 7—Age and Sex Distribution of Korean Immigrants, Fiscal Years 1970–1974

Age Group	Sex Ratio (number of males per 100 females)	Age Group Percentage of Total Immigrants
Total	61	100% (93,445)
Under 5	65	15
5–9	93	9
10–19	78	13
20–29	29	32
30–39	94	22
40–49	109	6
50–59	65	2
60 and over	48	2

Source: U.S. Department of Justice, Immigration and Naturalization Service, *Annual Reports*, 1970–1974.

with 22.5. Among Asian American groups, Koreans were considerably younger than the Japanese, 32.4, but about the same median age as the Chinese and Filipinos.

The proportion of children in the total Korean American population in 1970 was 12.4 percent, higher than in the total United States population with 8.4 percent and even among blacks, where the figure was 10.7 percent. The percentage of children among Koreans was higher than that of any other Asian group as well. Since 1970, however, the proportion has been increasing even more, reaching 15.6 percent of immigrants in fiscal year 1974. As Table 7 indicates, 15 percent of all immigrants between 1970 and 1974 were children under five. A study of Koreans in Chicago revealed that, along with this high proportion of children, there was a great tendency for Korean mothers to work outside the home. Researchers reasoned that this accounted for the great importance of day-care facilities to the Korean group in Chicago. [15]

There also exists among entering Koreans a high proportion of children under twenty years of age. Of all Korean immigrants between 1970 and 1974, 37 percent were under twenty. The implication of educational and other burdens on their parents should be studied.

Due to the recentness of Korean immigration, the proportion of people over sixty years of age has not been significant. In 1970 it was 4.6 percent, compared to 14.2 percent for the total United States population, 10.3 percent for blacks, 10.5 percent for the Japanese, and 10.9 percent for Filipinos. Actually, since 1970, this figure has declined. Of all the Koreans immigrating between 1970 and 1974, only 2 percent were over sixty. This low proportion, however, should not be taken at face value. Thomas Owan states that from 1969 through 1970, Asian Americans did not receive a single federal dollar for Project for the Aged. [16] Even the allocation for 1972 to 1974 showed just a minor increase. Even though their proportion is minimal, this age group seems almost totally dependent on their adult children for livelihood. The need for greater attention to the problems of the elderly will confront the Korean community in the near future.

Table 8 illustrates the changing dependency burdens borne by Korean Americans 20–59 years of age. The proportion of Korean immigrants aged 20–59 in 1973–1974 was not unusually low. Actually, it tended to be higher for Koreans than for other ethnic groups in the United States. The trend, however, has been toward steady decline since 1967, as Table 8 shows. This decline in the labor force population should have important implications for the general living standards of Korean Americans. These figures should be interpreted with caution because the count of Korean women married to Americans, and Korean orphans adopted by Americans, may have distorted

Table 8—Young and Old Dependency Among Korean Immigrants, 1967–1974

Year	Age 0–19	Age 20–59	Age 60+
	%	%	%
1967–1968	27.4	71.3	1.2
1969–1970	29.3	69.5	1.2
1971–1972	33.0	65.5	1.5
1973–1974	40.2	57.6	2.2

Source: U.S. Department of Justice, Immigration and Naturalization Service, *Annual Reports*, 1967–1974.

the dependency ratio found in the Korean community. These data are currently not available for homogeneous Korean households.

As a group, married women have been the dominant category among Korean Americans, although their numbers have declined. As mentioned above, this is due to the great number of American servicemen's wives among Korean immigrants. As the proportion of married women declines, the proportion of single persons of both sexes and of married men has risen. At present, however, single females seem to far outnumber single males. The sex ratio for immigrants between 1965 and 1972 was 79.6 males per 100 females. What this implies for the patterns of marriage and family among Korean Americans will be of considerable interest to many researchers (see Table 9).

Another notable pattern of marital behavior among Korean Americans has to do with the great proportion of Koreans marrying non-Koreans. Although the data in Table 10 are confined to Hawaii, which displays many atypical demographic features, the pattern seems too unique to ignore. Even if we explain away the high proportion of Korean women marrying non-Koreans, the case of Korean males remains puzzling. As to how prevalent this pattern is in the rest

Table 9—Korean Immigrants by Sex and Marital Status, 1965–1972

Year	Total	Male			Female		
		Single	Married	Other	Single	Married	Other
	%*	%	%	%	%	%	%
1965–1966	100	13.3	9.0	0.1	18.5	58.1	0.9
1967–1968	100	15.4	14.5	0.2	19.8	48.9	1.2
1969–1970	100	17.4	14.4	0.2	21.8	44.8	1.3
1971–1972	100	18.5	18.5	0.2	22.9	38.5	1.4
Total	100 (59,928)	17.5	16.4	0.2	22.0	42.7	1.3

Source: U.S. Department of Justice, Immigration and Naturalization Service, *Annual Reports*, 1965–1974.
*Due to calculations which include fractions, and omission of values smaller than 0.05, columns may not add up to 100 percent.

Table 10—Asian Marriages Within Own Subgroups in Hawaii, 1970

Groups	Male	Female
	%	%
Koreans	50	50
Japanese	93	85
Chinese	71	71
Filipinos	72	85
Hawaiians	62	59
Whites	84	87

Source: U.S. Department of Commerce, Bureau of the Census, PC(2)–4C.

of the United States and what its causes are, only further research can answer.

As was true of the variables in the previous section, education, income, and occupation are closely interrelated. Under the heading of education, three areas will be examined: mother tongue, school enrollment, and school completed.

In 1970, 76 percent of all Koreans enumerated in the census claimed Korean as their mother tongue. The proportion was, of course, higher for the foreign born at 91 percent, while 58 percent of native-born Koreans reported Korean as their mother tongue. Given the relatively late beginning of Korean immigration to the United States, this high proportion is understandable. Compare this figure with 76 percent for all Chinese, 62 percent for all Japanese, and 64 percent for all Filipinos, who have a longer history in this country. [17]

This linguistic handicap has been worsening, however, due mainly to the increase in Korean immigration in recent years. It is reasonable to assume that an overwhelming proportion of recent immigrants speak Korean as their mother tongue, and the 76 percent of the 1970 census figure might very well be too gross an underestimate to be useful at present.

Linguistic difficulty has many implications for the general status of Korean Americans. As a Department of Health, Education and Welfare study concludes, "English language facility is a major problem for all Koreans, hampering the ability of the adults to obtain a good job commensurate with their education as well as the performance of children in school." [18] Kim and Condon remark that in Chicago, "the Chinese and the Korean groups perceived and experienced most difficulties in the areas of language and life style differences." [19] In their survey, only 11.8 percent of male and 4.8 percent of female Korean respondents reported that they speak English fluently. This self-evaluation score was much poorer than that of most other Asian groups.

Table 11—School Enrollment and Years of School Completed for the United States Population and for White and Korean Americans of the United States, 1970

Percent Enrolled		United States	White	Korean
		%	%	%
14–17 years old:	Male	92.1	92.8	93.1
	Female	91.6	92.2	93.1
18–24 years old:	Male	36.8	38.1	50.7
	Female	26.7	27.1	25.5
25–34 years old:		5.7	5.8	14.4
Years of School Completed				
Total population		100.0	100.0	100.0
		(110 mil.)	(98 mil.)	(38,000)
No school years completed		1.6	1.4	2.8
Elementary:	1–4 years	3.9	3.1	2.8
	5–7 years	10.0	9.1	8.0
	8 years	12.6	13.0	5.5
High school:	1–3 years	19.4	18.6	9.7
	4 years	31.1	32.2	22.7
College:	1–3 years	10.6	11.1	12.1
	4 years or more	10.7	11.3	36.3
Median school years completed		12.7	12.1	12.9
Percent high school graduates		52.3	54.4	71.1

Source: U.S. Department of Commerce, Bureau of the Census, PC(1)–D1; PC(2)–1G.

As the upper panel of Table 11 shows, the percentage of Korean Americans enrolled in school is higher than that of other groups in all categories except females 18–24 years old. The proportion of Korean females in this category is not only smaller than for whites, it is only half the number of Korean males in the same age group who are enrolled in school. This may be due to Korean attitudes toward the education of daughters versus sons, to the early marriage of females, or to the high incidence of Korean women in this age group marrying American servicemen who tend to have a low level of education.[20]

The most salient difference, however, was found in the 25–34 category. While only 5.8 percent of white Americans of this age bracket are enrolled in school, the figure for Korean Americans is 14.4 percent. This shows a percentage difference of 8.6 percent, and means that Koreans of this age bracket are 148 percent more likely to be enrolled in school than their counterparts among white Americans. This high level of enrollment, continuing into middle age, appears to be one of the most conspicuous features of Korean American education.

The high aspirations for education this statistic reflects are apparently continuing among more recent Korean immigrants. Kim and Condon found that 35.5 percent of Korean male and 13.4 percent of Korean female respondents in Chicago gave "educational opportunity" as their primary reason for immigrating to the United States. For these males, this is the most frequently cited among nine possible reasons for immigration. Most females (17.7 percent) gave "better work opportunity" as their main reason for immigrating; education was the next most cited reason. For both groups, a higher proportion cited "educational opportunity" as the prime reason than did most other Asian groups.

The high proportion of school enrollment for the 25–34 age bracket, however, may not continue at the same level in the future. In Honolulu, where Korean immigration is long-standing, only 10.1 percent of this age group were enrolled in school. When Korean immigration to the mainland has lasted longer, this number may decline as it has in Hawaii.

Table 11 gives statistics on median years of school completed, comparing whites and Koreans within the total U.S. population. In the country as a whole, 52.3 percent of all adults have completed high school. Among Korean Americans, 71.1 percent have done so (over 80 percent in Los Angeles and New York). Of all Korean adults 36.3 percent have had some college education, while only 10.7 percent of the United States population have. The proportion of college graduates among Koreans is 240 percent of the proportion among the United States population generally and 220 percent greater than that of white Americans. Along with the high enrollment figures mentioned above, this reflects the unusually high educational aspirations of Koreans both in Korea and in America.

In Honolulu, however, an unusually low proportion of college graduates was revealed. Only 13.7 percent of Korean adults graduated from college. Although this percentage is considerably higher than that for the total United States population or that for whites, it is much lower than that for Korean Americans in general. The situation in Hawaii may point to reasons why the college graduate proportion for Korean Americans in general could decline in the future.

At present, however, enrollment, college graduation, and median level of education are much higher for Koreans than for other ethnic groups in the United States. The only notable exception may be the Jewish population, though the lack of data on Jews precludes demonstrating this.

Under occupation, three general areas will be dealt with: employment status, occupational characteristics, and business activities. Of 47,000 Koreans who were sixteen years old or older in 1970, 75.5 percent of all males and 41.5 percent of all females were in the labor force. Interestingly, these figures are almost identical with the percentages for the total United States population and for the white population. Unemployment statistics were also similar. Due to the current recession, however, these statistics may be outdated.[21] Given this problem and that the statistics on Koreans did not reveal anything visibly atypical, we will spend no more space here on this subject.

Of all Koreans who reported an occupation when they arrived in the United States, between 1965 and 1974, 67 percent stated that they had highly skilled backgrounds in professional, technical,

Table 12—Occupational Distribution of Korean Immigrants at Time of Entry, 1965–1974, and of the United States Population in 1970

Total Population	Korean Immigrants 100%[a] (29,000)	United States 100% (80 Million)
	%	%
Professional, technical, and managerial workers	67.0	22.6
Clerical and sales workers	7.5	24.9
Craftsmen and operatives	15.1	31.9
Laborers, farm and nonfarm	1.3	7.8[b]
Service workers, including domestics	9.1	12.8

Source: U.S. Department of Justice, Immigration and Naturalization Service, *Annual Reports*, 1965–1974.

[a] This total represents 26% of all Koreans who immigrated to the United States from 1965 to 1974. The remainder either did not have an occupation or did not report one. The total figure includes housewives and children.

[b] This includes farmers and farm managers.

and managerial occupations (see Table 12). This high proportion of professional and kindred workers among Korean immigrants is one of the most salient features of the Korean American occupational pattern. It appears, however, that this proportion has recently shown a downward trend. In 1971, 73 percent reported this type of occupation, followed by increasingly smaller proportions thereafter, 64 percent in 1972, 50 percent in 1973, and 42 percent in 1974. It appears, therefore, that this unusually high proportion of professional workers is gradually giving way to other types of occupations.

The most unfortunate aspects of the analysis of occupational characteristics of Korean Americans, from the researcher's standpoint, are that we only have data at the time of immigration, and that data from the census on the jobs Koreans obtained *after* they entered the United States are lacking.

Recent surveys, however, show the general tendency toward downward mobility to be of considerable significance for professional and managerial workers. These mobility patterns among Koreans were noted by comparing the respondents' current jobs with those held previously in their home country.[22] Dorothy Cordova and Lee Ick-whan elaborate on the downward mobility among health professionals of Korean origin in the Seattle area.[23]

As Table 13 indicates, business activities by Korean Americans in this country were not prominent up to 1972, relative to other Asian groups. There were only .012 firms per capita among Korean Americans, but .030 for Japanese, and .028 for Chinese. Only the Filipinos trail behind with 0.006.

It appears that the average size of Korean establishments, indicated by dollar receipts per firm, is more or less competitive with that of Japanese and Chinese businesses, and surpasses that of Filipino firms significantly. There seems to be an urgent need for more thorough study of small entrepreneurs of Korean origin in the United States, for their numbers seem to have increased since 1972.

It is considerably more difficult to establish income characteristics than other socioeconomic features of the Korean Americans. Almost no reliable data on them exist beyond the 1970 census. Given the

Table 13—Business Ownership of Asian Americans, 1972

	Koreans	Japanese	Chinese	Filipinos
Total population[a]	103,771	597,538	470,935	394,578
Number of firms	1,021	17,837	13,070	2,237
Firms per capita	.012	.030	.028	.006
$ Receipts ($1,000)	$64,839	$1,038,887	$1,186,907	$34,641
$ Receipts per firm ($1,000)	54	58	91	15

Source: U.S. Department of Commerce, Bureau of the Census, MB 72–3.
[a]Total population of each group was computed by adding the 1970 census figure and the immigration of the group to the United States in 1971 and 1972.

heavy immigration of Koreans since 1970 and the general economic turmoil in the United States from recession, unemployment, and energy crisis, any projection based on 1970 data should be viewed with great caution.

Even from the 1970 census, data with any research utility are rare. Existing published materials are either too general or tabulated with inconsistencies which make comparison impossible. For these reasons, our discussion will be general and the analysis based on only personal income.[24]

In 1970, the income levels of Korean Americans of both sexes were close to national levels. The median income of Korean males was about $650 less than that of U.S. males in general, while that of the females exceeded their U.S. counterparts by $260.[25]

The proportion of those of both sexes earning more than $10,000 was identical with that of the United States population as a whole, although doubt remains about the differences at a higher gradation, say, about $20,000. Fewer Korean females belong to this income category than their counterparts in other Asian groups (see Table 14).

The males and females of Korean origin whose income was under $4,000 were not only more numerous than those in the total United States population but also most numerous among Asian groups. The causes and consequences of this high proportion of Korean Americans in this category merit investigation by students of minority groups.

Also, in spite of the comparable median income level between Korean Americans and the United States population, the earnings of Koreans are in fact much lower than those of the total United States population when their high proportion of college educated and professional workers is considered.

Table 15 shows that the high level of education among Korean Americans has not paid off in high incomes. This imbalance appears

Table 14—Characteristics of Personal Income of the Total United States Population and of Asian Americans, 1970[a]

	United States	Koreans	Japanese	Chinese	Filipinos
% Under $4,000					
Male	31	43	30	41	40
Female	68	81	58	65	56
% $10,000 and Over					
Male	25	25	33	24	12
Female	3	3	5	5	5

Source: U.S. Department of Commerce, Bureau of the Census, PC(1)–C1; PC(1)–D1; PC(2)–1G.
[a] Percent of persons 16 years and over.

Table 15—Ratio of Persons Earning $10,000 or More to Persons with a College Education, 1970

United States	1.4
Koreans	.8
Japanese	1.2
Chinese	.7
Filipinos	.4

Source: U.S. Department of Commerce, Bureau of the Census, PC(1)–D1; PC(2)–1G.

prevalent among Asian groups, with the notable exception of the Japanese Americans. The median years of school completed and the proportion of college graduates are, however, higher for Koreans than for other Asian groups. The imbalance, therefore, may affect a greater number of Korean Americans than of other Asian groups. The question of whether this imbalance will persist and, if it does, how it will affect the high educational aspirations of Koreans remains a research interest.

The proportion of Korean American families headed by females in 1970 was 14.7 percent, which was considerably higher than the national proportion, 10.8 percent. While few persons reported themselves as divorced, separated, or widowed at the time of immigration (see above), this high proportion of female-headed households may indicate an increased level of family instability after immigration. No definitive statements, however, can be made at present due to a lack of reliable statistics.

Female-headed families tended to have children. One-quarter of the female-headed Korean families in the metropolitan areas of Honolulu, New York, and Los Angeles had children under six years of age. Outside these areas, 47 percent had small children. This phenomenon seems to point again to the urgent need for day-care facilities.

In 1970, 43.4 percent of Korean-occupied housing units were owned by Korean Americans, a percentage comparable to that of the other Asian groups.[26] A look at Table 16 shows certain interesting features about the housing of Korean Americans.

Korean Americans tend to live in more crowded surroundings than their fellow Asians. The average number of persons per housing unit was 4.8 for Koreans. Nearly 30 percent of all Korean-occupied housing units had 1.51 persons or more per room. Other Asians appeared to live in far less crowded units.

In purchasing homes, Korean Americans seem to spend less money relative to their income than other Asians. Thirty-seven percent of Koreans owning their homes in 1970 bought them at a value less

Table 16—Housing Characteristics of Asian Americans, 1970

	Koreans	Japanese	Chinese	Filipinos
Total population[a]	98,794	586,675	433,469	336,823
All occupied housing units	20,675	167,268	120,920	89,901
% owner occupied	43.4%	56.3%	43.9%	39.3%
Persons per housing unit	4.8	3.6	3.6	3.7
% Housing units w/1.51 persons or more per room	29.9%	2.3%	8.5%	12.4%
Median household income: Urban	$8,500	$11,000	$8,900	$8,300
Rural	4,300	9,200	10,700	6,700
Housing value-income ratio:[b]				
% less than 1.5	37.0	23.0	22.0	26.0
1.5–2.4	27.0	37.0	37.0	35.0
2.5–3.9	19.0	23.0	24.0	22.0
4.0 or more	14.0	16.0	16.0	15.0
Gross rent as % of income:				
% less than 15.0	23.0	30.0	28.0	35.0
15.0–24.0	27.0	27.0	28.0	27.0
25.0–34.0	13.0	12.0	13.0	12.0
35.0 or more	25.0	22.0	24.0	18.0

Source: U.S. Department of Commerce, Bureau of the Census, HC(7)–9.
[a]This table is constructed on a 15 percent sample and thus the population figures are at about 20 percent variance with other figures from census publications.
[b]This is based on "specified" owner-occupied units, which excludes some units which did not specify the requested information. Also, this is limited to one-family homes on less than ten acres with no business on property.

than 1.5 times their annual income, while 37 percent of Japanese and Chinese and 35 percent of Filipinos bought houses at a value between 1.5 and 2.4 times their annual income. This general difference, however, may have changed considerably since 1970.

In renting houses or apartments, Koreans appear to spend more conspicuously. In 1970, 38 percent of Koreans living in rental properties were paying 25 to 35 percent or more of their income for rental fees, highest among Asian groups. The implication of this differential between the buying and renting behavior of Korean Americans should be of interest to researchers of many fields.

We have seen in this brief study that the Korean American population is one of the most rapidly expanding groups in this country. Aside from its phenomenal growth rate, this group has many unique characteristics, the investigation of which may contribute much to the field of demography in general, as well as to other branches of sociology. The disparate sex ratio, dispersed settlement, high rate of exogamy, high educational levels and other social and economic characteristics of the Korean American population lend themselves greatly to potentially fruitful research. The problem has been, and is, that the kind of reliable, detailed data needed for more refined research is not yet available. Beginning with the 1980 census, the increasing quantity and quality of information on Korean Americans will, I believe, make such potentially valuable research possible.

Notes

1.   Philip M. Hauser and Otis D. Duncan, eds., *The Study of Population* (Chicago: University of Chicago Press, 1959), p. 3.

2.   Kim Hyung-chan, "Some Aspects of Social Demography of Korean Americans," in this volume.

3.   For population trends since 1970, one must review U.S. Department of Justice, Immigration and Naturalization Service, *Annual Reports,* and scattered published reports of the Bureau of the Census. Most of these data are general and give only national, regional, and selected state trends.

4.   Even in the four-year period from fiscal year 1971 to 1974, there was a 119.2 percent increase of Korean Americans over the 1970 census figures. Also, this does not take into account Koreans born in this country.

5. At the initiative of the Bureau of the Census, an advisory committee has been formed to improve the census counting of Asian Americans in 1980. The committee started work in 1976 and it promises to make available a greater range and quality of data on Asians in the United States.

6. Department of Health, Education and Welfare, "A Study of Selected Socio-Economic Characteristics of Ethnic Minorities Based on the 1970 Census: Asian Americans," unpublished study (Arlington, Virginia: Urban Associates, 1974), p. 3.

7. Jacob S. Siegel, "Estimates of Coverage of the Population by Sex, Race and Age in the 1970 Census," paper presented at the 1973 Annual Meeting of the Population Association of America, New Orleans.

8. Bok-Lim C. Kim and Margaret E. Condon, "A Study of Asian Americans in Chicago: Their Socio-Economic Characteristics, Problems and Service Needs: Final Report" (Urbana: University of Illinois, 1975), pp. 88–92.

9. The increase from 1971 to 1974 represents the absorption of 3 percent of the net population increase in South Korea for the same period. This percentage increase did not reflect the natural increase since the immigrants arrived in the United States.

10. Additional difficulty lies in the absence of the rate by which nonimmigrants decided to stay permanently.

11. On December 13, 1975, the Seoul government stated that in 1975, 26,444 South Koreans immigrated to the United States (*Korea Week,* December 30, 1975). This group included about 4,600 wives of U.S. servicemen and about 3,500 orphans adopted by American families. Since there were 42,000 American soldiers in South Korea, this means that one out of every nine American servicemen who entered Korea for a year of duty exited with a Korean wife.

12. Kim Sil-tong, "An Analysis of Problems of Asian Wives of U.S. Servicemen," unpublished monograph (Seattle: Demonstration Project for Asian Americans, 1975), p. 28.

13. Kim Hyung-chan, "Some Aspects of Social Demography."

14. Average life expectancy in Korea in 1975 was 66 for males and 70 for females (*Korea Week,* January 15, 1976).

15. Kim and Condon, "Study of Asian Americans," p. 88.

16. Thomas Owan, "Asian American: A Case of Benign Neglect and Bilingual-Bi-cultural Service of Delivery, Implications to Spanish Speaking Americans and Native Americans," paper presented at the 1975 National Conference on Social Welfare, San Francisco.

17. Moreover, close relations have existed between the United States and the Philippines since 1898.

18. Department of Health, Education and Welfare, "Study of Characteristics of Ethnic Minorities," p. 137.

19. Kim and Condon, "Study of Asian Americans," table 3.109, p. 89.

20. Kim Sil-tong, in his "Analysis of Problems of Asian Wives," p. 16, says that these women have only 7.6 years of schooling on the average.

21. CBS News, July 2, 1975, broadcast a four-minute feature on the Korean community in Los Angeles and found that their unemployment rate was about 20 percent (*Korea Week,* September 3, 1975).

22. Kim and Condon, "Study of Asian Americans," tables 3.2–4, p. 45.

23. Dorothy L. Cordova and Lee Ick-whan, "A Study of Problems of Asian Health Professionals," unpublished monograph (Seattle: Demonstration Project for Asian Americans, 1975), pp. 43–45.

24. Family income or income of unrelated individuals would be more useful for our purpose, but data on these are unavailable.

25. These median income figures are somewhat misleading. Median income for Koreans was computed for individuals sixteen years of age and over, while those

for the U.S. were for eighteen years and over. Thus, the figures for Koreans might be a little higher. The higher income of Korean females over the U.S. females may be more a function of overtime pay, the full to part-time job continuum, and the nature of hourly wages than a reflection of a genuine difference in income for similar work. At present, however, this is merely speculation.

26.   A survey of Koreans in Chicago revealed that 88.6 percent of the respondents lived in rented houses or apartments. The figure of 43.4 percent based on a 15 percent sample in 1970 appears somewhat overestimated.

Business Development
in Koreatown, Los Angeles

David S. Kim and Charles Choy Wong

WHILE THE HISTORY of Koreans in Los Angeles dates back to 1904, the Korean community there did not begin to grow measurably until after 1970.[1] The census of that year enumerated only 9,935 Koreans in Los Angeles County and only about 70,000 for the entire United States. By 1975, however, demographic experts claimed that there were at least 60,000 in Los Angeles (community estimates reach upwards to 75,000) and 200,000 in the nation.[2] Post-1970 immigration is the principal source for this tremendous rate of increase. In just four years, over 90,000 new quota immigrants entered the United States. This figure represents only those who were actually counted by the Immigration and Naturalization Service (INS). Many were not counted, chiefly illegal aliens and Korean wives of American citizens, especially military personnel. In addition, large numbers of "nonimmigrants" are admitted to the United States each year. Many of these persons become integrated into the immigrant community during their stay in America.

The Korean settlement in Los Angeles, historically the largest in North America, grew tenfold in just the eight years following 1968. As expected, the increasing numbers swelled the ethnic community's social structure.[3] Besides immigrant businesses, there are, for example, nearly 100 nonprofit organizations such as alumni clubs and trade associations, and at least 72 Korean churches, with Protestant denominations predominant.[4] Other inviting features of the Los

Angeles area include an abundance of public and private educational institutions, low central city resident density, a freeway close to the suburban ethnic enclave, and a mild climate.

Commonly known as "Koreatown" or the "Olympic Area" by Koreans and non-Koreans alike, a five-square-mile area in central Los Angeles harbors the heart of the Korean immigrant community and its commercial life. Olympic Boulevard, a wide commercial thoroughfare, is the symbolic artery of this growing immigrant community, whose territorial boundaries are now four major roads: Wilshire Boulevard to the north, Washington Boulevard to the south, Hoover Street to the east, and Crenshaw Boulevard to the west. Because Korean businesses are playing a crucial role in the rapid development of this mushrooming Koreatown, an exploratory study of Korean businesses was undertaken.

During the summer of 1973, the Department of Health, Education and Welfare (HEW) commissioned the Korean Field Study (KFS) in the aforementioned Olympic Area.[5] In order to provide a socioeconomic outline of the Korean community, the study's major findings are briefly summarized.[6]

Koreatown is almost exclusively a post-1965 immigrant community. Seventy-five percent of the surveyed Korean population arrived after 1970, and 93 percent arrived after 1966. According to the 1970 census, Koreans comprised only 2 percent of the Olympic Area's total ethnically mixed populace of 83,855 (see Table 1). By 1975 Koreans had already become one of the major ethnic groups in the area, though no accurate statistics are available.

The two largest age groups among Koreatown residents are 25–44 years of age and under 12 years. This indicates that the largest segment of the immigrant community is composed of young couples with children. Moreover, Koreatown immigrants manifest age characteristics virtually identical to those of the population at large (see Table 2).

Korean immigrants are highly educated. A full 58 percent of

Table 1—Ethnic Population of Olympic Area, 1970

	Number	Percent
Total population	83,755	100.0
Total Asian	12,151	14.5
(Korean)	(1,706)	(2.03)
Black	23,674	28.2
Spanish surname	21,681	25.9
Other	26,249	31.4

Source: U.S. Department of Commerce, Bureau of the Census, 1970 census.

Table 2—Age Distribution of Olympic Area Koreans, 1973

Age	Sample Population (%)*	Koreans Nationwide (%)	U.S. (%)
0–4	15.3	12	8
5–11	13.6	14	14
12–17	6.2	9	12
18–24	5.1	11	12
25–44	46.6	42	24
45–64	9.9	9	20
65–99	3.2	3	10

Source: U.S. Department of Health, Education and Welfare, Korean Field Study, 1973.
*Due to calculations which include fractions, and omission of values smaller than 0.05, columns may not add up to 100 percent.

Koreans 18 and over (excluding those currently enrolled in school) have completed at least a four year college degree. For those 25–44, the proportion is even greater—83 percent for men and 54 percent for women, or an average of 70 percent. Almost all (93 percent), however, received their degrees in Korea.

Three out of every ten Koreans speak no English at all. The other 70 percent have varying degrees of English language proficiency. Of these, only about 10 percent can speak English fluently. Korean is the primary language for 98 percent of Koreatown residents.

Underemployment is both severe and ubiquitous. In 1973, one out of every three (34 percent) working Koreans was employed as a "factory operator" (a garment seamstress, for example), and of those with professional degrees, such as physicians, pharmacists, and nurses, 49 percent were working as operatives, craftsmen, or salespeople. Only 25 percent were working in professional or semiprofessional capacities. The situation is even worse for those professionally qualified in the liberal arts, teachers, for example; only 7 percent were able to secure the kind of employment for which they were trained.

Unemployment is growing. The KFS found a 12 percent unemployment rate in the summer of 1973. By 1974, a Los Angeles mayor's report estimated the rate had increased to 18 percent.

The 1970 census described the Olympic Area as an economically very depressed neighborhood. While the Los Angeles-Long Beach Standard Metropolitan Statistical Area (SMSA) mean family income in 1970 was $10,300, the Olympic Area's mean family income was only $6,190. In 1973 the median household income for Koreans was between $582 and $594 a month. This is 17 percent below the $708 median level for the Los Angeles-Long Beach SMSA, based three years before on the 1970 census.

Thus, the Koreatown socioeconomic profile is one of recently immigrated, young, highly educated, language handicapped, under or unemployed, and low-income characteristics. The characteristics of Korean businessmen, as revealed in a survey administered to key business organizations and individuals, are virtually identical to those of the Olympic Area population at large. They are almost all post-1968 arrivals, under 40 years old, highly educated, and low in English language proficiency.

While earlier Asian immigrants were mostly of rural laboring backgrounds with little education and few technical skills, the Korean immigrants of today are of urban upbringing, college educated, and highly skilled. According to the Immigration and Naturalization Service, of all Koreans reporting an occupation upon entry into the United States between 1965 and 1973, almost three-fourths (72 percent) stated that they were professional, technical, or managerial workers back home.[6] This is the highest ratio among any of the post-1965 Asian immigrant groups (see Table 3). Consistent with this finding are the KFS and 1970 census data.

Yet many Koreans soon find themselves in menial, dead-end, low-paying secondary labor market jobs, or worse, no jobs at all.[7] In the face of their high aspirations, Koreans become intensely dissatisfied and frustrated and search eagerly for other avenues of mobility. They turn toward self-employment as the only means available for personal economic advancement.[8]

The reasons behind Korean self-employment are poverty due to underemployment and unemployment, institutionalized discrimination in licensing and hiring practices, and unfamiliarity with the English language. These conditions erect almost insurmountable barriers to the securing of jobs commensurate with Koreans' expectations and training. Testifying before the U.S. Civil Rights Commission in late 1974, Kuk Yŏng-il, vice-president of the Korean-American Political Association of Southern California, articulated the dire problem of status inconsistency, which has grown to alarming proportions:

> The Korean American community in Los Angeles would benefit not just from their [professional] services. If they are allowed to work with dignity in the profession of their training—instead of as restaurant busboys or gardeners' assistants—and to earn standard wages for their work, they would be in a position to give our community additional strength and leadership. This is important to all of us.[9]

In the meantime, while they are trying to eke out a living at one, or perhaps two, jobs, little time is left to devote to English classes and licensure examination classes, where permitted. The barrier encountered by Korean pharmacists is especially immense.

Table 3—Occupational Distribution of Asian Immigrants: 1965-1973 At Time of Entry

	Japan	China, Taiwan, and Hong Kong	Philippines	Korea
	(%)	(%)	(%)	(%)
All immigrants reporting an occupation	100	100*	100	100
Professional, technical and managerial workers	53	50	69	72
Clerical and sales workers	17	11	8	7
Craftsmen and operatives	8	16	6	12
Laborers, nonfarm workers	2	2	2	1
Service workers including domestics	17	2	9	8
Farm-related managers and workers	3	0.2	6	—
% of all immigrants with no occupation or not reporting an occupation (includes housewives and children)	75	63	55	73

Source: U.S. Department of Health, Education and Welfare, *A Study of Selected Socio-Economic Characteristics of Ethnic Minorities Based on the 1970 Census*, vol. 2, *Asian Americans* (Washington, D.C.: Government Printing Office, 1974), pp. 91, 141.
*As reported to author.

Foreign-trained pharmacists are not even allowed to take the California examination for licensure. According to the Korean Pharmacists Association of California, there are at least 300 experienced Korean pharmacists in Southern California alone. Yi Kong-mu, vice-president of the association, voices the angry frustration of all his colleagues:

> We never expected to lose our profession at the same time as we immigrated to this beautiful and wonderful country. Today, most of us find ourselves in a job which is inconsistent with our qualifications and experience. We are suffering from starvation wages.[10]

In actuality, then, the reasons for Korean entry into entrepreneurship ironically belie the idealistic precepts of American equality. For the majority of entrepreneurs today, whether native born or immigrant, self-employment is the calculated adaptive response most typically resorted to in the face of overt or institutional barriers blocking participation in the primary labor market. Immigrants do not go into business because they initially wanted to, but because they have no other viable occupational alternative in American society which will enable them to advance economically. This is clearly evident in the occupational mobility pattern of earlier Asian immigrants. First generation immigrants were frequently self-employed, while white-collar professional and technical employment was typical of the second and third generations.[11]

An extremely high proportion, 15 percent, of the Korean labor force is engaged in some form of self-employment.[12] This is 50 percent greater than the proportion of Chinese or the national average. Also, because most Korean enterprises, such as garment factories, maintenance companies, newspaper and other mass media, and food-related enterprises, employ other Koreans, the actual proportion of Koreans deriving their livelihood from Korean-owned businesses (in either operator or wage earner capacity) should be very high indeed.

Small business success is extremely problematic, however, in this advanced stage of corporate monopoly capitalism. Regardless of ethnic ownership, statistics show that one out of three new retail businesses fails within its first year and two out of three fail within six years.[13] Despite these figures, however, Small Business Administration officials, bank officials, and Korean businessmen alike agree that Koreans have been unusually successful in small business so far. Koreans are evidently succeeding even in the ghetto of central Los Angeles where many others have failed.

To obtain as comprehensive and accurate a listing and plotting of Korean-owned businesses in the Olympic Area as possible, a lengthy five-step procedure was utilized:

First, a list of Korean businesses located in the vicinity of the

Olympic Area was compiled mainly from the *Korean Business Directory* issued by the Los Angeles branch of the *Korean Times,* and from a few other minor sources.

Second, a complete listing of all businesses (not just Korean ones) located in the vicinity of the Olympic Area was made, utilizing the telephone directory, Haines Directory, and others. Two Korean real estate firms situated within the Olympic Area identified Korean businesses that they knew of.

Third, street by street visual verification of the list compiled from steps one and two was conducted. During this process, many new businesses were added, and some defunct ones were eliminated from the list.

Fourth, verification by telephone of those businesses that could not be verified by field observation was then conducted.

Fifth, the final list resulting from steps one through four was plotted on a map. The map and final list were updated to March 1975.

To obtain details concerning Korean firms, questionnaire interviews were administered to key informants who possessed acknowledged expertise on Olympic Area Korean business activities. Their names were raised in consultation with the Korean Chamber of Commerce and the Korean Town Development Association, two major organizations concerned with Korean business development. Our key informants included certified public accountants, insurance agents, real estate agents, and a number of other individuals representing a variety of public and private agencies. There were twenty-six in all.

By 1975, the number of Korean-operated businesses had visibly risen throughout Los Angeles. The largest concentration was in a three-mile stretch along Olympic Boulevard between Hoover Street and Crenshaw Boulevard. Lining either side of the broad thoroughfare are a multitude of Korean firms serving both ethnic and neighborhood needs. Symbolic of the extent of Korean commercial success, Cooke Sunoo observes, "Hardly a week goes by without the 'grand opening' of a new storefront with *han'gul* (Korean alphabet) signs proclaiming grocery stores, restaurants, barbershops, hamburger stands, gas stations, or other small business."[14] Indeed, on a few blocks along the stretch, bright red *han'gul* characters oversee every single establishment.

As noted above, Koreatown is generally accepted as the area bounded by Hoover Street, Crenshaw Boulevard, Washington Boulevard, and Wilshire Boulevard.[15] In constructing the Korean business map, however, a much larger area was first surveyed and investigated in order to determine the "exact" boundaries of concentrated Korean firms (see above). At present, Korean firms extend far beyond the previously recognized Wilshire Boulevard limit northward to Beverly Boulevard. On the other hand, southward expansion seems unlikely due to many factors which collectively create an unfavorable business climate. First, there is no migratory flow of existing Korean residents and merchants to the south as there is to the north. Second, the south harbors a smaller concentration of Koreans, less attractive land characteristics, and a lower socioeconomic environment than the north. Third, the south fosters a higher crime rate and, hence, higher insurance rates than the north.

The two other areas of Korean business concentration are smaller, but almost equally noticeable. One is located northwest of the Olympic Area, around Alvarado Street and Wilshire Boulevard. The other is along the Crenshaw Shopping Center.

A total of 278 Korean-owned firms were enumerated within the new Olympic Area. This deliberately represents a very conservative count because only those firms actually verified were included. For example, only one garment factory was verified. There are certainly many more Korean-owned garment shops in Koreatown. Korean subcontractors themselves estimate there are between fifty and one hundred Korean-owned shops in the city of Los Angeles. Also, some businesses located inside large office buildings, particularly along Wilshire Boulevard, were inevitably missed. The verified 278 firms were analyzed according to three separate dimensions: business types, according to retail and service fields and mode of business management; business location, according to subareas and streets; business operations, according to the number of employees, total assets, annual sales, and initial source of business capital.

Initially, the firms were dichotomized into retail and service-oriented categories. The largest type by far was food-related enterprises with 85, followed by professional and semiprofessional services with 61. These two classifications alone constitute over half (53 percent) of all Korean businesses in the investigated area. While it might be expected that food-related firms would be the predominant minority enterprises, due to ethnic-demand and low capital investment requirements, it was not anticipated that the professional and semi-professional service sector would make up 22 percent of all Korean-owned firms and 40 percent of all service-oriented firms. Such large numbers of physicians, lawyers, real estate agents, CPAs, insurance agents, and travel agents can only suggest the fluid and increasing supply of capital in the young immigrant community. The large number of service personnel can be attributed to the immigrants' English language handicaps, comfort in dealing with fellow countrymen who understand the immigrants' frame of reference, and possibly lower charges for the services rendered (see Table 4 for a breakdown of all Korean businesses).

Second, the 278 firms were analyzed in terms of small versus big business. By small business is meant only those enterprises that permit the personalized management of the business by the owner-operator. This definition eliminates institutionalized forms of management such as bureaucratic structures and makes no reference to the size or volume of the particular business. Instead, the definition emphasizes the responsibility of the owner-operator as the determining criterion. A review of Table 4 strongly complements the field observation that regardless of the type of business, the vast majority of Korean enterprises are small businesses.

The itemized profile of Korean businesses presented above clearly supports prior field observations that Central Olympic, with 133 firms, is the center of the Olympic Area, having both the widest range and the greatest number of firms. Located in the heart of the immigrant settlement are a profusion of authentic Korean restaurants and the largest concentration of Korean-oriented enterprises. A modified variant model of "concentric zone" expansion is indicated.[16] West Olympic, with the second highest number of businesses, more than any other subarea resembles Central Olympic. Wilshire Boulevard stands out ostentatiously as a high rent, high-rise commercial district with its large proportion of professional and semiprofessional firms. Upper Olympic, being farthest from the center of the Korean community, is dominated by American-oriented and food-related enterprises.

The 278 firms were distributed mostly along twelve streets, and the characteristics of the streets generally reflected the characteristics of the subareas in which the firms were located. Nevertheless, the streets housing the most Korean-oriented enterprises, ranked in order, were Olympic Boulevard, Western Avenue, 8th Street, Wilshire Boulevard, Pico Boulevard, and Vermont Avenue (see Table 5 for a breakdown of businesses by street).

Specific data concerning the number of employees, total assets, annual sales, and initial source of capital of 51 Korean-owned firms in the Olympic Area were obtained from our key informants. The authors do not suggest that these 51 firms provide a nonbiased representation of the 278 firms. The fact that such sensitive and specific data were ascertained at all is noteworthy. The following tables should be interpreted as providing useful information in evaluating and augmenting field observations.

Table 6 shows that 88 percent of the 51 firms have 10 or fewer employees and that 69 percent have 5 or fewer. This strongly confirms ethnographic observations that most Korean enterprises are small

Table 4—Number of Korean Businesses According to Categories

Retail trade

Grocery and related retail	40
Market	28
Liquor stores	10
Drugstores	2
Hardware-type retail	36
Electronics and appliances	8
Car dealers, sales and service	4
Sewing machines, sales and service	3
Office supplies, furniture	4
Gas stations	12
Other	5
Software-type retail	16
Wig stores	10
Shoe stores	3
Clothing stores	3
Other retail	9
Gift and jewelry stores	5
Books, stationery stores	2
Sporting goods stores	1
Other	1
Wholesale and trading companies	24
Wig wholesalers	6
Grocery wholesalers	3
Other	15

Service trade

Food and entertainment services	42
Restaurants	18
Coffee shops	3
Hamburger stands, donut shops	11
Nightclubs and bars	10
Semiprofessional services	32
Travel	14
Insurance	8
Real estate	8
Business consultants	2
Professional services	29
CPA, accounting, income tax	10
Physicians, dentists	13
Lawyers, architects	2
Herbalist, acupuncturist	4
Small scale services	26
Photography, art studio, gallery	6
Printing	5
Beauty shops	5
Shoe repair	4
Barbershops	2
Other	4

Table 4—*Continued*

Large scale services	10
Maintenance	4
Garage	2
Garment manufacturer	1
Other	3
Schools	9
Driving, music, language	5
Martial arts	4
Newspaper, television, theater	5

Table 5—Korean Businesses by Street

Street	Number of Businesses
Olympic Blvd	54
Western Avenue	42
8th Street	34
Wilshire Blvd	29
Pico Blvd	29
Vermont Avenue	26
3rd Street	11
Washington Blvd	10
6th Street	7
Beverly Blvd	6
Crenshaw Blvd	5
Venice Blvd	5

Table 6—Korean-Owned Firms in Olympic Area by Number of Employees

Number of Employees	Retail Firms	Service Firms	Subtotal
1–5	24	11	35
6–10	2	8	10
11–15	2	1	3
16–20	0	1	1
21–25	1	0	1
26–30	0	0	0
31–40	0	0	0
41–50	0	1	1
Total	29	22	51

in size and often employ unpaid family labor.

Table 7 shows that 82 percent of the 51 firms have assets of less than $50,000. Even more significant is the fact that over half (57 percent) have assets of less than $20,000. This supports the hypothesis that Korean successions of businesses start from enterprises requiring little capital, little English language ability, and little managerial expertise. Thus, for example, grocery stores and wig stores

Table 7—Korean-Owned Firms in Olympic Area, by Total Assets

Total Assets	Retail Firms	Service Firms	Subtotal
Under $20,000	17	12	29
20,000–50,000	6	7	13
50,000–100,000	5	2	7
200,000–300,000	1	1	2
Total	29	22	51

are often stepping-stones to restaurants, import trading companies, and other larger enterprises.

Table 8 shows that the mean annual sales of retail and service firms together is $283,000, and that the median is at the lower end of the $100,000 category. Of course, there is no necessarily direct relationship between gross sales and net income. Unless the commodity is an especially expensive item, turnover is the key to profit-making in any business. The preceding three tables together suggest that the typical Korean immigrant enterprise has a relatively high sales volume or turnover, employs a very small labor force, and occupies a small physical site which is leased or rented. Classic examples of such Korean businesses are the numerous wig shops, grocery stores, and eating places.

The predominant source of initial capital, according to our informants, was the entrepreneur's savings. Tied for distant second were loans from the Small Business Administration (SBA) and American banks. SBA records indicate that over 100 loans were consigned to Koreans in Los Angeles County between 1971 and 1974, with a combined amount of over $10 million. Table 9 shows that while food-related enterprises accounted for two-thirds of the loans ($6,106,550), the largest single loans were made to garment manufacturers, suggesting large-scale operations. Altogether, the SBA data testify to the importance Koreans place upon SBA as a source of initial capital.

Thus, Korean immigrant businesses are begun with capital that is either brought from overseas or with savings derived methodically from wage labor in the United States. The rest, if needed, is typically obtained from institutional sources such as the SBA, at lower interest rates than from commercial banks. Indeed, SBA and American bank officials consider Koreans low risks precisely because they already have a sizeable amount of their own money invested in the business. According to these officials and Korean businessmen alike, Koreans so far are more successful in business enterprises than any other ethnic group, even though most Korean immigrants have very little or no prior experience in business.[17] The reason for this extraordinary success rate in small business is, however, beyond the defined scope of this exploratory study.[18]

Table 8—Annual Sales Volume

Sales Volume	Retail and Service Detailed Data		Categorical Data from Trade Associations	Wholesale and Trading	Total
	Retail Firms	Service Firms			
$ 0–5,000		1			1
20,000–30,000		1			1
30,000–40,000	4				4
40,000–50,000	1			1	2
50,000–60,000	1		21		22
60,000–70,000	5	5		1	11
70,000–80,000		2	4	3	9
80,000–100,000		4		16	20
100,000–250,000	4	6	18	18	46
250,000–500,000	9	3	68	26	106
500,000–1 mill.	4			24	28
1 mill.–2.5 mill.				7	7
2.5 mill.–5 mill.	1			2	3
Over 5 million				2	2
Total	29	22	111	100	262

Table 9—Number and Amount of Korean Loans from Small Business Administration, 1971–1974

Business Category	Total Number in Each Category	Total Amount in Each Category
Liquor store	33	$ 2,850,550
Markets	18	1,713,400
Restaurant, Hamburger stand, Coffee shop, Donut shop, other	15	1,542,600
Garment manufacturing	5	2,260,600
Trading companies	4	660,000
Other service	14	346,000
Other retail	12	995,600
Total	101	$10,368,750

In summary, Olympic Area Korean businesses are mostly small and service enterprises outnumber retail enterprises. Moreover, the businesses are limited in scope and food-related, professional, and semiprofessional businesses dominate.

From the analysis of the location of Korean businesses, it is evident that the Olympic Area does not have a single uniform character throughout, but rather incorporates six identifiable commercial subareas. Central Olympic is the center of the Olympic Area and best represents the emergent Koreatown. The characteristics of the other subareas, however, reveal more complex aspects of the Olympic Area and provide the basis for better understanding of future commercial and community growth and direction.

From our key informants, important facts emerge. Businesses bought most often are grocery stores, liquor stores, hamburger stands, gas stations, and wig stores. Korean businesses that advertise most are markets, restaurants, nightclubs, jewelers, travel agencies, electronics firms, and to a lesser degree, insurance agencies. Businesses that are highly competitive but do not advertise much are garment factories, janitorial firms, wig wholesaling firms, and printing shops. Tables 6, 7, and 8 suggest that most Korean businesses rely upon high commodity turnover, low capital investment, and labor-intensive requirements for their business entry and success.

A comparison of Korean business development with earlier Chinese and Japanese immigrant experience can provide valuable insights into Koreatown's future directions. In the face of occupational barriers, all three Asian groups turned toward self-employment in large numbers. For the Chinese, the most prevalent enterprises were restaurants, laundries, grocery stores, import/export enterprises, and garment factories. For the Japanese, vegetable farming, gardening, grocery stores, and import/export enterprises were most numerous.

Both subsequently developed Chinatown and Little Tokyo tourism as a part of their ethnic subeconomies.

A review of post-1965 Korean occupational adjustment in Los Angeles reveals a similar pattern of immigrant small business development. The first Korean businesses to be established after 1965 were the import/export firms. They were all small operations with their trade limited to the United States and Korea. Gradually, Korean restaurants and grocery stores sprang up throughout the Olympic Area. About 1970, there suddenly emerged a mushrooming of wholesalers and retailers. Local Koreans quickly took advantage of the fact that Korea had become the principal supplier of the world's wig market. At hand was a ready-made vertical structure from manufacturing, to wholesaling, to retailing. The peak period of the local wig boom was 1973. More recently, Korean business acuity has taken advantage of the oil crisis by developing gas station dealerships. Steady and growing demand for gasoline, coupled with limited supplies, resulted in high profit margins for both oil corporations and their local franchisers.

By 1975, the *Korean Directory of Southern California* alone listed over 1,300 Korean-owned firms, the majority of which were aimed at a Korean clientele. By 1975 the most prevalent businesses were wig shops, restaurants, grocery stores, liquor stores, gas stations, maintenance companies, and a variety of other ethnic-demand and community-at-large enterprises. The total number of Korean-owned businesses in Los Angeles is simply not accurately known.

As with Chinatown and Little Tokyo, the specific direction of Koreatown development will be largely determined by the interests and policies of the Korean merchant class. At present, there are a number of competing development plans. The first plan, sponsored by the Korean Community Development Corporation (KCDC), calls for a high-density, centralized commercial and residential complex. If eventually implemented, this development would be similar to San Francisco's Japan Trade Center. The other major plan, sponsored by the Korean Town Development Association (KTDA), envisions a looser and more decentralized structure with emphasis on gradual development of the Olympic Area. Thus, even at this incipient stage of Koreatown development, the lines and factions of community interests are already being drawn.

Notes

1. Helen Lewis Givens, "The Korean Community in Los Angeles County" (M.A. thesis, University of Southern California, 1939); Kim Hyung-chan and Wayne Patterson, eds., *The Koreans in America, 1882–1974* (Dobbs Ferry, New York: Oceana Publications, 1974); Warren Y. Kim (Kim Wǒn-yong), *Koreans in America* (Seoul: Po Chin Chae, 1971); Lee Kyung, "Settlement Patterns of Los Angeles Koreans" (M.A. thesis, University of California, Los Angeles, 1969); John A. Thames, "Korean Students in Southern California: Factors Influencing their Plans Returning Home" (M.A. thesis, University of Southern California, 1971).

2. Yu Ǔi-yǒng, "A Comment on the Number of Koreans in the 1970 U.S. Census of Population" (Los Angeles: Korean Student Association of Southern California, 1974), pp. 35–36.

3. David Lee, "Organizational Activities of Korean Community" (M.A. thesis, University of California, Los Angeles, 1974).

4. Korean Association of Southern California, *The Korean Directory of Southern California, 1975* (Los Angeles: Key's Printing, 1975), pp. 276–79, 312–18.

5. The survey excluded the newly expanded area between Wilshire Boulevard and Beverly Boulevard, which we now include as part of the Olympic Area.

6. Department of Health, Education and Welfare, "Korean Field Study, Los Angeles, 1973" (Washington, D.C.: Government Printing Office, forthcoming).

7. Peter B. Doeringer, ed., *Programs to Employ the Disadvantaged* (Englewood Cliffs, New Jersey: Prentice-Hall, 1969), pp. 245–61.

8. The authors are aware of nonmonetary factors of self-employment. We are suggesting, nonetheless, that economic considerations are of primary importance in the case of Korean immigrants. Although illegal occupational pursuits are another alternative, penalties are especially serious for aliens.

9. U.S. Civil Rights Commission, "A Dream Unfulfilled: Korean and Filipino Health Professionals in California" (Washington, D.C.: Government Printing Office, 1975), p. 18.

10. U.S. Civil Rights Commission, "A Dream Unfulfilled," p. 18.

11. See, for example, Harry H.L. Kitano, *Japanese Americans: Evolution of a Subculture* (New York: Prentice-Hall, 1969); Gene Levine and Darrell Montero, "Socioeconomic Mobility Among Three Generations of Japanese Americans," *Journal of Social Issues* 29:2 (1973): 33–48; Ivan H. Light, *Ethnic Enterprise in America: Business and Welfare among Chinese, Japanese, and Blacks* (Berkeley: University of California Press, 1972); Betty L. Sung, *Mountain of Gold* (New York: Macmillan, 1967), later entitled *The Story of the Chinese in America* (New York: Collier Books, 1967).

12. *New Korea*, May 29, 1975.

13. Clifford M. Baumback et al., *How to Organize and Operate a Small Business*, 5th ed. (Englewood Cliffs, New Jersey: Prentice-Hall, 1973), p. 22.

14. Cooke Sunoo, "Koreans in Los Angeles: Employment and Education," *The*

New Americans Education and Employment Assistance Act Hearings (Washington, D.C.: Government Printing Office, 1974), p. 183.

15. See, for example, Cooke, "Koreans in Los Angeles"; Lee, "Organizational Activities of Korean Community."

16. Noel Gist and Sylvia Fava, *Urban Society*, 5th ed. (New York: Thomas Y. Crowell, 1964), pp. 95–117.

17. Data are from personal interviews.

18. The first step toward an analysis of Koreatown business development is a descriptive profile which establishes the basis for the second step, explaining differential business success. The authors are pursuing the latter research problem.

Notes on the Availability of Materials for the Study of Korean Immigrants in the United States

Arthur L. Gardner

THE CONFLUENCE WITHIN the past decade of interest by the United States in its own ethnicity and in the history and culture of its minority groups, and of steady and growing immigration from Korea under the provisions of the October 1965 immigration act has certainly stimulated academic interest in the almost three-quarters of a century old Korean American community. In pursuing this interest, however, even the most enterprising scholar finds himself confronted by obstacles to successful research. Unfortunately, Koreans are among the Asians described by Roger Daniels in a bibliographical essay on the views of American historians toward East Asian immigrants as having had "little of a historical nature published about them" and about whom "there is, as yet, no substantial literature to analyze."[1] While some helpful studies have recently been published and others are in progress at present, it is generally true that the search for an accurate account of the Korean American community's past is hampered by the paucity of reliable source materials upon which sound analysis and interpretation can be based.

The attempt here is not so much to systematically cover the entire field as to share information gained through the experience of searching for materials to be included in *The Koreans in Hawaii: An Annotated Bibliography.*[2] This work has apparently begun to serve its intended purpose of directing others to materials of possible assistance to them as they assemble data which will reveal the process

247

by which Koreans adjusted to and left their mark on American life. Implicit in the identification of certain materials available in Hawaii is the suggestion that, in other areas where Koreans have settled in considerable numbers, similar kinds of information could be tracked down and utilized.

The reasons for the dearth of primary materials and systematic records about Korean Americans are not hard to identify. The total Korean community in the United States, at least until very recently, has never been large. About 7,000 immigrants arrived in Hawaii in the short period of organized immigration between 1902 and 1905, and about half of them almost immediately moved to the United States mainland, settling predominantly in California but in various other states as well. Honolulu and Los Angeles were the only centers of any eventual concentration. Additions to the community, except through natural increase, were few. A number of students and political refugees were admitted; wives came to join Koreans already resident here; a number of Korean women who married Americans during and after the Korean War entered the country in the 1950s and 1960s. It has only been in the last decade that Korean communities have mushroomed in Los Angeles, Washington, D.C., New York, and a few other places. Until recently, then, the number of Koreans in any particular place was too small to permit the degree of cultural and social impact other immigrant groups have made.

Despite their relatively small numbers, Korean Americans have never been a united body of people mingling together in associations which enjoyed total community support. From early in their history, they were divided along political and, to a lesser extent, denominational lines. This has tended to inject a degree of partisan opinion into much that has been published by and about Koreans. Accordingly, scholars who work with the records that have been preserved must clearly understand the various currents of ideology and belief that Korean Americans became caught up in from time to time. The subjugation of Korea by the Japanese between 1905 and 1945 gave rise to a virulent nationalism on the part of Koreans, which expressed itself in a variety of movements to regain independence, several of which were based in the United States. Not only this drive for independence, but the factional struggles between contending bodies promoting different means to attain that independence drained the energies and the finances of two generations of Korean Americans and helped subvert any serious systematic recording of the process of adaptation to American society.

Reference works helpful to those who do undertake a study of Korean Americans include my *The Koreans in Hawaii*, already referred to, which contains items that relate to the entire Korean American community as well as those relating specifically to Koreans in Hawaii; *Asian Americans: An Annotated Bibliography,* compiled by Harry H.L. Kitano with E. Jung, C. Tanaka, and B. Wong; and *Asians in America: A Bibliography of Master's Theses and Doctoral Dissertations,* compiled by William Wong Lum.[3] A published account of proven value is Kim Wŏn-yong's (Warren Y. Kim) *Chae-Mi Hanin osimnyŏn-sa* [Fifty-year history of the Koreans in America], which is more a chronology than a true history.[4] Although comprehensive and containing a great deal of helpful information, few sources are given for the information provided, and verification becomes a major problem. Kim was intimately involved in various Korean community activities and writes from this background, but his work betrays a partisanship which makes verification important on many points. An abridged English-language version of this work appeared in Seoul in 1971 under the title *Koreans in America.*[5] Another basic chronology is the two volume work by No Chae-yŏn, *Chae-Mi Hanin saryak* [A concise history of Koreans in America], also written in Korean.[6] While again no sources of information are provided, the entries seem quite reliable and appear to be drawn largely from the newspaper *Shinhan Minbo* (see below). A more recent chronology, covering the period from 1882 to 1974, is that by Kim Hyung-chan and Wayne Patterson.[7] This volume also includes a section of useful documents.

An unpublished work that has been widely used by those writing on Korean Americans up to this time is the master's thesis of Bernice B.H. Kim, "The Koreans in Hawaii," submitted in 1937 to the sociology department of the University of Hawaii. Data collected at that time, through extensive fieldwork and interviews, are still extremely valuable, but the work was never intended to be a historical study and its usefulness as such is limited. The main purpose of the study was to examine the adjustment of Korean immigrants to the American social and economic environment and the effects of that adjustment on individuals and the group. Those interested in studying the adaptation process and its problems in the larger perspective might find Judith Rubano's *Culture and Behaviour in Hawaii: An Annotated Bibliography* helpful both for information and for ideas.[8] Those who want to study the Koreans as part of the immigration to the United States by East Asians in general should refer to the previously mentioned essay by Roger Daniels, "American Historians and East Asian Immigrants," for the best published material available.

Recent years have seen the publication of several articles in English on Korean Americans which, unlike the majority of occasional pieces printed in former years, appear to have been soundly researched and are meticulously referenced. The emergence of true scholarship is apparent in the authors' careful analysis and preliminary steps toward interpretation.[9] A growing number of theses and dissertations on the topic are also appearing but few subsequently find their way into print. Kim and Patterson refer to several of these in their introduction and bibliography, and several others have recently been published by R. and E. Research Associates of San Francisco.[10] This company openly solicits scholarly studies on immigration, accultura- tion, and ethnic minorities fields, and anyone with serious interest in this area should have his name added to the company's mailing list for information relating to new publications. For those who read Korean, a growing number of full-length works and journal articles are appearing in publications in the Republic of Korea and should not be overlooked.[11]

The best source of continuous information about the Korean community in the United States from its beginning to the present is undoubtedly the newspaper, *Shinhan Minbo* (New Korea). Although published first in San Francisco then in Los Angeles and primarily serving those communities' needs, the paper has always given attention to developments in the Korean communities in Hawaii and in other parts of the country. Through all these years the paper has remained the official organ of the Korean National Association (Kungmin-hoe) on the U.S. mainland, but has not exhibited the extreme partisan nature of some of the periodicals and newspapers published in Hawaii, where political divisions were more intense. When the Korean National Association was organized, on February 1, 1909, to unite most of the smaller Korean organizations in Hawaii and North America, it established its first headquarters in San Francisco. Two newspapers published there at that time, *Kongnip Sinbo* (Public News) and *Taedong Kongbo* (Great Unity News) were absorbed. *Shinhan Minbo* sees itself as the successor to *Kongnip Sinbo* and still prints on its masthead as the date of its establishment November 22, 1905, the date of the first issue of *Kongnip Sinbo*. The newspaper is predominantly in Korean but since 1937 has printed portions of its content in English. The most complete holdings of the paper are in the possession of the Korean National Association in Los Angeles. All issues of *Kongnip Sinbo* and *Shinhan Minbo* are there except for those published in 1948.[12] The collection has been microfilmed and is available in that form to the researcher located in other than the Los Angeles area. Unfortunately, there is no index to the newspaper and this impedes efficient use. This is an obvious need which will, it is hoped, be filled in the near future.

There is no file for other newspapers comparable to that available for *Shinhan Minbo*. *Kungmin-bo* (Korean National Herald) was published in Honolulu from 1913 until late 1968, when support for a Korean-language newspaper proved insufficient to warrant further financial investment by the Korean National Association in Hawaii, for which the paper had long served as official organ. Despite the major influence of the paper through its fifty-five-year history, the surviving holdings are meager. The Honolulu headquarters of the Korean National Association has preserved a continuous file only from January 1942. *T'aep'yŏngyang Chubo* (Korean Pacific Weekly), published by the Tongji-hoe, an organization which generally competed with the Korean National Association for the loyalties of Hawaii's Koreans, has suffered little better fate. As the official organ of Tongji-hoe, it appeared regularly from December 1930 until February 6, 1970, and the issues from 1939 through 1941 and from December 1949 until termination of publication, as well as a few other random issues, are preserved at the society's Honolulu headquarters.[13] As in the case of *Shinhan Minbo,* there is no index to either of these papers. From January 1942 to February 1944, the two rival newspapers were jointly published, as a wartime exigency, using the combined title *Korean National Herald-Pacific Weekly.*

The concentration of Koreans in Honolulu and their accompanying impact on the Territory (later state) of Hawaii, which has long accentuated its own ethnic diversity, makes the files of the *Honolulu Advertiser* and other Hawaii newspapers of particular interest to the researcher.[14] Similarly useful information, though probably to a lesser extent, should be traceable in newspapers in mainland urban areas such as San Francisco and Los Angeles, where Koreans were organizationally active. Recent years have seen a proliferation of newspapers in both Korean and English published to supply the real or imagined needs of the contemporary Korean community in the United States. Many of these have a very limited circulation and few, if any, are indexed. All of them will certainly contain some information of value to anyone researching contemporary patterns and attitudes within the Korean community. In newspapers in Korea itself, references to Koreans abroad have naturally appeared from time to time. *Hwangsŏng Shinmun* (The Imperial Palace News) published in Seoul from 1898 to 1910, is being reissued in facsimile form and could supply some interesting references to early emigration. Of the other papers, *Tong-a Ilbo* (East Asia Daily) has been most continuously in operation and has the advantage of partial indexing.

United States census reports published by the Bureau of the Census are a basic source for statistics on social organization, including comparative racial and ethnic statistics. The chief difficulty in tracing continuous statistical data on Korean Americans is that after being identified as a distinct ethnic category for the censuses of 1910, 1920, and 1930, Koreans were from 1940 included in the "all others" category in ethnic breakdowns. The only exceptions were for certain data collected in Hawaii. Due to the rapid increase in the number of Koreans being admitted to the country as immigrants after 1965, they were again listed as a separate ethnic group in the 1970 census reports. Annual reports by the Immigration and Naturalization Service are the other major source for continuous statistical data relating to Koreans in the United States. If the present rate of immigration from Korea continues or accelerates, the statistical breakdowns for those states to which large numbers of Koreans are gravitating, such as California, Hawaii, Virginia, Maryland, and New York, should prove increasingly enlightening. While Hawaii was still a territory of the United States, federal organizations such as the Department of Commerce and Labor and the Department of the Interior periodically published statistics relating to the labor force, movement to and from the mainland, school population and educational status, and so forth. Boards established for internal administration by the territory published their own rather complete statistical reports also, and the state of Hawaii continues that practice today.[15]

Unpublished materials present their own special problems, not the least of which are difficulties of locating and access. Of potential value but difficult as yet to accurately assess are the archives of organizations which have played important roles in the Korean community in the past. Most of these organizations are now struggling for survival and undergoing a serious reevaluation of their role in the contemporary Korean community.[16] In my efforts to locate materials for inclusion in *The Koreans in Hawaii*, I was eventually given sufficient access to the archives of most organizations in Hawaii to at least determine the extent and nature of materials being preserved. It was a rather discouraging experience. The records were generally quite inadequately housed with no systematic arrangement at all. I was able to do little more than describe as accurately as I could the various items in the collections. There is urgent need for these materials to be not only preserved but arranged and indexed in such a way that anyone doing research could have access to those records relevant to their inquiry. Unfortunately, the present financial situation of the societies and, to a lesser extent, their program priorities make unlikely the initiation of this task from within the organizations themselves. They are now largely dependent on volunteer help, and in some cases their present interests have become divorced from the historical background out of which they emerged. Until this work is done, however, the records remain unproven potential rather than a confirmed resource for scholars.

Religion, particularly the Christian religion, played a major role in the lives of the early Korean immigrant communities. The church buildings served as much more than locations for religious activities. They were social centers, political arenas, and educational institutions for the community. A great deal of organizational fragmentation occurred through the years, often because of the American parent denomination's lack of sympathy for perpetuating the ethnically distinctive congregation. Many of the splinter organizations failed to survive. The files of the Korean churches in Hawaii yielded such things as business meeting and conference minutes, annual congregational and committee reports, membership records and directories, records of births, baptisms, marriages and deaths, financial records, some historical sketches, and assorted programs and bulletins.[17] The archives of the national headquarters for the United Methodist church, which assumed pastoral care for the bulk of the early Koreans in Hawaii subsequent to an agreement worked out with the Hawaiian Mission Board in 1905, might well yield further helpful information.

The identification of so many of the first Korean immigrants with the sugar plantations in Hawaii suggests a careful search through plantation records. Many of the old plantations are no longer operating and their files are presumably kept at the Hawaiian Sugar Planters' Association library in Honolulu. This is a private institution and access to all holdings cannot be presumed. Probably little information relative to Koreans is included in the older company files, given the fact that the mass immigration of Koreans did not take place until after the annexation of the Hawaiian Islands by the United States, with the resulting tightening of controls over labor and immigration. Records available for inspection at the Ewa Sugar Plantation in 1969 included sets of personnel records showing the arrival date at the plantation of each worker and his previous employment. Individual cards contained information such as the worker's name, birthdate, birthplace, family members, date of arrival in Hawaii, and so forth. The plantation has since closed its milling and office operations. These and similar records from other plantations could provide the basis for some firm data on early immigrant origins and plantation worker mobility. The Hawaiian Sugar Planters' Association's *Census of Hawaiian Sugar Plantations,* published annually from 1931 to 1957, is quite generally available.

Positive effects from the many involved legal battles engaged in by various politically oriented factions within Hawaii's Korean community are not plentiful, but an examination of the records of the Circuit Court of the First Judicial District of the Territory of Hawaii reveals a great deal of information about Hawaii's Koreans. In addition to insights into the power struggles, important data incidentally inserted into the court records are preserved there as exhibits. Organizations of historical importance involved in these legal proceedings include the Korean National Association, the Tongji-hoe, the Korean National Independence League (Tae-Choson Tongnip-dan), the Korean Residents Association (Tae-Hanin Kyomin-dan), and the Korean Christian Missions Board. These materials are available for general inspection.

The sociology department of the University of Hawaii has custody of the Romanzo Adams Social Research Laboratory confidential research files. The personnel of the laboratory, which operated until 1963, encouraged students of all ethnic backgrounds to write first-person accounts of their family life and experiences. The resulting manuscripts, mostly student papers and reports of interviews with family members and elderly relatives, are largely descriptive but do provide material that would be difficult to duplicate today. Access is limited both by the circumstances of confidentiality under which many of the papers were written, and by the incomplete cataloging of the laboratory files. Along with the student reports and papers there is a wide selection of clippings and assorted documents which have been accumulated and partially classified and indexed.

The Archives of Hawaii (Honolulu) is the major depository for the archival records of the former Kingdom of the Hawaiian Islands, annexed by the United States in 1898 before the first Korean immigrants arrived there. Official references to the Koreans are generally found in United States federal government documents rather than in papers unique to the archives. However, pertinent items are there for the diligent researcher to discover as both Deborah Church and Wayne Patterson have shown in their preliminary studies utilizing, in part, documents from the archives. These items are scattered through governors' correspondence, customs office records, folders of newspaper clippings, and miscellaneous other reports.

The locating and evaluating of first-person accounts of developments in the Korean community is a difficult and time-consuming task. Divisions within the community resulted in a great deal of bitterness and stirred up deep personal animosities. In the case of some manuscripts, the families of the writers are reluctant to make the papers freely available to scholars. The late Henry C. Kim, a resident of the United States from 1909 until his death in 1967, editor at different times of both *Shinhan Minbo* and *Kungmin-bo,* and former president of the Korean National Association of Hawaii, left his autobiography and several other manuscripts under the collective title "Biographical Sketches of Friends and Foes." Included are biographies of Syngman Rhee, Pak Yong-man, and Kim Hong-gi, all of whom at one time played prominent roles in the Korean American community.[18] Hyŏn Sun's "My Autobiography" tells about his brief stay in Hawaii from 1904 to 1907 and of a longer stay after 1923, when he was a pastor and, later, a businessman.[19] Hyŏn's Korean-language work, *P'owa yuram-ki* [Memoirs of my Hawaiian sojourn], is being increasingly used by Korean scholars interested in this portion of Korean immigration.[20] Chŏng Tu-ok of Honolulu, who was associated at one time or another with most of the politically active groups in Hawaii, has written a rather personalized account of his experiences and perceptions. Yi Chung-kŭn and Yi Hong-gi both spent most of their lives on the island of Kauai working on a sugar plantation. Both have written autobiographical accounts of their experiences, covering the period 1905 to 1950.[21] Continued investigation is certain to uncover other valuable firsthand accounts such as these.

A final source of information not to be neglected is the memory of the individual community members. Most Korean Americans are cooperative in discussing their family backgrounds and sharing their personal recollections and opinions when the interviewer reveals genuine interest in the subject matter and sensitivity to the interviewee's concerns about the ways in which the information gained might be used. The collecting of this kind of information is no easy task and most of its value will emerge only when such records are available in quantity sufficient to narrow individual distortions of events. The techniques involved are rather specialized and require much more than possession of a tape recorder and a few addresses. Interviews of this kind should not be restricted to the elderly. The concerns and observations of newly arrived Korean Americans, recorded early in their residence, will provide helpful data for future studies on the acculturation and adaptation of the wider community.

Notes

1. Roger Daniels, "American Historians and East Asian Immigrants," *Pacific Historical Review* 43:4 (November 1974): 470.

2. Arthur L. Gardner, *The Koreans in Hawaii: An Annotated Bibliography* (Honolulu: University of Hawaii, Social Science Research Institute, 1970).

3. Harry H.L. Kitano, E. Jung, C. Tanaka, and B. Wong, *Asian Americans: An Annotated Bibliography* (Los Angeles: University of California, Asian American Studies Center, 1972); William Wong Lum, *Asians in America: A Bibliography of Master's Theses and Doctoral Dissertations* (Davis: University of California, Asian American Research Project, 1970).

4. Kim Wŏn-yong (Warren Y. Kim), *Chae-Mi Hanin osimnyŏn-sa* [Fifty-year history of the Koreans in America] (Reedley, California: Charles Ho Kim, 1959).

5. Warren Y. Kim (Kim Wŏn-yong), *Koreans in America* (Seoul: Po Chin Chae), 1971.

6. No Chae-yŏn, *Chae-Mi Hanin saryak* [A concise history of Koreans in America], 2 vols. (Los Angeles: American Publisher, 1951, 1963).

7. Kim Hyung-chan and Wayne Patterson, eds., *The Koreans in America, 1882–1974* (Dobbs Ferry, New York: Oceana Publications, 1974).

8. Judith Rubano, *Culture and Behaviour in Hawaii: An Annotated Bibliography* (Honolulu: University of Hawaii Press, 1971).

9. Lee Houchins and Chang-su Houchins, "The Korean Experience in America, 1903–1924," *Pacific Historical Review* 43:4 (November 1974): 548–75; Kim Hyung-chan, "Korean Emigrants to the U.S.A., 1959–1969," *Korea Journal* 11:9 (September 1971): 16–24, 31; Kim Hyung-chan, "Some Aspects of Social Demography of Korean Americans," in this volume; Ko Sŭng-je, "A Study of Korean Immigrants to Hawaii," *Journal of Social Sciences and Humanities* 38 (June 1973): 19–33; Koh Kwang-lim and Koh Hesung C., eds., *Koreans and Korean-Americans in the United States: A Survey of Three Conference Proceedings, 1971–73* (New Haven: East Rock Publishing, 1974); Linda Shin, "Koreans in America," in Amy Tachiki, Eddie Wong, and Franklin Odo, eds., *Roots: An Asian American Reader* (Los Angeles: University of California, Asian American Studies Center, 1971); Song Johng-doo, "Educational Problems of Korean Children in the United States," *Korean Observer* 6:3 (Summer 1975): 231–44.

10. Theses referred to by Kim and Patterson are Cho Kyŏng-suk Gregor, "Korean Immigrants in Gresham, Oregon: Community Life and Social Adjustment" (M.A. thesis, University of Oregon, 1963); Lee Kyung, "Settlement Patterns of Los Angeles Koreans" (M.A. thesis, University of California, Los Angeles, 1969); Helen Lewis Givens, *The Korean Community in Los Angeles County* (San Francisco: R. and E. Research Associates, 1974), master's thesis dating from 1939; Kim J. Sangho, *A Study of the Korean Church and Her People in Chicago, Illinois* (San Francisco: R. and E. Research Associates, 1975); Lee Don-chang, *Acculturation of Korean Residents in Georgia* (San Francisco: R. and E. Research Associates, 1975). Also see Chang Won H., "Communication and Acculturation: A Case Study of [the] Korean Ethnic Group in Los Angeles" (Ph.D. diss., University of Iowa, 1972).

11. Two fairly recent publications are Ko Sŭng-je, *Han'guk imin-sa yŏn'gu* [A study on the history of Korean emigration] (Seoul: Changmungak, 1973); Sŏ Kwang-un, *Miju Hanin ch'ilsimnyŏn-sa* [Seventy-year history of Korean emigrants in the United States] (Seoul: Kyop'o Munje Yŏn'guso, 1973).

12. This was true in early 1973. The 1948 issues are available at the National Central Library in Seoul and a few random issues from that year are in the University of Hawaii library's Hawaiian and Pacific Collection.

13. Further detail on availability is given in the author's *The Koreans in Hawaii*.

14. The State of Hawaii, Office of Library Services, has published *Index to the Honolulu Advertiser and Star-Bulletin, 1929–1967* (Honolulu, 1968) in five volumes. The *Advertiser* began publishing as the *Pacific Commercial Advertiser* in 1856 and the *Star-Bulletin* began publishing in 1912.

15. Territory of Hawaii boards which published pertinent reports include the boards of immigration, labor and statistics, prison directors, health, and public instruction. Current demographic data without analysis are released by the State of Hawaii, Department of Planning and Economic Development, through its *Statistical Report* series and its Census Tract Committee reports.

16. Principal organizations are the Korean National Association (1909–) in Honolulu and Los Angeles, the Hŭngsa-dan (1913–) in Los Angeles, and the Tongji-hoe (1921–) in Honolulu. The last seems to have settled for the uncomplicated role of a benevolent society.

17. For further details see the author's *The Koreans in Hawaii*, pp. 32–33.

18. Copies of all manuscripts referred to in this section are deposited at the Center for Korean Studies, University of Hawaii.

19. Hyŏn Sun, "My Autobiography," University of Hawaii, Social Science Research Institute.

20. Hyŏn Sun, *P'owa yuram-ki* [Memoirs of my Hawaiian sojourn] (Seoul: Hyŏn Kong-yŏm, 1909).

21. Both accounts are located at the Social Science Research Institute, University of Hawaii.

Contributors

Wayne Patterson is a member of the Department of Political Science, Saint Norbert College, West De Pere, Wisconsin.

Yun Yŏ-jun is chief correspondent, Bureau of Political Affairs, *Kyŏnghyang Daily*, Seoul, Korea.

Kim Hyung-chan is a member of the Department of Education, Western Washington State College, Bellingham, Washington.

Chang Won H. is a member of the School of Journalism, University of Missouri, Columbia, Missouri.

Lee Don-chang is a member of the Division of Social Sciences, Georgia Southwestern College, Americus, Georgia.

Yu Chae-kŭn, formerly with the University of Washington, is now in private business.

Cha Marn J. is a member of the Department of Political Science, California State University, Fresno, California.

Ryu Jai P. is a member of Loyola College, Baltimore, Maryland.

David S. Kim and Charles Choy Wong are both graduate students at the University of California, Los Angeles.

Arthur L. Gardner is a member of the Department of History, Graceland College, Lamoni, Iowa.

Index

Index

The Korean Diaspora was copy edited by Paulette Wamego,
proofing by Barbara Philips,
text design by Shelly Lowenkopf.
Composition by Edwards Brothers, Inc., Ann Arbor, Mich.
on a Linotron 505C crt phototypesetter
using Baskerville text and Univers tabular.
Printing and binding also by Edwards Brothers.
Text is 55# Book Natural bulking at 390 p.p.i.
Cover, designed by Jack Swartz, prints over Kivar 6 cambric finish
and is applied to standard boards and endsheets.